Cognitive Exploration of Language and Linguistics

# Cognitive Linguistics in Practice

A text book series which aims at introducing students of language and linguistics, and scholars from neighboring disciplines, to established and new fields in language research from a cognitive perspective. Titles in the series are written in an attractive, reader-friendly and self-explanatory style with assigments, and are tested for classroom use at university level.

## Executive Editor

Günter Radden
University of Hamburg
radden@rrz.uni-hamburg.de

## Editorial Board

René Dirven
University of Duisburg, Essen

Suzanne Kemmer
Rice University

Kee Dong Lee
Yonsei University

Klaus-Uwe Panther
University of Hamburg

Johanna Rubba
California Polytechnic State University

Ted J.M. Sanders
University of Utrecht

Soteria Svorou
San Jose State University

Elżbieta Tabakowska
Cracow University

Marjolijn H. Verspoor
University of Groningen

## Volume 1

Cognitive Exploration of Language and Linguistics, 2nd rev. ed.
René Dirven and Marjolijn Verspoor, Editors

# Cognitive Exploration of Language and Linguistics
## Second Revised Edition

Edited by

René Dirven
University Duisburg, Essen

Marjolijn Verspoor
University of Groningen

In collaboration with

Johan De Caluwé, Dirk Geeraerts, Cliff Goddard, Stef Grondelaers,
Ralf Pörings, Günter Radden, Willy Serniclaes, Marcello Soffritti,
Wilbert Spooren, John R. Taylor, Ignacio Vazquez, Anna Wierzbicka,
Margaret E. Winters

John Benjamins Publishing Company
Amsterdam/Philadelphia

TM The paper used in this publication meets the minimum requirements of American National Standard for Information Sciences — Permanence of Paper for Printed Library Materials, ANSI Z39.48-1984.

Library of Congress Cataloging-in-Publication Data

Cognitive exploration of language and linguistics / [edited by] René Dirven and Marjolijn H. Verspoor; in collaboration with Johan De Caluwé... et al.--2nd rev. ed.

p.   cm. --  (Cognitive Linguistics in Practice, ISSN 1388-6231 ; v. 1)
Includes bibliographical references and indexes.
1. Linguistics. 2. Cognition. I. Dirven, René. II. Verspoor, Marjolijn. III. Series.
P123 C567      2004
410--dc22                                                                    2004045509
ISBN   978 90 272 1905 3 (EUR) / 978 1 58811 485 3 (US) (HB; alk. paper)
ISBN   978 90 272 1906 0 (EUR) / 978 1 58811 486 0 (US) (PB; alk. paper)
ISBN   978 90 272 9541 5 (EB)

John Benjamins Publishing Company • P.O. Box 36224 • 1020 ME Amsterdam • The Netherlands
John Benjamins North America • P.O. Box 27519 • Philadelphia PA 19118-0519 • USA

# Table of contents

# Preface

Language is one of our most articulated means of expressing ideas and thoughts. This introduction to language and linguistics as the science of language will mainly look at language from the perspective of "expressing ideas and thoughts". This approach to the study of language is known as the cognitive perspective. The cognitive perspective also holds that language is part of a cognitive system which comprises perception, emotions, categorization, abstraction processes, and reasoning. All these cognitive abilities interact with language and are influenced by language. Thus the study of language, in a sense, becomes the study of the way we express and exchange ideas and thoughts.

This *Cognitive Exploration of Language and Linguistics* is firmly rooted in cognitive linguistics. One of the great assets of this new understanding of language and linguistics is that its foundations and most theoretical constructs are so solid that they are still valid after a quarter of a century. The evolution within cognitive linguistics rather tends to go in depth: scholars reveal ever deeper insights into the nature and functioning of language and its relation to cognition, culture, and communities. Since this book is an introduction, this second edition must stick to the great basic insights of (cognitive) linguistics and can only reflect a few insights gained in the newer evolutions within cognitive linguistics such as construction grammar (see Goldberg 1995, 1996), mental space theory (see Fauconnier 1997; Fauconnier and Sweetser 1996), blending theory (see Coulson 2000), image schema research (see Hampe 2004) or embodiment studies (see Lakoff/Johnson 1999; Zlatev et al. Forthcoming).

It was originally planned that this introduction should be accompanied by a second part, covering interdisciplinary areas such as language acquisition, language processing, applied linguistics and language learning, sociolinguistics, discourse study, cultural studies, language and ideology, linguistic anthropology, etc. Since cognitive linguists are now working in all these areas, books on these topics are in preparation for the Cognitive Linguistics in Practice series of which this is the first volume. For an overview we refer to the forthcoming *Handbook of Cognitive Linguistics*, edited by Geeraerts and Cuyckens.

This book is part of a more ambitious project comprising introductions in eight other languages: Dutch, French, German, Greek, Italian, Korean, Polish, and Spanish. The idea behind the project is to create the possibility for students participating in international exchange programmes to find a similar syllabus in the host country. The authorship of this Introduction was also multilingual and multicultural. The authors and their university affiliations are, in alphabetical order,

> De Caluwé, Johan (Ghent, Belgium)
> Dirven, René (Duisburg-Essen, Germany)
> Geeraerts, Dirk (Leuven, Belgium)
> Goddard, Cliff (Armidale, Australia)
> Grondelaers, Stefan (Leuven, Belgium)
> Pörings, Ralf (Duisburg-Essen, Germany)
> Radden, Günter (Hamburg, Germany)
> Serniclaes, Willy (Brussels, Belgium)
> Soffritti, Marcello (Bologna, Italy)
> Spooren, Wilbert (Amsterdam, The Netherlands)
> Taylor, John (Otago, New Zealand)
> Vazquez-Orta, Ignacio (Zaragoza, Spain)
> Verspoor, Marjolijn (Groningen, The Netherlands)
> Wierzbicka, Anna (Canberra, Australia)
> Winters, Margaret (Wayne, Detroit, Mich., USA)

As this list of contributors shows, this book is indeed the product of an intensive, collective, international authorship. Each chapter was written by one or more original authors. The first and second drafts were extensively discussed by all authors and then rewritten by the original authors (named first). The editors reworked the chapters to varying degrees, from slight to complete adaptions, in order to keep the book consistent in style and coherent in contents. At all stages of their growth, the project and the book have profited very much from Günter Radden's rich teaching experience, deep insights in linguistics, alert sense of accuracy, and his intensive contact with students giving feedback for many improvements. Another rich source for important changes, especially in Chapter 10, were the remarks by Ulrike Claudi and her colleagues at Cologne University, Germany. We owe them all our deepest gratitude.

The chapters were written by the following original authors (before //) and revised by the authors after //:

| | |
|---|---|
| Chapter 1: | Dirven and Radden |
| Chapter 2: | Geeraerts and Grondelaers // Dirven and Verspoor |
| Chapter 3: | De Caluwé // Dirven and Verspoor |
| Chapter 4: | Verspoor, Dirven and Radden |
| Chapter 5: | Taylor // Serniclaes |
| Chapter 6: | Goddard and Wierzbicka // Dirven |
| Chapter 7: | Vazquez-Orta // Dirven, Pörings, Spooren, Verspoor |
| Chapter 8: | Spooren |
| Chapter 9: | Winters // Dirven |
| Chapter 10: | Soffritti // Dirven |

Coordinators of the project were Ulrike Kaunzner (Bologna, Italy) and Ralf Pörings (Duisburg-Essen, Germany). The language counselling was carried out by Jane Oehlert (Sevenoaks, England). The drawings were the work of Tito Inchaurralde (Barcelona, Spain). They all deserve our sincere thanks for their skilful and conscientious work. This new edition has not only been reformatted, corrected, and updated, but has also been improved in many details; particularly Chapter 10 has been rethought and reformulated.

The Editors  
René Dirven and Marjolijn Verspoor

*Note for teachers*

The key to the Assignments is available at  
www.benjamins.com/jbp/additional/cellsol.pdf

## Some conventional signs used in this book

| | |
|---|---|
| * | The asterisk in front of a sentence or word means either that the given expression is not correct or has been reconstructed |
| ? | The question mark in front of an expression means that its acceptability is dubious |
| ?? | The double question marks in front of an expression point to extremely dubious acceptability |
| '…' | Single quotation marks are used for the meaning of an expression in language |
| "…" | Double quotation marks are used for concepts, and also for highlighting something or for quotations |
| /…/ | In the representation of pronunciation, slashes indicate a broad, phonemic transcription |
| […] | Square brackets in pronunciation represent a narrow, phonetic transcription |

## Some frequent abbreviations

DCE     Longman's Dictionary of Contemporary English
Collins  Collins Dictionary of the English Language
OED     Oxford English Dictionary
SOED    Shorter Oxford English Dictionary

# 1    The cognitive basis of language
## Language and thought

## 1.0  Overview

This first chapter introduces the reader to some fundamental aspects of language and linguistics. First it will look at language as a system of communication. Like all communication systems, language makes use of signs. The systematic study of signs is included in the field of semiotics, which analyzes verbal and non-verbal systems of human communication as well as animal communication.

Semiotics distinguishes between three types of signs: indices, icons and symbols. These three types of signs represent three different structural principles relating form and content. Human language stands out among sign systems in using all three structuring principles, but especially symbolic signs.

Secondly, this chapter will look at how language not only enables communication, but also reflects mankind's conceptual world. The conceptual world consists, amongst others, of conceptual categories, which are far richer than the system of linguistic signs. A great many, but by no means all, of the conceptual categories give rise to linguistic categories. Linguistic categories not only enable us to communicate, but also impose a certain way of understanding the world.

## 1.1  Introduction: Sign systems

As humans, we are social beings and want to share information with others about what goes on in our minds: What we see, believe, know, feel, want to do or are doing now. We can achieve this in many ways. We express our surprise by raising our eyebrows, we can draw the outline of a woman by using our hands, and we can express our thoughts by speaking. All these methods of expression are meaningful to us as "signs" of something. In its widest sense, a **sign** may be defined as a form which stands for something else, which we understand as its meaning. For example, raising one's eyebrows is understood as a sign of surprise, whereas blowing one's nose is usually not taken to be a meaningful sign, but it may become one if it is intended as an expression of protest. The three examples given above are illustrations of three possible different types of signs, i.e. indexical, iconic and symbolic signs.

An **indexical sign**, or **index**, points to something in its immediate vicinity, as is suggested by the etymology of the Latin word *index* 'pointing finger'. The clearest case of an indexical sign is a signpost for traffic pointing in the direction of the next town such as Bath. The signpost has the meaning: "Go in this direction to get to Bath." But facial expressions such as raising one's eyebrows or furrowing one's brows are also indexical signs: They "point" to a person's internal emotional states of surprise or anger.

An **iconic sign**, or **icon**, (from Greek *eikon* 'replica') provides a visual, auditory or any other perceptual image of the thing it stands for. An iconic sign is similar to the thing it represents. The road sign that warns drivers to look out for children near a school pictures two or three children crossing the road on a zebra crossing. The image is of course only vaguely similar to reality since, at a particular moment, only one or any number of children may be running across the street, but its general meaning is very clear nevertheless. The idea of danger caused by animals on roads is also pictured by iconic signs such as images of cows, deer, geese, horses, toads, etc. Pictures of lorries, cars, tractors, cycles, cycling paths, rivers, bridges, falling rocks, bends in the road, hairpin bends, etc. are usually represented iconically. The above-mentioned gestural drawing of a woman's shape with one's hands or the tracing of a spiral staircase with one's finger are, of course, also iconic signs.

Unlike indexical and iconic signs, a **symbolic sign**, or **symbol**, does not have a natural link between the form and the thing represented, but only has a conventional link. The traffic sign of an inverted triangle is one such symbol: It does not have a natural link between its form and its meaning "give right of way". The link between its form and meaning is purely conventional. The same applies to military emblems, the pound sign £, almost all flags and, of course, most of language. Thus, there is no natural link at all between the word form *surprise* and its meaning. The term *symbolic* as used in linguistics is understood in the sense that, by general consent, people have "agreed" upon the pairing of a particular form with a particular meaning. This sense of *symbolic* goes back to the original meaning of the Greek word *symbolon* 'a token of recognition' used between two guests or friends, e.g. a ring broken into two halves, which allowed them to identify each other after a long time by matching the two parts and checking whether they fit together. The two halves of the ring are inseparable, just like the form of a word and its meaning.

The scholarly discipline that studies systems of signs in all their manifestations is **semiotics** (from Greek *semeîon* 'sign'). Human language is, of course, the most elaborate system of signs to be studied, but semiotics also looks at other forms of human and non-human communicative behaviour such as gestures, clothing, keeping distances, baring one's teeth, etc. Animals have very sophisticated sign systems, too. For example, bees communicate by complex patterns of dances signalling to other bees the direction, the distance and the quantity of a source of nectar; monkeys make use of a system of nine different cries to express how far and how big a possible danger is; whales use a system of songs, although biologists have not yet been able to decode their signs. These systems of communication are almost exclusively indexical. For example, a honey bee can indexically communicate to another bee about nectar sources that are in its proximity, and signalling the quantity of the nectar occurs by iconic knocking on a surface: the more knocking, the more nectar. But there is no flexibility in the system: the bees' indexical range of signs is limited to the horizontal dimension. An experiment in Pisa has shown that bees were not able to inform other bees at the bottom of the tower of Pisa about the nectar source that had been put at the top.

There is a hierarchy of abstraction amongst the three types of signs. Indexical signs are the most "primitive" and the most limited signs in that they are restricted to the "here" and "now". Yet, indexical signs are very wide-spread in human communication, for example in body language, traffic and other signs and areas such as advertizing. Most commercial products are too prosaic to be attractive in themselves; they need to be associated with more attractive surroundings. For example, Marlboro cigarettes are indexically related to the adventurous life of the American cowboy.

Iconic signs are more complex in that their understanding requires the recognition of similarity. The iconic link of similarity needs to be consciously established by the observer. The image may be fairly similar as with ikons, which are pictures of a holy person venerated in the Russian or Greek Orthodox Church, or they may be fairly abstract as in stylized pictures of men and women on toilet doors, or of cars or planes in road signs. Icons are probably not found in the animal kingdom.

Symbolic signs are the exclusive prerogative of humans. People have more communicative needs than pointing to things and replicating things; we also want to talk about things which are more abstract in nature such as events in the past or future, objects which are distant from us, hopes about peace, etc. This can only be achieved by means of symbols, which humans all over the world have created for the purpose of communicating all possible thoughts. The most elaborate system of symbolic signs is natural language in all its forms: The most universal form is spoken language; at a certain phase of civilization and intellectual development a written form of language develops; and people who are deaf have developed a sign language, which is largely based on conventionalized links between gestures and meanings.

The three types of signs may be represented as in Table 1 and reflect general principles of coping with forms and meanings.

Table 1.  Links in the three types of signs

| I n d e x | | I c o n | | S y m b o l | |
|---|---|---|---|---|---|
| Form | Meaning | Form | Meaning | Form | Meaning |
| contguity | | similarity | | convention | |

Indexical signs reflect a more general principle, whereby things that are contiguous can stand for each other. For example, we strongly associate a piece of art with the artist and, hence, can say things like *I am curious to see the Turners*. Iconic signs reflect the more general principle of using an image for the real thing. Farmers have applied this strategy for centuries by putting up scarecrows in their fields, which the birds take for real enemies. Symbolic signs allow the human mind to go beyond the limitations of contiguity and similarity and establish symbolic links between any form and any meaning. Thus, a rose can stand for love and the owl for wisdom. These three principles of indexicality, iconicity and symbolicity underlie the structuring of language, which will be the subject of the next section.

## 1.2   Structuring principles in language

As we saw in the previous section there are three types of signs: indexical, iconic, and symbolic. Almost all language is symbolic as the relationship between words and their meanings is not based on contiguity or similarity (except perhaps in words for animal sounds), but on convention. However, within this complex system of symbols, called language, we can also recognize indexal, iconic and symbolic principles. For example, we can recognize words whose sole function it is "to point". Some sentence patterns iconically show "similarity" with the order of things in reality. And finally, once arbitrarily chosen word forms (symbols) may be put together to form new words whose meaning is transparent.

### 1.2.1   The principle of indexicality in language

The **principle of indexicality** means that we can "point" to things in our scope of attention. We consider ourselves to be at the centre of the universe, and everything around us is seen from our point of view. This **egocentric** view of the world also shows in our use of language. When we speak, our position in space and time serves as the reference point for the location of other entities in space and time. The place where we are is referred to as *here*, and the time when we speak is *now*. If I said, *My neighbour is here now,* my listener would know that "here" is the place where I am, and "now" is the time when I am speaking. This would even hold true for a transatlantic telephone conversation, in which the speaker's, and not the hearer's, place and time are meant. Spaces other than ours are described as *there* or, when they are even further from us, as *over there*. Similarly, times other than our present time are referred to as *then*, which may be either past time as in *Then they got married* or future time as in *Then they will have children*.

Words such as *here, there, now, then, today, tomorrow, this, that, come* and *go* as well as the personal pronouns *I, you* and *we* are described as deictic expressions. **Deictic expressions** (from Greek *deiktis* of *deiknumi* 'show') relate to the speaking EGO, who imposes his perspective on the world. Deictic expressions depend for their interpretation on the situation in which they are used. Without knowing the situational context, the request for joining a demonstration printed on a leaflet found on a train *Massive demonstration tomorrow at ten; meet here!* is rather meaningless.

The EGO also serves as the "deictic centre" for locating things in space as in *The house is in front of me*. Far bigger things than oneself may be located with respect to the speaking ego. In saying *The Empire State Building is right in front of me*, we pretend that the person speaking, rather than the skyscraper, is the stable reference point of this world. It is also possible to take the hearer's perspective while looking at things. This is what guides on sight-seeing buses do all the time when they say for example *As we approach St. Paul's now, the Tower is to your left.*

The ego furthermore serves as the deictic centre for locating things with respect to other things. Thus, when the speaker says, *The bicycle is behind the tree,* he draws an imaginary line from himself to the tree and locates the bicycle behind the tree, as shown in Figure 1a. When the speaker moves to the other side of the street, his **deictic orientation** changes too and the bicycle is now in front of the tree, as shown in Figure 1b. Trees are different from artefacts such as buildings and cars, whose fronts and backs are easily identifiable due to their inherent nature. Therefore, the position of the bicycle with respect to the car does not change with the speaker's perspective, as shown in Figures 1c and 1d on the next page. Whatever the speaker does in Figure 1c, the bicycle remains behind the car, because we associate that area of the car as 'the back'.

The **inherent orientation** that we give artifacts such as the car in Figures 1c and 1d is an extension of our human body: The front of the car coincides with the driver's front side as does the back, the left and right hand side. Just as we speak of our bodily front and back, top and bottom, left and right side we conceive of shirts, chairs, cars, houses and other artefacts as having intrinsic fronts and backs, tops and bottoms and left and right sides.

At a more general level, we transpose our egocentric orientation onto the human being as such. Our psychological proximity to fellow humans leads to an anthropocentric perspective (from Greek *anthropos* 'man'). Our **anthropocentric** perspective of the world follows from the fact that we are foremost interested in humans like ourselves: Their actions, their thoughts, their experiences, their possessions, their movements, etc. We, as human beings, always occupy a privileged position in the description of events. If a human being is involved in an event, he or she tends to be named first, as the subject of the sentence. The examples with a human subject in 1 illustrate the normal way of expressing events or states.

a. *the bicycle behind the tree*        b. *the bicycle in front of the tree*

c. *the bicycle behind the car*        d. *the bicycle in front of the car*

**Figure 1.** Deictic orientation (a, b) and inherent orientation (c, d)

(1) a.  *She* knows the poem by heart.
    b.  *He* would like some more milk in his coffee.
    c.  *I* lost my contact lenses.

It is only with special focus on an object that a non-human entity is preferred over a human entity and becomes the subject of the sentence. Thus, when a teacher takes a mental distance from her students, she might say *By tomorrow this poem must be known by heart by everybody*, but since it is not likely that we take distance from ourselves, we are unlikely to say *\*This poem is known by heart by me* (note: An asterisk before a linguistic expression means that it is not correct).

The human being is given special prominence in other areas of grammar, too. English has special personal pronouns for males and females (*he* and *she* as opposed to *it*), special interrogative and relative pronouns that refer to humans as opposed to things (*who, whose,* and *whom*, as opposed to *which*) and a special possessive form for humans (*the man's coat* but not *\*the house's roof*).

The following sentences illustrate a less conspicuous instance of anthropocentricity:

(2) a.  His house got broken into.
    b.  ?The house got broken into.
    c.  ??The house got burnt down.

These sentences with the *get*-passive display a scale of acceptability: The *get*-passive is fully acceptable in (2a) but, as the question marks in front of a sentence suggest, less acceptable in (2b) and hardly acceptable in (2c). What determines our judgement of acceptability of the *get*-passive is the degree of human involvement in the event.

### 1.2.2 The principle of iconicity in language

The **principle of iconicity** in language means that we conceive a similarity between a form of language and the thing it stands for, e.g. the name of a bird may imitate the sounds it seems to make, i.e. *cuckoo*. Iconicity may manifest itself in three sub-principles, i.e. those of linguistic expressions related to sequential order, distance and quantity.

The **principle of sequential order** is a phenomenon of both temporal events and the linear arrangement of elements in a linguistic construction. In its simplest manifestation, the principle of iconicity determines the order of two or more clauses as in Julius Caesar's historic words, *Veni, vidi, vici* 'I came, I saw, I conquered' or in the advertizing slogan *Eye it, try it, buy it*. Here reversing the order would produce nonsense. But in other contexts this is perfectly possible. By changing the linear arrangement of the co-ordinated clauses of (3a), we automatically get a different sequence of events (3b):

(3)  a.  Virginia got married and had a baby.
     b.  Virginia had a baby and got married.

The conjunction *and* itself does not tell us anything about the sequence of events; it is only due to the arrangement of the two clauses that the natural order of the events is mirrored. But if, instead of *and*, we used the temporal conjunction *before* or *after*, we may describe the event either in an iconic way (4), where the linear order is related to the order of events, or in a non-iconic way (5), where the linear order is unrelated to the order of events:

(4)  a.  Virginia got married *before* she had a baby.
     b.  *After* she had the baby, Virginia got married.

(5)  a.  *Before* she had a baby, Virginia got married.
     b.  Virginia had a baby *after* she got married.

Sequential-order iconicity is also found within the structure of a sentence. Thus, the sentences below have the same words but convey different meanings because of the different order of the adjective *green*:

(6)   a.   Bill painted the *green* door.
      b.   Bill painted the door *green*.

In (6a), the door was already green and then painted over again, but we do not know what colour it was painted. In (6b), we do not know the original colour of the door but we know that it came out green. The normal position of adjectives in English is in front of the noun they modify as in (6a); the position after the noun in (6b) iconically reflects a resulting and, hence, later state in the door's colour.

The iconic principle also determines the sequential order of the elements in "binary" expressions which reflect temporal succession:

(7)   a.   now and then, now or never, sooner or later, day and night
      b.   cause and effect, hit and run, trial and error, give and take, wait and see, pick and mix, cash and carry, park and ride.

All these binary expressions are irreversible. As a rule, we do not speak of *then and now* or *effect and cause*; such reversals would only occur for special communicative effects, e.g. drawing attention to the expression. The first group of these binary expressions refers to purely temporal sequences; the second group describes events which routinely occur in the order in which they are expressed.

Further evidence of this iconic principle is also found in the **word order** of subject, verb and object in a sentence. In almost all the languages of the world, the subject precedes the object. The subject (S), the verb (V) and the object (O) of a sentence can theoretically be ordered in six different ways: SVO, SOV, VSO, OSV, OVS, VOS. The first three patterns establish the most widely used orders (note: The English sentences in (8b,c) are word-for-word translations of the non-English sentences):

(8)   a.   SVO:   The lawyer wrote the letter.
      b.   SOV:   *(Er weiß, daß) der Anwalt den Brief schrieb.*
                   He knows that the lawyer the letter wrote.
      c.   VSO:   *(Endlich) schrieb der Anwalt den Brief.*
                   Finally   wrote the lawyer the letter.

English and the Romance languages have fixed word order and only allow SVO. German, Dutch and the Scandinavian languages also have the two other word order possibilities: they have SVO in main clauses (8a), SOV in subordinate clauses (8b), and VSO after adverbs or adverbial clauses (8c). The overwhelming occurrence of the subject before the object in the world's languages is motivated by the way humans perceive the internal structure of events: Events typically describe actions in which one entity acts upon another. The acting entity is expressed as the subject of the sentence; its action occurs before its effect, the object, is realized.

The **principle of distance** accounts for the fact that things which belong together conceptually tend to be put together linguistically, and things that do not belong together are put at a distance. This principle explains the grammatical contrast in the following pair of sentences:

(9)   a.   A noisy group *was* hanging around the bar.
      b.   A group of noisy youngsters *were* hanging around the bar.

In sentence (9a), the singular noun *group* agrees with the singular verb immediately following it. In sentence (9b), the noun *group* is put at some distance from the verb, which now agrees with the plural noun *youngsters* adjacent to it. With certain quantifying expressions as in *a number of students* and *a lot of people*, plural agreement has become the grammatical norm.

The principle of distance also accounts for the various types of subordinate clauses following the verb of a main clause. English has, amongst others, three types of clauses after a main verb: A clause without *to* (10a), a clause with *to* (10b), and a clause with *that* (10c):

(10)   a.   I made *her* leave.
       b.   I wanted *her to* leave.
       c.   I hoped *that she would* leave.

In (10a), the subject *I* has direct influence on the other person and, therefore, there is minimal distance between the two verbs. In (10b), the subject's desire may have some indirect impact on the other person and, therefore, the distance between the verbs is greater. In (10c), there is no impact whatsoever on the other person and, hence, the distance between the verbs is greatest.

As a final example of iconic distance let us consider the choice between the indirect object construction and the *to*-phrase in English, which is known as "dative alternation", as in:

(11)   a.   Romeo sent *his girlfriend* a Valentine card.
       b.   Romeo sent a Valentine card *to his girlfriend*.

The smaller linguistic distance between *sent* and *his girlfriend* in (11a) means that she actually received the Valentine's Day card, while the greater distance between the verb and the *to*-phrase in (11b) leaves the meaning unclear as to whether she ever received the card.

The iconic **principle of quantity** accounts for our tendency to associate more form with more meaning and, conversely, less form with less meaning. By stretching the o-sound of *long* as in *That's a looooong story* we iconically express the idea of an "extremely long" story. The same principle is applied by young children, who express the notion of plurality as in *trees* by repeating the word *tree* several times: *Look, daddy, a tree and another tree and another tree.*

This repetition strategy is systematically exploited in many languages: Thus in the pidgin language *Tok Pisin*, *cow-cow* means 'cows', *wilwil* (wheel-wheel) means 'bicycle', and in Afrikaans, *plek-plek* (place-place) means 'in various places'. This iconic device of repetition is known as **reduplication**. Reduplication is, of course, not a very economical way of expressing the idea of "more quantity". Most languages have developed more efficient symbolic ways of expressing plurality.

The quantity principle also shows up in politeness strategies, according to the motto "being polite is saying a bit more". Thus, the increasing quantities of language forms in the following examples are meant to convey increasing respect for the hearer:

(12)  a.  No smoking.
      b.  Don't smoke, will you?
      c.  Would you mind not smoking here, please.
      d.  Customers are requested to refrain from smoking if they can.
          (notice at Harrods)
      e.  We would appreciate if you could refrain from smoking cigars and
          pipes as it can be disturbing to other diners. Thank you.
          (notice at Clos du Roi, Bath)

The use of wordy phrases also illustrates the way in which people try to attach more importance to a subject matter:

(13)  a.  I obtained the privilege of his acquaintance.
      b.  In my opinion it is a not unjustified assumption that …

Pretentious diction and "meaningless wordings" such as these have repeatedly been criticized by literary critics and purists of language. Orwell, who in his essay on "Politics and the English language" cites sentence (13b) as an illustration of language abuse, says that it is easier to say such sentences than to say *I think*.

The quantity principle also implies that less meaning requires less form. This is precisely what happens with information that is felt to be redundant. Thus, we use the less explicit form (14a) rather than the more explicit version (14b):

(14)  a.  Charles said that he was short of money and *so did* his girl-friend.
      b.  Charles said that he was short of money and his girl-friend *said that she was short of money, too.*

The form *so did* in (14a) replaces the whole verbal expression following the subject *girl-friend*. A number of syntactic phenomena such as the use of pronouns and the reduction of full sentences are due to the operation of the quantity principle. Conversely, if such redundant sentences are used as in (14b), they express the same idea as the shorter form, but on top of that they tend to express emphasis, irony or a negative attitude.

### 1.2.3  The principle of symbolicity in language

The **principle of symbolicity** refers to the conventional pairing of form and meaning, as is typically found in the word stock of a language. The concept of "house" is rendered as *house* in English, *Haus* in German, *huis* in Dutch, *casa* in Italian and Spanish, *maison* in French, *talo* in Finnish, *dom* in Russian, etc. There is, of course, nothing in the forms of these words that makes them suitable to express the concept of "house". They might even express something quite different in another language: for example, the form *kaas* in Dutch, which sounds like Italian *casa*, means "cheese", and the German word *Dom* does not mean "Haus", but "church of a bishop". This is one of the reasons why the link between the form and the meaning of symbolic signs was called **arbitrary** by the founding father of modern linguistics, Ferdinand de Saussure. Often signs which originally made sense have become arbitrary in the course of time: Telephones no longer have dials for selecting telephone numbers but key-pads in which we "punch" a number, and receivers are no longer hung up but put down, but without giving these changes any thought we still speak of *dialling a phone number* and *hanging up the phone*.

However, while the notion of arbitrariness certainly holds true for most of the simple words of a language, it is at odds with our general human disposition of seeing meaning in forms. If we look at the whole range of new words or new senses of existing words, we find that almost all of them are **motivated**. New words are, as a rule, built on existing linguistic material and, as such, are meaningful to us. For example, the newly coined word *software* was formed by analogy to the existing word *hardware*. The compound sign *hardware* consists of two simple words, *hard* and *ware*, which are both arbitrary. But the compound is no longer arbitrary because the combination of the two parts leads to a more or less transparent meaning. The original meaning of *hardware* is 'equipment and tools for the home and the garden'. This meaning was extended to refer to the machinery and equipment of a computer, and by analogy, the programmes running the computer were called *software*. The word *software* is still a symbolic sign in that there is only a conventionalized connection between the form and its meaning, but it is not arbitrary, since the pairing of its form and meaning is motivated. As a linguistic term, **motivation** refers to non-arbitrary links between a form and the meaning of linguistic expressions. The factor of motivation is at work both in the hearer and the speaker. The hearer wants to make sense of linguistic expressions, particularly the new ones. In some cases, he will even overuse his search for meaning and create "folk etymologies". Thus the English word *crayfish* is a folk-etymological interpretation of the French word *écrevisse*, which in its turn goes back to Germanic *krebiz* (German *Krebs*). Similarly, the opaque Spanish-Caribbean word *hamaca* 'hanging bed' was borrowed and assimilated in English as *hammock*, but in Dutch it was made transparent by folk etymology as *hangmat* 'hanging carpet', and from there it was borrowed into German as *Hängematte*.

## 1.3  Linguistic and conceptual categories

### 1.3.1  Conceptual categories

The semiotic framework developed so far has concentrated on the link between the form and meaning of signs as they are realized in words. Language resides, not in dictionaries, but in the minds of the speakers of that language. Therefore, in order to understand the nature of language, we will also have to look at our conceptual world and how it has shaped the signs. Language only covers part of the world of concepts which humans have or may have.

The notion of **concept** may be understood as "a person's idea of what something in the world is like". More specifically, concepts can relate to single entities such as the concept I have of my mother or they can relate to a whole set of entities, such as the concept "vegetable". This type of concept has structure, in that it includes certain entities such as carrots, cabbages, lettuce, etc and excludes others such as apples and pears. Such concepts which slice reality into relevant units are called categories. **Conceptual categories** are concepts of a set as a whole. Whenever we perceive something, we automatically tend to categorize it. For example, when we hear a piece of music, we automatically categorize it as rock or as classical music or as something else. Thus, the world is not some kind of objective reality existing in and for itself but is always shaped by our categorizing activity, i.e., by our human perception, knowledge, attitude, in short, by our human experience. This does not mean that we create a subjective reality, but as a community we agree about our intersubjective experiences.

Conceptual categories which are laid down in a language are **linguistic categories**, or, linguistic signs. Any linguistic sign has a form and a meaning, which roughly speaking is identical with a concept. A meaning or concept relates to some entity in our experienced world. A more comprehensive view of language as a system of signs must also include the human "conceptualizer" and the world as it is experienced by him. The human conceptualizer, conceptual categories and linguistic signs are interlinked as shown in Table 2.

**Table 2.**  Model of the conceptual world

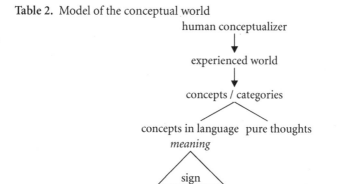

As illustrated in Table 2, a sign consists of a form and a meaning, which reflects a conceptual category, which is ultimately based on a human conceptualizer and his/her experience of the world; the meaning thus relates to an entity in the experienced world. This model of the conceptual and linguistic worlds also accounts for the possibility that different people may categorize the same thing in the world differently and even the same person may do so at different times. One person may describe a half-filled glass of wine as *half full* and another person may describe the same thing as *half empty*. Each person's choice between various alternatives is called **construal**. The notion of construal becomes even more evident, if we compare the names for the same object in various languages. Thus what English construes as *horseshoe* (i.e. 'shoe for horse') is construed in French as *fer à cheval* 'iron for horse', and as *Hufeisen* 'hoof iron' in German. All these signs are motivated: English and French see a relationship between the animal as a whole and the protecting device, while German relates the protecting device to the relevant body part of the horse. Moreover, French and German highlight the material the protecting device is made of, whereas English by using *shoe* takes an anthropocentric view of the scene. These various ways of construing the same thing are reflected in Figure 2.

Some other examples of the ubiquitous difference in construal are *grand piano* and *pavement*. English *grand piano* focuses on the size, while in French *piano à queue* 'tail piano' and German *Flügel* 'wing (piano)' a metaphorical similarity with animal parts is construed. In English *pavement* the focus is on the material, whereas its French equivalent *trottoir* 'pavement', derived from *trotter* 'to rush, to trot' focuses on the function and German *Bürgersteig* 'part of the road for civilians' stresses the people who use it.

So far we have looked at conceptual categories as they are laid down in words, or technically, as lexical categories. Conceptual categories may also show up as grammatical categories. The different ways of saying more or less the same thing in the following sentences result from using different grammatical categories:

(15)   a.   Look at that rain!
       b.   It's raining again.
       c.   And the rain, it raineth every day.

In all three sentences we have chosen the same lexical category *rain*, but it is construed as two different word classes, as a noun in (15a), as a verb in (15b) and both as a noun and a verb according to Shakespeare in (15c). Word classes are

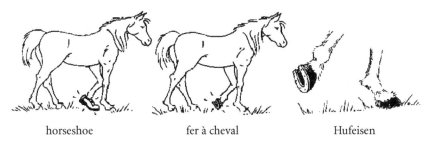

horseshoe                    fer à cheval                    Hufeisen

**Figure 2.** Different construals of the concept "horseshoe"

grammatical categories. These examples show another important fact of language: In the structure of a sentence, each lexical category is at the same time a grammatical category. Lexical categories are defined by their specific content, while grammatical categories provide the structural framework for the lexical material. Thus, the lexical category *rain* can either be framed into the grammatical category of a noun or a verb. For clarity's sake, lexical and grammatical categories will be discussed separately.

### 1.3.2  Lexical categories

The conceptual content of a **lexical category** tends to cover a wide range of instances. Think of the many different types and functions of vases. They may vary greatly in height or in width, but as long as we can put flowers in them, we are willing to categorize them as vases. Chairs also come in a variety of types as illustrated in Figure 3.

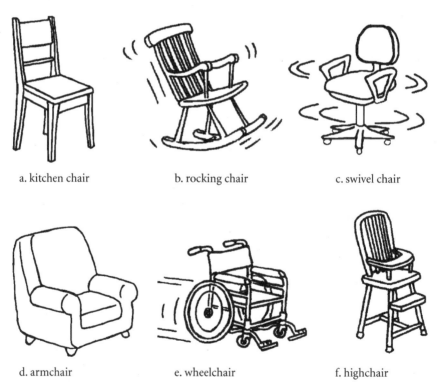

a. kitchen chair        b. rocking chair        c. swivel chair

d. armchair        e. wheelchair        f. highchair

**Figure 3.**  Some members of the lexical category "*chair*"

The best member, called the **prototypical member** or most prominent member of a category, is the subtype that first comes to mind when we think of that category. When we are asked to draw a picture of a chair, we are most likely to draw a picture of a kitchen chair and not an armchair. The choice of a prototypical chair also relates to its functions: It is a type of chair which we sit on, not one we lie on. Also the shape and the material plays a part. Therefore a prototypical chair has four legs, a seat and a back so as to be able to sit on it firmly and comfortably. A rocking chair or a swivel chair is somewhat less prototypical than a kitchen chair. However, all the items in Figure 3 are chairs, so that alongside prototypical members of a category and less prototypical ones, we also have more **peripheral** or **marginal members** such as the armchair or wheelchair, and even dubious cases such as the highchair. A stool is definitely not a member of the category of chairs: It lacks most of the properties of a kitchen chair: It has no back, it does not have four legs, it is higher than a usual chair and it is usually not made of wood. But the boundaries between a chair and a stool are far from absolute, and what some people call a stool is a chair for others. In general we find that the center of a lexical category is firmly established and clear, while its boundaries are **fuzzy** and tend to overlap with the boundaries of other lexical categories.

If lexical categories were not firmly established but ad hoc or haphazard, they might look like the category of "animals" as jokingly put together in the following quotation from an imaginary Chinese encyclopaedia:

(16)   On those remote pages it is written that animals are divided into (a) those that belong to the Emperor, (b) embalmed ones, (c) those that are trained, (d) sucking pigs, (e) mermaids, (f) fabulous ones, (g) stray dogs, (h) those that are included in this classification, (i) those that tremble as if they were mad, (j) innumerable ones, (k) those drawn with a very fine camel's hair brush, (l) others, (m) those that have just broken a flower vase, (n) those that resemble flies from the distance.
(J.L. Borges. 1966. *Other Inquisitions.* New York: Washington Square Press, p. 108).

This category of "animals" with its imaginary members makes no sense because it lacks systematicity. We can still imagine that there is some cultural reason for putting together the members (a), (b) and (c), but we would certainly not expect to find (d) as a specific member and even less so the remaining imaginary members.

### 1.3.3  Grammatical categories

The structural frameworks provided by **grammatical categories** include abstract distinctions which are made by means of word classes, number (singular and plural), tense, etc. Here we will only look at the grammatical category of word classes. Each **word class** is a category in itself. Depending on definitions used for each word class, English can be said to have eight or ten different word classes, as shown in the following list:

(17)  Word classes

| | | |
|---|---|---|
| a. | *noun* | mother, bird, pleasure |
| b. | *pronoun* | I, you, she, someone, which |
| c. | *determiner* | the, a, this, two |
| d. | *verb* | say, cry, consider |
| e. | *adjective* | big, rich, happy |
| f. | *adverb* | happily, merely, very |
| g. | *preposition* | at, on, during, amongst |
| h. | *particle* | (hang) up, (hand) in |
| i. | *conjunction* | and, because, after, before |
| j. | *interjection* | alas!, oops!, wow! |

Most of the word classes were first introduced and defined by Greek and Roman grammarians. They gave them the name *partes orationis,* which was literally translated into English as *parts of speech* and also gave rise to the verb *to parse* 'to analyze a sentence into its parts'. The grammatical category of word classes is still used today, but the notional definitions given to them by traditional grammars are often at odds with linguistic evidence. Even modern dictionaries still rely on traditional definitions and would define a noun as "a word or group of words that refers to a person, place or thing", a pronoun as "one of a class of words that serves to replace a noun or noun phrase", etc. (*Collins Dictionary*). It is easy to find counterexamples which disprove these definitions: For example, in the sentence *Someone has stolen my wallet,* the pronouns *someone* and *my* cannot be said to "replace" a noun or a noun phrase.

Traditional definitions of word classes were based on the erroneous assumption that the word classes are clearly definable in the first place and that all the words of a language can be neatly grouped into one of them. In the same way that prototypical and peripheral types of chairs are subsumed under the lexical category "chair", different types of words are subsumed under a grammatical category.

Thus, the category "noun" subsumes, amongst others, the following disparate types of nouns:

(18)  a.  We needed a new *telephone*.
      b.  We called the telephone *company*.
      c.  They installed it in the *afternoon*.
      d.  But they did a lousy *job*.
      e.  I am still amazed at their *stupidity*.

A word such as *telephone* is a prototypical noun: It denotes a concrete, physical, three-dimensional thing. The noun *company* is less prototypical: It denotes a non-concrete entity, i.e. an institution which, however, has some kind of concrete existence. The temporal noun *afternoon* has no concrete existence and is an even less prototypical member of nouns. The noun *job* refers to an action and, hence, is more verb-like in its meaning, while the noun *stupidity* refers to a property and is more adjective-like in meaning.

The meanings traditionally associated with word classes only apply to prototypical members; the meanings of peripheral members run over into each other. Yet, there is, after all, a good reason for having word classes in language. Protoypical nouns denote time-stable phenomena, while verbs, adjectives and adverbs denote more temporary phenomena. In using *job* and *stupidity* in (18d,e) as nouns rather than verbs or adjectives, the speaker "construes" actions and properties as time-stable, thing-like phenomena and, in saying the sentences (18d) and (18e), lends greater weight to his expression of discontent.

A lot of confusion about Latin-inspired word classes arose because the single word classes may have a different status as a grammatical category in a particular language. All languages have nouns and verbs, most languages also have adjectives, but the remaining word classes may not be represented overtly. For example, English and the Romance languages mark the difference between adjectives and adverbs, but the other Germanic languages do not:

(19)  a.  *adjective*:  She is *beautiful*.      –Sie ist *schön*.
      b.  *adverb*:     She sings *beautifully*.  –Sie singt *schön*.

The word class of particles plays an important role in English, but is not found in the Romance languages. For example, whereas French has a one-word verb to express the action of "taking" and the resulting place of this taking, English expresses these two concepts with two words, a verb and a particle.

(20)  a.  He picked up the paper.
      b.  Il ramassait le journal.

The English particles are very similar to prepositions, but they behave different-ly: Particles (21a) may be moved after a noun (21a′), but prepositions (21b) may not (21b′).

(21)  a.  He picked up the paper.
     a′. He picked the paper up.
     b.  He climbed up the tree.
     b′. *He climbed the tree up.

What this brief discussion has shown is that grammatical categories are not as clear-cut as traditionally has been assumed. Also, grammatical categories may be very language-specific.

## 1.4  Summary

Any communication, whether it is between animals or humans, takes place by means of signs and is studied in **semiotics**. **Signs** always stand for something else, which we call their meaning. The relation between a sign and its meaning can be of three different kinds. **Indexical signs** or **indices** "point" to what they stand for; **iconic signs** or **icons** provide images of what they stand for; and **symbolic signs** or **symbols** involve a purely conventional relationship between the form of the sign and its meaning. This set of signs results from cognitive principles which help humans to organize their worlds and experiences in it.

Within the symbolic system called language, we may recognize principles that are similar to the different types of signs: The **principle of indexicality** occurs when we use "pointing" words, which often reflect our **egocentric** and **anthropocentric** view of the world. The EGO is the centre for **deictic expressions** and for the **deictic orientation** of objects. But some objects like chairs or cars have **inherent orientation**. The **principle of iconicity** shows up in similarities between the order of events and the **word order** in the sentences we use to describe them; it is reflected in various sub-principles: The **principle of sequential order**, the **principle of distance**, and the **principle of quantity**. The **principle of symbolicity** accounts for the purely conventional relation between the form and the meaning of signs. This is known as the **arbitrary** nature of symbolic signs or the arbitrariness of language. The large number of arbitrary lexical signs should not underestimate the value in language of non-symbolic signs, i.e. indexical or iconic. In particular, most of the complex forms of a language, such as complex words or sentences are — as we shall see later — not arbitrary, but transparent or **motivated**.

Linguistic signs are part of the conceptual world of the human mind. We have many more **concepts** and thoughts than linguistic expressions. But those concepts that we have "fixed" in language constitute the meaning of language. Concepts which structure our world of thought are **conceptual categories**, i.e., concepts of a set as a whole. Conceptual categories may also be expressed as **linguistic categories**. Most linguistic signs denote specific conceptual content and show how we **construe** this content. These appear as **lexical categories**, while the smaller number of **grammatical categories** provides the more general structural framework of language. The members of a category tend to have a different status: Some are **prototypical members**, others are more **peripheral members**. The further one gets away from the centre of a category to its periphery, the more the category tends to become **fuzzy**.


## 1.5  Further reading

The work by the founding father of modern linguistics is Saussure (1966 [1916]). Recent introductions to linguistics are Taylor (2003) and Ungerer and Schmid (1996). Theoretical foundations of the cognitive basis of language are explored in Lakoff (1987), Langacker (1987, 1993), Talmy (2000), Rudzka-Ostyn, ed. (1988), Janssen and Redeker, eds. (1999), Taylor (2002), and Croft and Cruse (2004). The relation of language to human cognition is analyzed by Talmy (1988, 2000).

A good introduction to the various types of signs in animal and human communication is Nöth (1990). Studies of the iconic principle in language are Haiman (1985), Posner (1986) and Ungerer and Schmid (1996). Recent studies on motivation are offered in Cuyckens, Berg, Dirven and Panther, eds. (2003) and in Radden and Panther, eds. (Forthcoming). Word order phenomena in many of the world's languages are studied in Greenberg, ed. (1963, 1966). The psychological basis of categories and prototypicality is experimentally explored in Rosch (1977, 1999).

## Assignments

1.  What types of sign (iconic, indexical, symbolic) are involved in the following cases?

    a.  inverted triangle as a road sign
    b.  sign depicting falling rocks
    c.  morse signs
    d.  frozen window panes of a car
    e.  speedometer in car
    f.  burglar alarm going off
    g.  baby crying
    h.  dog wagging its tail
    i.  animal drawings in cave dwellings
    j.  a wedding ring
    k.  a clenched fist in the air
    l.  a ring in the nose (human)

2.  In what way are the following expressions iconic? (sequential order, distance, quantity)

    a.  The Krio word for 'earthquake' is *shaky-shaky*.
    b.  Department store ad: We have rails and rails and rails of famous fashion.
    c.  Police warning: Don't drink and drive!
    d.  Japanese *ie* 'house', *ieie* 'houses'
    e.  See Naples and die.
    f.  I swear by Almighty God that what I am about to say is the truth, the whole truth, and nothing but the truth.

3.  In what way do the indexical principles, egocentricity and anthropocentricity, play a role in the ordering of the following irreversible pairs of words?

    a.  come and go, this and that, here and there
    b.  women and wine, king and country, people and places
    c.  man and beast, man and dog
    d.  friend or foe, win or lose, live or die

4.  Sentence (a) is more likely to occur than (b), which does not make much sense at first sight. Which indexical principle is not respected in (b)? If (b) were to occur, what would it mean?

    a.  The results of the study depart from our expectation.
    b.  <sup>??</sup>Our expectation departs from the results of the study.

5.  The expressions in italics are peripheral members of their particular grammatical
    category such as noun, adjective, adverb, etc. Why?

    a.  The approach has to be simple and *low cost*.
    b.  This is the *very* man.
    c.  the *then* president

6.  In English, the same form may sometimes be a member of up to five different word
    classes. Specify the word class of *round* in each of the following examples.

    a.  My friend is coming *round* the corner.
    b.  That was the first *round* table I saw.
    c.  She came *round* when she got something to drink.
    d.  Let's *round* off with an exercise.
    e.  After school we can play a *round* of golf.

# 2   What's in a word?

## Lexicology

## 2.0  Overview

The next three chapters offer a systematic study of the meanings of linguistic expressions as they are related to one another and to entities in our conception of the world. This field of linguistics is called **semantics**, which deals with lexicology (Ch. 2), morphology (Ch. 3), and syntax (Ch. 4). In the present chapter the meanings and the structure of words are studied. This is lexicology, i.e., the systematic study of the meanings (or senses) of words. In this approach we can go from the form of a word to the various senses. Or we can adopt the opposite approach: Take a given concept and then see what different words are available as synonyms to refer to the entities in our conceptual world.

In both approaches the same general route will be followed. First of all, we will look at the central members of a category and at prototype effects; then we will look at the links between the different members of a category; and finally, we will look at the marginal members at the periphery and their "fuzzy" character. Categories are clear-cut at the centre but tend to be more fuzzy towards the periphery.

## 2.1  Introduction: Words, meanings and concepts

In Chapter 1 we saw that language helps us categorize our experiences of the world. Therefore, the answer to the question in the title "What is in a word" is relatively simple: "The whole world", or at least all the experiences we have of our world that have somehow been categorized linguistically. These are probably the experiences that have more prominence in a given cultural community.

In one very naïve way, one might be tempted to expect that for each conceptual category we have just one linguistic category, or word, and, conversely that each word stands for one conceptual category or one meaning. But this is not the way that language works. On average, a word form has three to four senses. A word with different, related senses is a **polysemous** word (from Greek *poly* 'many' and *sema* 'sign, meaning'). A good dictionary usually lists several senses for one lexical item. Here is part of a slightly adapted example of the item *fruit* from the DCE:

(1)  fruit /fruːt/ n plural *fruit* or *fruits*

    a.  something such as an apple, banana, or strawberry that grows on a tree or other plant and tastes sweet: *Fresh fruit and vegetables, a bowl of fruit*

    b.  *technical* the part of a plant, bush, or tree that contains the seeds

    c.  *The fruit/fruits of sth* the good results that you have from something after you have worked very hard

    d.  *The fruits of the earth/nature* all the natural things that the earth produces such as fruit, vegetables, or minerals

    e.  *old-fashioned slang* an insulting way of talking to or about a man who is a homosexual

    f.  (not in DCE) *fruit of the womb* offspring

As the example shows, a dictionary starts from a word form and lists the various senses and therefore follows a semasiological approach. Semasiology (from Greek *sêma* 'sign') is thus an approach to the lexicon which describes the polysemy of a word form and the relationship between these various senses. The two literal senses in (1a,b) come before the figurative one in (1c). The most common senses in (1a–d) are in contrast to the less common ones as in (1e,f), and so on. Sometimes the same form may in reality stand for two entirely different words, as in *Pole,* used for inhabitants of Poland and for the North and South Pole. This is called **homonymy**, which means that two different words have the same form.

But we can also follow the opposite approach. This second approach is the onomasiological approach (from Greek *ónoma* 'name'). In onomasiology we start from a concept such as "fruit/fruits" and see which other words or expressions we can use as synonyms to denote the same or similar concepts. This is what a **thesaurus** does. A thesaurus is "a book in which words are put into groups with other words that are related in meaning" (DCE). *The Cambridge Thesaurus of American English* gives the following synonyms and other related words for the literal meanings (2a) and figurative meanings (2b) of *fruit*:

(2)   fruit, n.
    a.   berry, vegetable, grain, nut, root, tuber, crop, harvest, produce, product, yield
    b.   result, outcome, consequences, aftermath, effect, profits, pay, benefit, return, yield, harvest

An onomasiological approach in a thesaurus goes from a concept or meaning to the various synonyms which can be used to denote that concept. Onomasiology thus deals with the fact that different words may express similar meanings like *rich* and *wealthy*, called **synonymy**; with the fact that words have opposite meanings like *rich* versus *poor*, called **antonymy**; and with the fact that the meanings of groups of words are related, like *richness, affluence, wealth, poverty*, called a **lexical field**. This is summarized in Table 1.

Table 1.  Word forms and meanings or concepts

| Semasiology | Onomasiology |
| --- | --- |
| Word form (e.g. *fruit*) | Concept (e.g. "fruit") |
| senses a, b, c, d, etc. in (1) | words a, b in (2) |
| polysemy; homonymy | synonymy, antonymy |

*Definitions of four terms used in Table 1:*

**Polysemy**
The fact that a word may have two or more related senses as illustrated in (1); sometimes even more than ten senses are possible, as in the case of the preposition *over*.

**Homonymy**
The fact that two words of different origin have the same form, e.g. *Pole* as in the sense of 'Polish' and *Pole* as used in 'North Pole'.

**Synonymy**
The fact that two words have the same or nearly the same meaning, e.g. *happy, joyful, pleased*.

**Antonymy**
The fact that two words have the opposite or nearly the opposite meanings, e.g. *large* and *small*, *thick* and *thin*, to *buy* and to *sell*.

Thus, given the nature of the lexicon, we can use a semasiological approach, concentrating on the many different senses of words, or an onomasiological approach, concentrating on what is common or different between the various words in capturing the essence of our experiences. These two paths will now be systematically explored in Sections 2.2 and 2.3. In Section 2.4, however, we will see that these approaches interact and overlap.

## 2.2  From words to meanings: Semasiology

Let us suppose you want to communicate to someone else that you can see an apple. As already discussed in Chapter 1, you can make this clear in three different semiotic ways. You can point to it (indexical sign), you can draw a picture that resembles the thing (iconic sign), or you can say the word *apple*, which is a symbolic sign. In the last case, how does the word that I pronounce [æpəl] relate to the thing I see? The word itself is of course not the thing itself, but only a symbol for the thing. A symbolic sign is a given form which symbolizes or stands for a concept (or a meaning) and this concept is related to a whole category of entities in the conceptual and experiential world. The relationship between these three elements (a) form, b) concept or meaning, and c) **referent** or entity in the conceptual and experiential world) was presented in a triangle in Chapter 1, Table 2 and is reproduced here as Table 2 for the sake of clarity.

**Table 2.**  The semiotic triangle

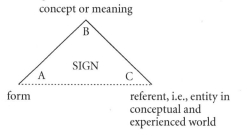

form

referent, i.e., entity in
conceptual and
experienced world

Although many different interpretations have been proposed for this semiotic triangle since it was devised by its inventors Ogden and Richards (1923), the interpretation proposed here is generally acceptable. There is a direct, though conventional link between A (form) and B (concept, meaning) and between B (concept) and C (referent, i.e., entity in conceptual and experienced world). But there is only an indirect link between A (form) and C (referent or entity in world), indicated by the interrupted line AC. This semiotic triangle is a further elaboration of the views of the Swiss linguist Ferdinand de Saussure, who introduced two essential terms: The word form is the *signifiant* (that which signifies), and the meaning of the word is the *signifié* (that which is signified). We will refer to the former simply as **word form** or **word** and put it in italics, and to the latter as **meaning** — or if a word form is polysemous, as its **senses** — and put it in single quotation marks. For example, the word (form) *apple* stands for the meaning 'a kind of fruit'.

As the dictionary entry of the word *fruit* in Section 2.1 shows, this word has more than one meaning. Next to the basic, every-day sense 'sweet and soft edible part of a plant' as in (1a), illustrated in Figure 1a, it has various other senses. In its technical sense (1b) 'the seed-bearing part of a plant or tree', the word refers to things that are not usually included in its every-day use, as shown in Figure 1b. It also has a more general use in an expression like *the fruits of nature* (1d), which refers to 'all the natural things that the earth produces' (including, for instance, grains and vegetables). In addition to these literal senses, there is a range of figurative senses, including the abstract sense in (1c) 'the result or outcome of an action' as in *the fruits of his labour* or *his work bore fruit*, or the somewhat archaic senses in (1e) 'homosexual' or in (1f) 'offspring, progeny' as in the biblical expressions *the fruit of the womb, the fruit of his loins*.

Each of these different uses represents a separate sense of *fruit*. In turn, each sense may be thought of as referring to a different set of things in the outside world, a set of referents. For example, when we use the word *fruit* with the basic sense 'sweet and soft edible part of a plant', we refer to a set of referents that includes apples, oranges, bananas, and many other sweet and soft edible objects as in Figure 1a. If we use *fruit* in its second sense 'seed-bearing part of plant', we think of the fruit's function as a seed for future plants, typically shown by the seeds or the referents in the middle of the melon in Figure 1b.

But the seed-bearing part may be the whole fruit as is the case with a walnut, which is "technically speaking" a fruit (in the second sense), but it is probably not a fruit in the every-day sense. Thus in the case of a walnut, the referent is the whole seed-bearing part. In the case of the melon (in the second, technical sense), the referent is rather the core with the seeds. However, in the every-day sense, it is rather the edible part. A referent can be defined in a

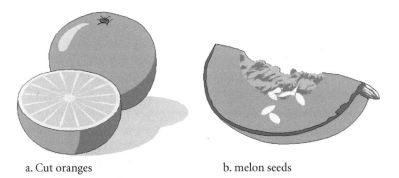

a. Cut oranges                    b. melon seeds

Figure 1.

simplified way as an entity or part of an entity evoked by words. Each word sense evokes a member of a different conceptual category. In the *fruit* example, the category members happen to be material objects, but in the case of verbs, they could be actions and in the case of adjectives, they could be properties.

There is no precondition that the "things" in the category need exist in the real world. The category "fruit" contains all real and imaginary apples and oranges that *fruit* could possibly be applied to, in the same way in which *goblin* will have a set of members associated with it, regardless of whether goblins are real or not.

In the next sections we will look more closely at the relationships among members of a category. We will look at which member is considered the most central or salient one (2.2.1), how the members are linked to each other in meaning (2.2.2), and how meanings are fuzzy, i.e. cannot always be distinguished clearly (2.2.3).

## 2.2.1  Salience: Prototypical word senses and referents

In Chapter 1.3.1, it was shown that categories, e.g. the category "chair", have **prototypical** or central members and more marginal or peripheral members. This principle does not only apply to the members of a category, but also to the various senses of a word form. The question then is: How can we tell which sense of a word form like *fruit* is the most central? There are three interrelated ways that help us determine which sense of a word is the most central. In order to establish the **salience** of a sense, we can look at what particular sense comes to mind first, we can make a statistical count as to which use is the most frequent, or we can look at which sense is the more basic in its capacity to clarify the other senses.

When you hear someone say "I like fruit", probably the first thing that comes to everybody's mind, not only to the dictionary maker's, is the 'sweet and soft edible part' sense and not the archaic 'offspring' sense. The technical sense of 'seed-bearing part of a plant or tree' would not occur to us as immediately, unless we were talking about *fruit* in that sort of context. If you were to count the types of senses where a word like *fruit* is used in every-day language, you would probably discover that the 'edible part' sense is used far more frequently than the other senses. From this we may infer that the sense 'edible part' is much more central or salient in our conception of *fruit* than the 'seed-bearing part' sense and certainly more salient than the archaic 'offspring' sense. Another reason for regarding both the 'edible part' and also the 'seed-bearing part' sense as more central than the other senses is the fact that these senses are a good starting-point for describing the other senses of *fruit*. For example, suppose you don't know the expression *fruit of the womb*. This sense can be understood more easily through the central 'seed-bearing part' sense of *fruit* rather than the other way round. In other words, the most salient, basic senses are the centre of semantic cohesion in the category: They hold the category together by making the other senses accessible to our understanding.

Thus **centrality effects** or **prototypicality effects** mean that some elements in a category are far more conspicuous or salient, or more frequently used than others. Such prototypicality effects occur not only at the level of senses but also at the level of referents. As we saw earlier, *fruit* has many different referents. When Northern Europeans are asked to name fruits, they are more likely to name apples and oranges than avocados or pomegranates whereas Southern Europeans would name figs. Also, if we were to count the actual uses of words in a Northern European context, references to apples or oranges are likely to be more frequent than references to mangoes.

## 2.2.2 Links between word senses: Radial networks

The fact that some word senses are more salient and others more peripheral is not the only effect under consideration here. Word senses are also linked to one another in a systematic way through several cognitive processes so that they show an internally structured set of links. In order to analyze these links and the processes that bring them about, let us consider the senses of *school* in (3).

(3) *school*
   a. 'learning institution or building'   Is there a school nearby?
   b. 'lessons'   School begins at 9 a.m.
   c. 'pupils and/or staff of teachers'   The school is going to the British Museum tomorrow.
   We must hand in the geography project to the school in May.
   d. 'university faculty'   At 18 she went to law school.
   e. 'holiday course'   Where is the summer school on linguistics to be held?
   f. 'group of artists with similar style'   Van Gogh belongs to the Impressionist school.

| | | |
|---|---|---|
| g. | 'views shared by a group of people' | There are two schools of thought on drinking red wine with fish. |
| h. | 'a group of big fish swimming together' | A school of whales followed the boat. |

The first sense of *school* in (3a) is in fact not just 'learning institution', but it can also be the place or building where the learning institution is housed. Thus in the sentence *She left school at the age of 14*, the word *school* can only mean 'learning institution', but in *She left the school after 4 p.m.*, *school* can mean both, and in *The school was burned down* only the building is meant.

The last case in (3h) is a problem. As stated before (see definition of *homonymy*) there are, historically speaking, two words *school*. The senses in (3a–g) of *school* go back to a Latin word *schola;* the last meaning (3h) is not an extension of the other senses but it stems from a different word form, i.e. Old English *scolu* 'troup' and has its own development. Still, in the present use of the meaning of *school* as 'group of big fish', the language user appeals to folk etymology and may rather see this meaning as a metaphorical extension of the other senses. Accordingly we will treat the 'group of big fish' sense of *school* as a process of folk etymology, taking all the senses of this word to be related to each other.

So, these eight senses appear to form a cluster that is structured in the shape of a radial network, i.e. a centre with radii going in various directions. For the radial network representing the senses of *school* we find four main directions as represented in Table 3.

What are now the processes that constitute the links within this radial network? It is clear that the central meaning of *school* has to do with 'learning by a group of (young) people'. There are four different processes that allow us to focus on one or more components in this general category. The first is metonymy. In **metonymy** (from Greek *meta* 'change' and *onoma* 'name') the basic meaning of a word can be used for a part or the part for the whole. For instance, *school* as a 'learning institution for a group of people' allows us to focus upon each subset (the pupils, the staff) of this complex category and we can take the subset (e.g. the head of the school) for the whole category. In metonymy the semantic link between two or more senses of a word is based on a relationship of contiguity, i.e. between the whole of something, i.e. *school* as an "institution for learning in group" and a part of it, e.g., the lessons. In fact, the expression *the school* can metonymically stand for each of its components, i.e. the building itself, the lessons, the pupils, the staff, the headmaster etc. More generally, contiguity is the state of being in some sort of contact such as that between a part and a whole, a container and the contents, a place and its inhabitants, etc.

**Table 3.** Radial network of the senses of *school*

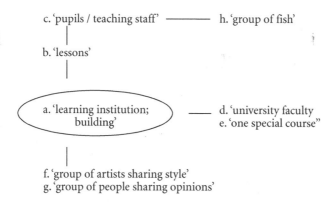

For example, in English and most languages we may say something like *He drank the whole bottle*. With such an expression we mean of course the contents in the bottle and not the bottle itself. Because the bottle and its contents are literally in contact with each other, this is considered a metonymic link. As we will see in Chapter 3.3, however, the concept of contiguity does not apply only to real physical or spatial contact, but also to more abstract associations such as time or cause.

The link which language users as folk etymologists make between the sense of *school* as a 'group of pupils/teaching staff' and its most peripheral sense as 'a group of fish swimming together' is based on the process of metaphor. Metaphor (from Greek *metapherein* 'carry over') is based on perceived similarity. Referring to the bottom part of a mountain as *the foot of the mountain* is based on a conceived similarity between the structure of the human body and a mountain and hence a transfer is made from the set-up of the human body to that of the environment. Even the interpretation of a homonym such as *school* in the sense of 'group of fish' can be related to the senses of *school* as 'group of pupils' and may thus be motivated by the relation of similarity which language users perceive between a group of pupils following a master and a group of fish swimming together and following a leader. But the similarity is completely in the eyes of the beholder: If he wants to see the similarity, it is there. But the link is never objectively given as in the case of metonymy, where the relation of contiguity always involves some objective link between the various senses of a word. In metaphor one of the basic senses of a form, the source domain, e.g. elements of the human body, is used to grasp or explain a sense in a different domain, e.g. the elements of a mountain, called the target domain.

The other senses of *school* are based on the processes of specialization and generalization. The process of specialization is found with the senses of *school* as in (3d) 'a university faculty' and (3e) 'one special course'. In a process of specialization the word's original meaning is always narrowed down to a smaller set of special referents. Thus from the general meaning of *school* as 'an institution for learning', English has narrowed the sense down to that of an 'academic unit for learning' (3d) and even further down to 'any specialized institution for learning one specific subject' as is usually the case in a summer school (3e), or a dance school, a language school, etc.

Another example of specialization is the English word *corn*, which was originally a cover-term for 'all kinds of grain'. Later it specialized to the most typical referent in various English-speaking countries such as 'wheat' in England, 'oats' in Scotland, and 'maize' in the USA. The word *queen* also went through a specialization process. Originally, it meant any 'wife or woman', but now it is highly restricted to only one type of wife as in 'king's wife' or 'female sovereign'. Each language abounds with cases of specialization. Thus *hound* now denotes 'a dog used in hunting', but it used to denote 'any kind of dog', like the German or Dutch words *Hund, hond* 'dog'. Similarly *deer* originally meant 'any animal' like German or Dutch *Tier, dier* 'animal', *fowl* meant 'any kind of bird' like German or Dutch *Vogel* 'bird', *to starve* meant 'any form or way of dying' like Dutch *sterven*, German *sterben* 'to die'.

The opposite of specialization is generalization, which we find in the senses of *school* as in (3f) 'group of artists' or (3g) 'group of people sharing opinions'. Here the meaning component of 'an institution for learning' has been broadened to that of 'any group of people mentally engaged upon shared activities or sharing views of style or opinions'. Some other examples of generalization are *moon* and *to arrive*. The word *moon* originally referred to the earth's satellite, but it is now applied to any planet's satellite. The verb *to arrive* used to mean 'to reach the river's shore' or 'to come to the river bank', but now it means 'to reach any destination'.

In summary (see Table 4), the different senses of a polysemous word like *school* form a cluster of senses which are interrelated through different links: metonymy, metaphor, specialization and generalization. The various senses of a word are thus systematically linked to one another by means of different paths. Together, the relations between these senses form a radial set as shown in Table 3, starting from a central (set of) sense(s) and developing into the different directions. In addition, Table 4 offers a survey of the possible processes that have led to the meaning extensions of *school*.

Table 4. Processes of meaning extension of *school*

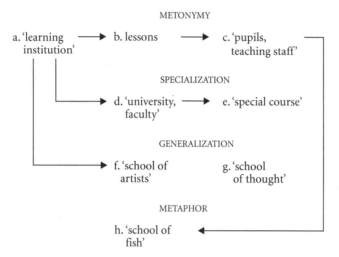

## 2.2.3 Fuzziness in conceptual categories and word senses

So far we have talked about the senses of a word as if they are clearly separate from each other. But we saw in Chapter 1 that meanings reflect conceptual categories. Categories may have clear centres, but their boundaries may not be clear-cut, and categories may overlap. As already discussed in Chapter 1.3.1, this phenomenon is called fuzziness, i.e. the boundaries of any category may be unclear or fuzzy. Since senses symbolize conceptual categories, it is no surprise that they cannot be defined in such a way that they include all the referents that should be included and exclude those that do not belong to the category. As an illustration, let us consider the question whether the central sense of *fruit* can be delimited in a straightforward fashion. Such a delimitation would take the form of a classical definition, a definition that lists all the necessary and sufficient conditions for something to be a member of a category. Such a classical definition is possible for any mathematical category, e.g. the category of "triangle", which is defined as 'a flat shape with three straight sides and three angles' (DCE). A condition is necessary in the sense of naming characteristics that are common to all triangles, and it is sufficient in the sense that it distinguishes a category, e.g. a triangle from any other category, e.g. a shape like ⌃⌄. This shape has three lines, but only two angles. So both elements "three lines" and "three angles" are necessary conditions, but at the same time also sufficient conditions: A flat shape with three lines and three angles can only be a triangle. But things are different with most natural categories.

If we try to give the necessary conditions or characteristics for *fruit*, characteristics such as *sweet, soft,* and *having seeds* may come to mind as good candidates. But these are not always necessary since lemons are not sweet, avocados are not necessarily soft, and bananas do not contain parts that are immediately recognizable as seeds. There are of course a number of characteristics that are necessary. All fruits "grow above the ground on plants or trees" rather than in the ground. They have "to ripen" before you can eat them, and if you want to prepare them rather than eat them raw, you would primarily use sugar, or at least use them in dishes that have a predominantly "sweet taste". Taken together, however, these obligatory features are not sufficient since they do not exclude almonds and other nuts or a vegetable like rhubarb, which grows above the ground and is usually cooked with sugar.

We must conclude, then, that the central sense of *fruit* cannot be defined in a classical sense, satisfying both necessary and sufficient conditions and covering all the eventualities of what speakers understand by *fruit*. However, this does not mean that our conceptualization of fruit, our mental picture of fruit, what we call to mind when we think of fruit, is necessarily fuzzy or ill-defined. It could very well be that the image that spontaneously comes to mind when we think of fruit is very clear-cut. Indeed, when we ask people to name a few examples of fruit, they will come up with very much the same list. But all the same, we also have to accept that such a mental image does not fit all fruits equally well.

## 2.3  From concepts to words: Onomasiology

Whereas semasiological analysis starts with a word and tries to discover the various senses it may have, onomasiological analysis starts from a given concept and investigates the words that are used to name that particular concept. What is the purpose of onomasiological analysis? First of all, it can help us find out where (new) lexical items come from and which mechanisms are used to introduce different words for the same concept into the vocabulary of a language. The main purpose of onomasiological analysis is to discover patterns in a group of conceptually related words, called a lexical field. A lexical field is a collection of words that all name things in the same conceptual domain. Thus words such as *breakfast, lunch* and *brunch* are related and belong to the same lexical field because they all name things in the domain of "meals". A conceptual domain, in its turn, can be defined as any coherent area of conceptualization, such as meals, space, smell, colour, articles of dress, the human body, the rules of football, etc., etc.

The question is: What is the position and status of single words in a lexical field delimited by a more general word like *meal*? Other typical examples of lexical fields are found in conceptual domains such as disease, travel, speed, games, knowledge, etc. As we will show in the next sections, the conceptual relations that occur between words in a lexical field are very analogous to those between the senses of a word identified in the section on semasiology: salience effects, links and fuzziness.

## 2.3.1 Salience in conceptual domains: Basic level terms

Just as there are **salience effects** in semasiology, which tell us which one of all the senses of a word or which one of the referents is thought of first and used most often, there are salience effects in onomasiology. For example, in a group of words like *animal, canine,* and *dog,* the hierarchical order goes from more general to more specific. If faced with something that barks at you, probably a word like *dog* would come to mind first. This would be one type of salience effect. Another type of salience effect may occur in a group of words that are at the same level of a hierarchy, such as *labrador, Alsatian, German shepherd,* and so on. Some names for dog breeds may occur more often than others. Both types of salience effects are discussed below.

According to anthropologist Brent Berlin, popular classifications of biological domains usually conform to a general organizational principle. Such classifications consist of at least three — for Berlin's investigation even five — levels, which go from very broad or **generic** to very narrow or **specific**. Thus in conceptual domains (see Table 5) with several levels, the most general category is at the highest level, and the most specific one is at the lowest level. A basic level term is a word which, amongst several other possibilities, is used most readily to refer to a given phenomenon. There are many indications that basic level terms are more salient than others. For example, while learning a language, young children tend to acquire basic level terms such as *tree, cow, horse, fish, skirt* before generic names like *plant, animal, garment, vehicle, fruit* or specific names such as *oak tree, labrador, jeans, sports car* and *Granny Smith*. From a linguistic point of view, basic level terms are usually short and morphologically simple. From a conceptual point of view, the basic level constitutes the level where salience effects are most outspoken. At the basic level category, individual members have the most in common with each other, and have the least in

**Table 5.** Folk classifications of conceptual domains

| Levels | Conceptual domains | | | | |
|---|---|---|---|---|---|
| *Generic level* | plant | animal | garment | vehicle | fruit |
| *Basic level* | tree | dog | trousers | car | apple |
| *Specific level* | oak tree | labrador | jeans | sports car | Granny Smith |

common with members of a related basic level category. In the domain of garment, items such as trousers, skirts, and coats may be considered basic level members. All members of the category "skirt" have in common that (1) they are normally restricted to female wearers, (2) they do not cover the legs separately, (3) they cover the body from the waist down, and (4) they usually are no shorter than the upper thighs. Features that "skirt" has in common with "trousers" or "sweater" are much more difficult to find. On the other hand, members of categories at the generic level such as *garment* have only one rather general characteristic in common: They all represent "a layer of clothing".

This basic level model is useful in that it predicts to a certain extent which level is the most salient in a folk classification. However, it cannot predict which term among the terms at the same level is preferred and used most often. Imagine you are looking at a magazine and you see a very short skirt with two loose front panels that are wrapped. Is it both a *wrap-over skirt* and a *miniskirt*? What are we most likely to call it? A detailed analysis of such terms has shown that fashion journalists prefer the term *miniskirt* in such a case. If there are several equally descriptive terms at one level, what criteria are applied in the choice of one term over another? (See Figure 2.)

We can explain this fact with the notion of entrenchment. This concept was first introduced by Ronald Langacker to explain how new expressions may be formed and then remain deeply rooted in the language. For example, in the past the two words *by* and *cause* formed the new compound *because*. This newly formed compound was used so often that people were no longer aware of its origin. In other words, a word group may develop into a regular expression, until it is so firmly entrenched in the lexicon that it has become a regular, well-established word in the linguistic system. A similar process may apply to the choice of one particular member of a category rather than the other. The name *miniskirt* is highly entrenched since it is used much more often than the name *wrap-over skirt* or another more general or more specific name.

| wrap-over skirt | pleated skirt | miniskirt | culottes |

**Figure 2.** Some women's garments

## 2.3.2 Links in conceptual domains: Taxonomies

In Section 2.2.2 on the links between the senses of a word (semasiology), we saw that words may develop new senses through the processes of metonymy, metaphor, specialization, and generalization. These processes may also be applied in onomasiology. As we saw earlier, onomasiology deals with the relations among the names we give to categories. These categories, in turn, are not just there in isolation, but they belong together according to a given conceptual domain.

Within a conceptual domain, we not only find a distinction between a generic level, a basic level and a specific level, as illustrated in Table 5, but these levels may also form a **hierarchical taxonomy,** as illustrated in Table 6. In a hierarchical taxonomy the higher level is the **superordinate level,** e.g. *vehicle,* which is a **hypernym** and subsumes all the concepts below it, e.g. *car.* But *car* is itself a superordinate category or hypernym, if compared with *sports car*, which is a **hyponym** of car. Thus Table 6 combines two things, i.e. a folk classification and a hierarchical taxonomy. A hierarchical taxonomy is also a special instance of a lexical field in that the lexical items are now hierarchically ordered. Thus in all cases of a lexical field, e.g. "article of dress", we can always distinguish between three hierarchical levels: Going up in the taxonomy is generalization, going down in the taxonomy is specialization. As the third group of words like

**Table 6.** Hierarchical taxonomy

LEVELS

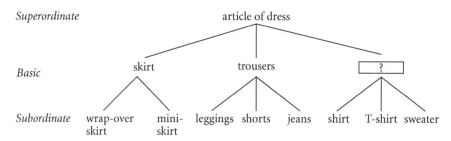

*shirt*, *T-shirt*, *sweater*, etc. shows, in a number of cases there may be a **lexical gap**, i.e. there is no basic level term available where we might expect one.

Other links between conceptual domains are made by means of metaphor and metonymy. We often use a whole conceptual domain to structure our understanding of some other domain. Thus, in our anthropocentric drive, we have used the domains of the human body to structure our view of the parts of a mountain. The lower part of the mountain is the foot of the mountain, the higher curving part is its shoulder and the top of the mountain is, in many languages, seen as its "head" or "crown". Here the process of metaphorization does not just apply to a given sense of a word as was shown for *school* in the sense of 'a group of fish' in Table 3. In the case of mountain a whole conceptual domain such as the human body is used to structure another conceptual domain such as the shape of a mountain. George Lakoff, who recognized this thought process, calls this use of metaphor a **conceptual metaphor**. Our understanding of abstract, conceptual domains such as reasoning and emotions is particularly affected by many conceptual metaphors. Thus Lakoff proposes an underlying conceptual metaphor ARGUMENT IS WAR for all the concrete metaphors found in English to denote arguing, such as *to win or lose an argument, to give up an indefensible position, to attack someone's views*, and many more. Likewise, emotions are conceptualized as HEAT OF A FLUID IN A CONTAINER, so that we can *boil with anger*, or *make someone's blood boil, reach a boiling point,* or *explode.*

Just as a conceptual metaphor restructures a conceptual domain like mountains in terms of another conceptual domain such as the human body, a conceptual metonymy names one aspect or element in a conceptual domain while referring to some other element which is in a contiguity relation with it. The following instances are typical of conceptual metonymy.

(4)   Instances of conceptual metonymy
    a.   PERSON FOR HIS NAME:               *I'm* not in the telephone book.
    b.   POSSESSOR FOR POSSESSED:           *My* tyre is flat.
    c.   AUTHOR FOR BOOK:                   This year we read *Shakespeare*.
    d.   PLACE FOR PEOPLE:                  *My village* votes Labour.
    e.   PRODUCER FOR PRODUCT:              My new *Macintosh* is superb.
    f.   CONTAINER FOR CONTAINED:           This is an excellent *dish*.

In each of these instances, the thing itself could be named. Thus in (4a) we could also say *My name is not in the telephone book*, in (4b) *The tyre of my car is flat*, in (4c) *This year we read a play by Shakespeare*, etc. By the use of the metonymical alternative, the speaker emphasizes the more salient rather than the specific factors in the things named.

Table 7 summarizes the conceptual relations we find in semasiological and onomasiological analyses. In both we discern hierarchical relations (from more salient to more specific), relations based on contiguity and relations based on similarity.

Table 7. Conceptual relations in semasiological and onomasiological analysis

| Conceptual relations | In semasiology (how senses of one word relate to each other) | In onomasiology (how concepts and words relate to each other) |
|---|---|---|
| 1. hierarchy (top/ bottom) | generalizing and specializing e.g. *school of artists* vs. *school of economics* | conceptual domain: Taxonomies (e.g. *animal, dog, labrador*) and lexical fields: e.g. *meals* |
| 2. contiguity (close to sth.) | metonymic extensions of senses (*school* as *institution* → *lessons* → *teaching staff*) | conceptual metonymy, e.g. CONTAINER FOR CONTAINED |
| 3. similarity (like sth.) | metaphorical extensions of senses (*win an argument*) | conceptual metaphor, e.g. ARGUMENT IS WAR |

## 2.3.3  Fuzziness in conceptual domains: Problematical taxonomies

In Section 2.2.3 we saw that whenever categorization of natural categories is involved, there is by definition some **fuzziness** at the category edges. Tomatoes, for example, can be categorized as either vegetables or fruit, depending on who is doing the categorizing. The same goes for the onomasiological domain.

For example, when we look at the basic level model introduced in 2.3.1, we might feel that if we "puzzle" long enough we will discover a clear, mosaic-like organization of the lexicon where each item has a clear "place" in a given taxonomy. However, there are several reasons to question this apparent neatness. For one thing, as Table 8 shows, there are problems of overlap in actual language data: Since shorts, jeans, and trousers are generally worn by both men and women, the taxonomy in Table 8 shows overlapping areas if women's and men's garment criteria are taken into account.

**Table 8.** Taxonomy with fuzzy areas

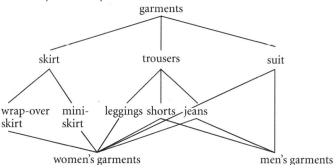

Another problem is that it is not always possible to decide exactly at which level one should place a lexical item in the hierarchy. A detailed analysis of clothing terms provided the following problem: At which level of the taxonomy in Table 8 would the item *culottes* (see Figure 2 on page 39) have to be placed? Is it a word at the more generalized, higher end of the taxonomy, alongside "trousers" and "skirt", that is, as a basic level term (Table 9a), or do *culottes* belong one level below these terms as a subordinate category, at the more specific level (Table 9b)?

**Table 9.** Culottes

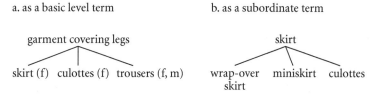

The fact that we cannot determine exactly at which level an item should be put relates to semasiological salience effects. As we saw earlier, those category members that are preferred and occur the most are the most salient. For example, words like *trousers* and *skirt* occur much more often than *culottes*. By nature, such salient category members are better category members than non-salient members. We may conclude that if it is unclear whether *culottes* are a pair of "trousers" or a "skirt", it is also unclear where to put it in the taxonomy. Different languages may even tend to classify the items differently. For example, the Dutch equivalent for culottes, i.e. *broekrok* (literally 'trouser skirt'), emphasizes the "skirt" aspect. The definition in the DCE for *culottes*, i.e. "women's trousers which stop at the knee and are shaped to look like a skirt", emphasizes the "trouser" part even more. From this viewpoint it would be at the same level as *leggings, shorts,* and *jeans* as represented in Table 8.

Also, contrary to what the basic level model might suggest, the lexicon cannot be represented as one single taxonomical tree with ever more detailed branchings of nodes. Instead, it is characterized by multiple, overlapping hierarchies. One could ask oneself, for instance, how an item like *woman's garment*, clothing typically or exclusively worn by women, would have to be included in a taxonomical model of the lexicon. As Table 8 shows, such a classification on the basis of sex does not work because some items may be worn by both men and women. Consequently, the taxonomical position of *woman's garment* itself is unclear because it cross-classifies with *skirt/trousers/suit*.

## 2.4  Conclusion: Interplay between semasiology and onomasiology

Up to now we have looked at semasiological and onomasiological matters from a theoretical point of view. To round off this chapter on lexicology, let us concentrate on meaning and naming with a more practical purpose, and ask ourselves the question "which factors determine our choice of a lexical item" or, in other words, "why does a speaker in a particular situation choose a particular name for a particular meaning". The basic principles of this "pragmatic" form of onomasiology are the following: The selection of a name for a referent is simultaneously determined by both semasiological and onomasiological salience. As we argued earlier, semasiological salience is determined by the degree to which a sense or a referent is considered prototypical for the category, and onomasiological salience is determined by the degree to which the name for a category is entrenched.

Semasiological salience implies that something is more readily named by a lexical item if it is a good example of the category represented by that item. Let's take motor vehicles as an example. Why do we in Europe call the recently issued type of motor vehicle like the Renault's *Espace*, which is somewhere between a van and a car, a *car* rather than a *van*. The preference for *car* as a name for these vehicles probably follows from the fact that — although they have characteristics of both vans and cars — they are still considered better examples of the category *car* because they are owned by individuals to transport persons. Typical European vans, on the other hand, transport goods. In other words, these vehicles are called *cars* because they are considered more similar to prototypical cars than vans. (Note that in the US, though, where these types of vehicles have been around longer and vans have been used as family vehicles, the name *mini-van* has become entrenched.)

Onomasiological salience may now be formulated as follows: A referent is preferably named by a lexical item *a* instead of *b* when *a* represents a more highly entrenched lexical category than *b*. So in the situation where our "mini-wrap-over skirt" is as much like a "wrap-over skirt" as a "miniskirt" — and there is no semasiological motivation for preferring one or the other category — the name *miniskirt* will still be chosen as a name for the hybrid skirt if *miniskirt* is a more highly entrenched word than *wrap-over skirt*.

In short, the choice for a lexical item as a name for a particular referent is determined both by semasiological and onomasiological salience. This recognition points the way towards a fully integrated conception of lexicology, in which both semasiological and onomasiological approaches are systematically combined.

## 2.5  Summary

We can see two almost opposite phenomena when studying words and their meanings. On the one hand, words are polysemous or have a number of different related senses. On the other hand, we use many different words, sometimes synonyms, but sometimes generic or specific words, to refer to the same thing, which is the referent. Such words are collected in a thesaurus. Next to relations of polysemy and synonymy, there is also antonymy and homonymy. The two basic approaches to the study of words and their senses or meanings are known as semasiology, and onomasiology, respectively. Although they are fundamentally different approaches to the study of the senses of words and the names of things, they are also highly comparable in that we find similar phenomena with respect to prototypicality or centrality effects, links between senses or words, and fuzziness.

Amongst the various senses of words, some are always more central or prototypical and other senses range over a continuum from less central to peripheral. The sense with the greatest saliency is the one that comes to mind first when we think of the meanings of a word. All the senses of a word are linked to each other in a radial network and based on cognitive processes such as metonymy, metaphor, generalization and specialization. In metonymy the link between two senses of a word is based on contiguity, in metaphor the link is based on similarity between two elements or situations belonging to different domains, i.e. a source domain, e.g. the human body, and the target domain, e.g. the lay-out of a mountain. The borders between senses within a radial network and especially between the peripheral senses of two networks such as *fruit* and *vegetable* are extremely fuzzy or unclear so that classical definitions of word meanings are bound to fail, except in highly specialized or "technical" definitions, in dictionaries.

Amongst the various words that we can use to name the same thing, we always find a prototypical name in the form of a basic level term such as *tree*, *trousers*, *car*, *apple*, *fish*, etc. Instead of a basic level term such as *trousers* or *skirt* we can also use superordinate terms such as *garment* or subordinate terms such as *jeans* or *miniskirt*, but such non-basic terms differ in that they are less "entrenched" in the speaker's mind. Entrenchment means that a form is deeply rooted in the language. If no word is available for a basic level category, we have a lexical gap. Words are linked together in lexical fields, which describe the important distinctions made in a given conceptual domain in a speech community. When a whole domain is mapped on to another domain, we have a conceptual metaphor; when part of a domain is taken for the whole domain or vice versa, we have a conceptual metonymy. Finally, it must be admitted that the hierarchical taxonomies in lexical items do not neatly add up to one great taxonomy of branching distinctions, but that fuzziness is never absent.

## 2.6 Further reading

The most accessible work on linguistic categorization and prototypes in semantics is Taylor (2003). The technical analysis of terms of clothing on which this chapter very strongly draws is Geeraerts, Grondelaers and Bakema (1994). Studies on basic level terms have been carried out by Berlin (1978), Berlin *et al.* (1974) for plants and Berlin and Kay (1969) for colour terms. Studies of metaphor and its impact on the extension of meanings are offered in Lakoff and Johnson (1980). Volumes grouping a large number of cognitive studies of metaphor and/or metonymy and their relevance for the lexicon are Panther and Radden (1999), Barcelona (2000), Dirven and Pörings (2002), Panther and

Thornburg (2003), and Ruiz de Mendoza (2003). A study of lexical relations, taxonomies, antonyms, etc. is Cruse (1986, 1991). A critical appraisal of the classical definition of word meaning in terms of "necessary and sufficient conditions" is offered in Geeraerts (1987), of prototypicality in Geeraerts (1988), and of fuzziness in Geeraerts (1993). Critical approaches to a number of cognitive insights in the lexicon such as polysemy, radial networks, relations between senses is Cuyckens, Dirven, and Taylor, eds. (2003). Lexical field studies are discussed in Lehrer (1974, 1990), Lehrer and Lehrer (1995). Generalization and specialization studies are found in Ullmann (1957).

## Assignments

1. From the large number of senses and contexts for the word "head" DCE mentions over sixty. We offer a small selection here:
   a. the top part of the body which has your eyes, mouth, brain, etc. *salient*
   b. the mind: *My head was full of strange thoughts.* *mytonmy*
   c. understanding: *This book goes over my head.* *metaphor*
   d. the leader or person in charge of a group: *We asked the head for permission.* *metonym*
   e. the top or front of something: *Write your name at the head of each page.*
   f. calm: *Keep one's head cool.* *mytonmy* *metaphor*
   g. (for) each person: *We paid ten pounds a head for the meal.* *mytonomy*

   Using Table 4 in this chapter as an example, explain what the processes of meaning extensions are for "head" and point out which of these meanings are metaphors and which are metonymies.

2. The following are some of the different senses of *skirt(s)* as adapted from the DCE dictionary item quoted below in (a–d) and extended by further contexts (e–i):
   a. A piece of outer clothing worn by women and girls which hangs down from the waist
   b. The part of a dress or coat that hangs down from the waist
   c. The flaps on a saddle that protect a rider's legs
   d. A circular flap as around the base of a hovercraft
   e. *A bit of skirt:* an offensive expression meaning 'an attractive woman'
   f. *Skirts of a forest, hill or village etc.:* the outside edge of a forest etc.
   g. *A new road skirting the suburb*
   h. *They skirted round the bus.*
   i. *He was skirting the issue* (= avoid).

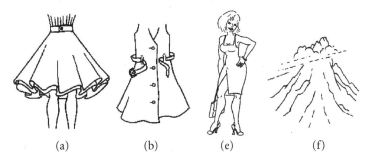

(a)                (b)                (e)                (f)

**Figure 3.** Some senses of *skirt*

    i.    What is likely to be the prototypical meaning and point out which process of meaning extension (generalization, metaphor, metonymy, specialization) you find in each of the other cases. Give reasons for your answers.

    ii.   How are the meanings in (f, g, h, i) related to the prototypical meaning? What is the difference between (f) versus (g, h, i)?

    iii.  Which of these meanings would lend themselves for a classical definition? Which of them would not? Give reasons for your answers.

    iv.  Draw up a radial network for the senses of *skirt*.

3.   Draw up a radial network for the different senses of *paper*.

    a.   The letter was written on good quality *paper*.

    b.   I need this quotation *on paper*.

    c.   The police officer asked to see my car *papers*.

    d.   The examination consisted of two 3 hour *papers*.

    e.   The professor is due to give his *paper* at 4 o'clock.

    f.   Seat sales are down, so we'll have to *paper* the house this afternoon. (Theatrical slang: 'to give away free tickets to fill the auditorium')

4.   The equivalents of the two first senses of English *fruit* in German and Dutch are expressed as two different words:

Fruit

    a.   sweet, soft and edible part of plant   = E. *fruit* G. *Obst*, D. *fruit*

    b.   seed-bearing part of plant or tree   = E. *fruit* G. *Frucht* D. *vrucht*

Which of these illustrates a semasiological solution, and which an onomasiological one for the same problem of categorization? Give reasons for your answer.

5.   In the thesaurus entry for *fruit* quoted in example (2) in this chapter we find the items *harvest* and *yield* both under the literal meanings of (2a) and under the figurative ones of (2b). Which of these can be related to *fruit* by the process of metonymy, and which by the process of metaphor? Give reasons for your answer.

6.  Below is a list of expressions with the word "red". In each case, try to find a plausible motivation for the use of the word and argue whether we have more to do with a "linguistic" metaphor or metonymy as with "school" (see Table 4) or more with a conceptual metaphor or metonymy as with "foot of the mountain" (see Section 2.3.2).

    a.  redhead (= someone with red hair)
    b.  red herring (= something that is not important, but distracts one from things that are important)
    c.  He was caught red-handed (= in the act of doing something wrong).
    d.  He was beginning to see red (= he was getting very angry).
    e.  This was a red-hot (= very exciting) project.
    f.  red politics (= extremely left-wing, communist ideas)

7.  For the notion of *footwear* think of or find as many words as you can, including such terms as *boots, slippers, trainers, pumps, flipflops, mountain boots, shoes, wellingtons* and add terms such as *indoor footwear, sportswear*, etc.

    a.  Which of these words are superordinate terms, and which ones subordinate terms?
    b.  Which of these words could be considered "basic level terms?" Give reasons for your answer.
    c.  Which of these words are highly entrenched, and which ones aren't? Give reasons for your answer.
    d.  For this set of words, draw up a hierarchical taxonomy as in Table 6 or Table 8 in this chapter.

8.  When young children first acquire language, they are known to call any male "dadda", any round object "apple", or any bigger animal "woof, woof" (BrE) or "bow bow" (AmE). Using the information given in Chapters 1 and 2, try to give an account for this phenomenon.

# 3 Meaningful building blocks
## Morphology

## 3.0 Overview

In Chapter 2, we saw that words or lexical items may have several, often related senses, forming a network. In Chapter 3 we will see that morphemes, the smallest meaningful elements in language, are like words in that they may have prototypical senses and peripheral senses, together forming a radial network of senses.

**Morphology** is the study of **morphemes**, i.e., building elements used to form composite words or grammatical units. In one sense, morphology can be defined as the study of the internal structure of composite words; in an other sense, as the study of the elements needed to consturct syntactic groups and sentences. A morpheme can be either a simple word or an affix. Simple words can occur on their own and thus are independent morphemes. For this reason they are called "free morphemes". In contrast, affixes cannot occur on their own and are therefore called "bound morphemes".

The formation of composite words is called **word formation**. The most important processes of word formation are compounding, e.g. *apple tree*, and derivation, e.g. *breathless*. Other processes of word formation are conversion (*clean* → *to clean*), backderivation (*typewriter* → *to typewrite*), blending (*motor* + *hotel* → *motel*), clipping (*a miniskirt* → *a mini*) and acronyms (*European Union* → *EU*).

Grammatical morphemes are used to link words in a grammatical unit. They function as building elements for syntactic groups (e.g. *many* books) or for sentence construction (e.g. *He* worked).

## 3.1  Introduction

After introducing the traditional distinctions made in morphology, we will look at factors that may play a role in word formation when we name things.

### 3.1.1  Two kinds of building blocks: Words and affixes

In Chapter 2 we concentrated on words. Now we will also look at elements which can be put on to words in order to build composite words such as *bookish* or in order to build grammatical units as in *(he) is coming*. It is convenient to have a common term for both a simple word form like *book* or *come* and for the affix *-ish* or the participial form *-ing* added to the verb. The term introduced for this purpose is **morpheme**, from Greek *morphè* 'form'. A morpheme is defined as the smallest meaningful unit in the language. We can distinguish between lexical morphemes, also called **lexemes**, and grammatical morphemes. We must further distinguish between **free morphemes** or simple words, and **bound morphemes** or affixes. They allow us to build composite words and composite grammatical units.

We will first look at the way words are composed from morphemes. Composite words can be formed in mainly two ways. We combine two "free" morphemes as in *fruit juice*, or we combine a "free" morpheme with a "bound" morpheme as in *fruitless*.

These two main ways of building composite words are known as compounding and derivation. In the simplest case, a **compound** consists of two free morphemes, whereas a **derivation** consists of a free morpheme and a bound morpheme (Table 1). Bound morphemes which are used to build derivations are called **derivational morphemes** and this branch of morphology is known as **derivational morphology**.

Table 1. Composite words

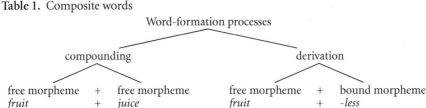

These two types of **word-formation processes** are not the only possibilities, of course. Different word-formation processes may be involved in forming one composite word. In the following examples, more complex types of composite words are analyzed by means of brackets (whereby m = morpheme) and by diagrams.

- *wheelchair patient*: (free m + free m) + free m

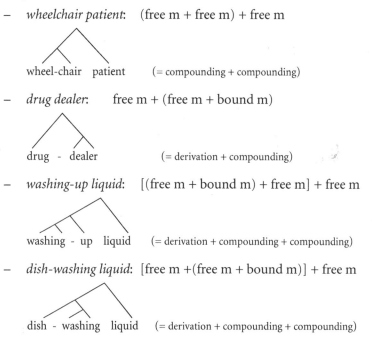

    wheel-chair   patient     (= compounding + compounding)

- *drug dealer*:    free m + (free m + bound m)

    drug  -  dealer     (= derivation + compounding)

- *washing-up liquid*:   [(free m + bound m) + free m] + free m

    washing - up   liquid   (= derivation + compounding + compounding)

- *dish-washing liquid*:  [free m +(free m + bound m)] + free m

    dish - washing   liquid   (= derivation + compounding + compounding)

In derivation some bound morphemes come after the free morpheme as in *fruitless*, some come before it as in **unkind**, and some even in the middle as in *speedometer*. The first type is called **suffix**, the second **prefix**, and the third **infix**; a cover term for the three forms is **affix** (from *to affix* 'to fasten, to stick together').

Morphology is not only operative in the lexicon but also in grammar. Thus the form for building the regular plural in English — the suffix *-s* — is a grammatical building element just like the *-y* in the derivation *fruity* is a lexical building element. At a more general level we call this plural *-s* the **plural morpheme**, which may have several different forms such as *-s* in *books*, *-en* in *oxen*, a change of the vowel as in *mouse* vs. *mice* or *goose* vs. *geese*. Morphemes such as the plural morpheme with nouns, or the present tense morpheme *-s* with verbs as in *he steps* or the past tense morpheme *-ed* as in *he stepped* are all grammatical morphemes.

Within **grammatical morphemes** we can also make a further distinction between two types: Free morphemes like the particle *to* in **to** *go* and bound morphemes like the 3rd person ending -s in *he likes*. Free grammatical morphemes are also referred to as **function words**. In a sense, they are less free than items such as *book* or *like*, which are known as **content words**. A function word and one or more content words can be linked together in a **syntactic group**, such as *a (very) (nice) present*.

Words combined with bound grammatical morphemes are referred to as **inflected forms** and constitute the part of morphology known as **inflection**. Therefore bound grammatical morphemes are also called **inflectional morphemes** and this branch of morphology is called **inflectional morphology**. The set of grammatical morphemes is summarized in Table 2.

Table 2. Types of grammatical morphemes

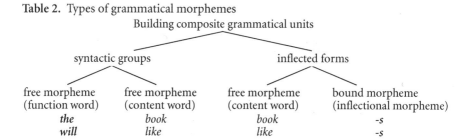

| free morpheme (function word) | free morpheme (content word) | free morpheme (content word) | bound morpheme (inflectional morpheme) |
|---|---|---|---|
| *the* | *book* | *book* | *-s* |
| *will* | *like* | *like* | *-s* |

### 3.1.2 Word formation and name-giving

We have now seen three different ways of forming new expressions for concepts: compounding, derivation, and syntactic grouping. This raises the question: Why is one name and not the other accepted in the language? There are several possibilities available and it can never be predicted which one will eventually be generally accepted. Let us look at a recent example.

The engineers in a big electronic firm are sitting around the table to discuss a new type of telephone not fixed to a plug which can be carried around. They might find all sorts of names for it like *mobile telephone, cellular telephone, pocket telephone, digital phone, portable phone*, etc. Each name reflects a different construal and highlights one salient aspect of the phone. In American English the name which has been accepted is based on the internal cellular system and it is called *a cellular phone, a cell phone*, or just — in its reduced form — *a cellular*. In British English the emphasis is placed on the movable quality of such a phone and it is called *a mobile phone*. In German, the "useful and simple to use" aspect is stressed and the device is named *ein Handy*, which is an instance of German word formation with English elements. In French its movability is stressed and it is called *un portable*. In Flemmish it is called *een gsm* (an acronym standing for 'global system for mobile communication') and in Dutch *een mobiel*. The word *portable* also exists as an older French loan-word in English, but it is nearly always associated with a television set as illustrated in (1).

(1)  We swapped our colour television, and bought a black and white *portable.*

When a name like *portable TV* has been around for some time, it becomes entrenched and accepted. Part of it may even be clipped, so that *portable* stands for the whole concept and is no longer available for a new concept, at least not in English.

As Dutch shows, acceptability of new composite words differs not only across languages, but also across varieties of the same language. In both British English (BrE) and American English (AmE), *car* refers to a vehicle with a fuel engine. However, *car* is more usual in BrE than in AmE, where the general name *automobile* or specific names such as *sedan* or *convertible* are frequently used. A place to park a car in BrE is *a car park*, in AmE *a parking lot* if outside, or *a parking garage* if it is an enclosed building. Obviously, the choice of a new composite word or expression for the many new things in our cultures is the result of an "onomasiological struggle", something which is also present in the way British and American English differ in the naming of kitchen gadgets.

(2)  *BrE*                          *AmE*

    oven                          cooker

    tap                           faucet (*loan from older French*)

    washing-up liquid             dish-washing liquid

    tin-opener                    can-opener (*from Dutch* kan)

    cutlery                       silverware

    fish-slice                    spatula (*loan from Spanish*)

    (electric) ring               burner (*warning lamp on fridge*)

    bin                           waste-basket

    tea-towel                     dishcloth

As the etymological origin of some American English items shows, name-giving in American English reflects to some extent the multicultural composition of the American population and the diverse onomasiological resources of American English. The study of name-giving or onomasiology is therefore closely linked to the culture prevailing within a given variety of a language and this is even more apparent if we look at different languages. Summarizing the various onomasiological possibilities of English, we have now encountered six types of name-giving, as shown in Table 3, where a number of the items of (2) are listed in six different classes.

**Table 3.** Various types of lexical forms

| a. simple words | b. compounds | c. derivations | d. complex types | e. syntactic groups | f. others, e.g. acronym |
|---|---|---|---|---|---|
| oven | silverware | cooker | dish-washer | electric ring | gsm |
| tap | fish-slice | cutlery | parking lot | | |
| bin | tea-towel | burner | tin-opener | | |

In the following sections, we will first investigate the two main types of word formation: compounding (3.2), and derivation (3.3). We will then look at other types of word formation (3.4), and finally at grammatical morphemes (3.5). In each section we will also consider the different senses morphemes may have and what roles they may play in naming things.

## 3.2  Compounding

After looking at the different patterns of compounds and analyzing the distinction between compounds and syntactic groups, we will look at the types of compounds that get accepted and the functions compounding has.

### 3.2.1  Basic patterns of compounds

Compounds have highly strict patterning. The first element in the compound receives the main stress, but it is generally the second element that determines the compound's new word class. Thus in *blackbird* the second element (*bird*) is a noun and the compound as a whole remains a noun. This element is called the **head** of the compound. The head of a compound belongs to one of the three major word classes: noun, verb, or adjective. The first element can also be any one of these three. Thus we have three patterns of compounds, each with three members.

(3)  Noun compounds
   a.  *noun + noun*      =    kitchen chair, wheel-chair
   b.  *verb + noun*      =    rocking chair, swivel chair
   c.  *adjective + noun*   =    highchair, easy chair

The meanings of these **noun compounds** are to some extent dependent on the basic meanings of the three word classes. As discussed in Ch. 1.3.2 nouns tend to denote time-stable things, whereas verbs denote a class of non-stable, temporal relations and adjectives tend to go either way. But to a very large extent, compounds result from a process of **conceptual blending.** In such a process elements from two concepts are selected and "blended" into a new, more complex concept. At this point, it is appropriate to introduce the notion of **frame**. By *frame* we understand all the elements that constitute a given concept. Thus the kitchen frame comprises utilities for cooking, washing up, eating, sitting down, etc. Part of the kitchen frame is its furniture, e.g. a chair. In its turn, the chair frame comprises ways of sitting defined by various domains, e.g. eating, taking a nap, working, etc.

Thus a *kitchen chair* is a blend of the chair frame and the working domain, i.e. it is typically designed and used for kitchen activities, hence solid and not particularly comfortable; a *rocking chair* is a blend between the chair frame and tho domain of resting, by the fact that it can rock up and down, it helps to bring about the nap; a *highchair* is a more complex blend, because the chair frame and the eating domain frame offer too little input to explain the meaning of this blend so that we must assume that in this blend new elements are generated, i.e. a special construction raised high enough for the baby to sit safely at the height of the table level.

Two of the most common elements chosen from the conceptual domains that enter a blend are those of provenance, i.e. where something comes from or what it is made of as in (4a,b), or of purpose , i.e. the activity it is mase for as in (4c–e).

(4)  a.  leather shoes      'shoes made of leather'
     b.  alligator shoes    'shoes made of alligator skin'
     c.  tennis shoes       'shoes to be used for tennis'
     d.  horse shoes        'metal protection for horse hoofs'
     e.  snow shoes         'wooden frames for walking in snow'

Our cultural knowledge, that is, our knowledge of frames and domains, determines the way in which we interpret such compounds. Since the frame of alligators tells us we cannot have a dressing domain (they don't wear shoes), it is most likely to be the "provenance" relation but not of the alligator as a whole, but of one element in the alligator frame only, i.e. its skin. In *tennis shoes* the purpose domain is clear. In *horse shoes* and *snow shoes* the purpose relation is self-imposing, too. There we have the elements of protecting or supporting for the feet: These the only elements that fit into the 'horse' frame and the 'snow' frame, respectively. As a consequence of this conceptual blending, the words that enter the compounding process do not necessarily keep their original meaning, but may undergo widening (generalization) or narrowing (specialization).

Since verbs and adjectives denote relations, the blends in these compounds are more straightforward because the kind of relation is overtly expressed.

(5)  Verb compounds
a.  *noun + verb*        = to vacuum-clean, to manhandle
b.  *verb + verb*        = to sleep-walk, to blow-dry
c.  *adjective + verb*   = to dry-clean, to highlight

**Verb compounds** usually denote an event in the head of the compound, and the first element in the blend suggests the instruments with which, or circumstances in which the event takes place: In (5a) we have an instrumental interpretation, in (5b) a circumstantial one (*you walk in your sleep*) and in (5c) again an instrumental one (*you clean something by blowing it dry*).

(6)  Adjective compounds
a.  *noun + adjective*       = colour-blind, duty-free
b.  *verb + adjective*       = soaking wet, stinking rich
c.  *adjective + adjective*  = dark-blue, pale yellow

Here the head of the **adjective compound** is further specified by the first element. The noun in (6a) denotes the area or field to which the adjective as the head applies. The verb denotes the degree (6b) to which the property holds and therefore means "very". The adjective in (6c) denotes a shade in the property denoted by the head element: The blue can be very dark or move towards the light end of the spectrum.

### 3.2.2  Compound versus syntactic group

A **syntactic group**, also called a **phrase,** is a composite syntactic unit such as *a black bird*, which is a **noun phrase** and consists of a determiner, an adjective, and a noun. The phonological difference with a compound like *blackbird* is that a compound has one main stress, usually on the first element, whereas a syntactic group like *a black bird* has two stresses: Primary or main stress (´) and secondary stress (`), and the main stress of these two is on the second element. Compare:

| (7) | *Compound* | | (8) | *Syntactic group* |
|-----|------------|---|-----|-------------------|
| a. | a ´blackbird | | a. | a `black ´bird |
| b. | a ´paper basket | | b. | a `paper ´basket |
| c. | an ´atom bomb | | c. | an a`tomic ´bomb |
| d. | ´small talk | | d. | a `small ´talk |

This phonological difference is accompanied by a fundamental difference in meaning. Compounds have meanings of their own: The sum of the meanings of the composing elements is not equal to the meaning of the compound. A blackbird need not necessarily be black, but might in the imagination of a speaker be any colour so that we could even have "a brown blackbird". Actually, we do talk of *brown blackbirds*, which are in fact the females of the species. In other words, in (7a) we only mean one kind of bird, but in (8a) we may mean any kind of bird that is black. Also in (7b) and (8b) this difference is very outspoken: A ´*paper basket* is a basket in which to throw used paper, but a `*paper ´basket* is any basket made of paper. In some cases there is no difference as in (7c) and (8c). On the whole, compounds are like simple words, but in spite of their idiosyncratic meaning, the meaning of a compound is to a large extent transparent.

Some compounds such as *cranberry* or *daisy*, however, are no longer transparent or analyzable. They are therefore called **darkened compounds**. In the example *cranberry* the first element *cran* does not evoke any meaning although it is etymologically relatable to the name of a bird, i.e. *crane*. Sometimes we do not even realize that a word was originally a compound as in *daisy*, which derives from the "day's eye", i.e. a flower opening up early in the morning, or in *window*, derived from *wind* and *auge* 'eye', i.e. "the eye (in the wall, like an eye in the face) for the wind to fan". What such darkened compounds show is that during the course of time a compound gets "entrenched" so deeply in the language that it is no longer analyzed and not felt to be different from a simple word any longer.

We can conclude that there are different degrees of transparency and productivity with compounds. At the fully **productive** end of the continuum, compounds are not only very easy to produce and hence so frequent, but they are also transparent as already discussed in Chapter 1.2.3. Compounds are fully transparent if both component parts and the link between them are unequivo-cally analyzable and hence immediately transparent, e.g. *apple tree*. They are partially transparent if the component parts are analyzable, but the link between them is insufficient to see which subcategory is meant as in *blackbird*. This name could also have been given to a different species of bird. Compounds are no longer transparent if metonymical or metaphorical processes are involved as in *red tape*. This noun compound does not describe a type of tape but 'obstruc-tive official routine or bureaucracy'. It derives metonymically and metaphori-cally from something most people have never seen, i.e. the pinkish red tape used to bind official documents.

### 3.2.3  The role of compounds in naming things

Compounds play a major role in developing taxonomies in the lexicon. As discussed in Chapter 2.3 taxonomies contain basic level terms with, above them, superordinate terms, and, beneath them, subordinate terms. It is the main function of a compound to "name" a subordinate category of a given type. Thus, as discussed in Chapter 2, *a sports car* is a subtype of a *car*, *a miniskirt* a subtype of a *skirt*, and *a minivan* a subtype of a *van* (at least in American English). When a new type of road for (motor)cars was built without normal level crossings, a new name, i.e. *motorway* (BrE), or an existing word, *highway* (AmE), was applied to it.

The large number of composite words are needed to name new subcatego-ries and to show the relation between these new hyponyms and their hypernyms as in the pair *motorway/highway* and *way*. If we invented a new simple form for each conceptual subcategory, we would overburden our memory capacity and no longer have a clearly hierarchically structured lexicon. It would become almost impossible to name the thousands of phenomena that arise every year. For instance, a printed newspaper used to be our only access to news, but we can now read an *electronic journal* on a *website*, on the *internet*. We do not have to send letters by *surface mail*, but can send them by *electronic mail* or *e-mail* as it is commonly abbreviated. Communication and transfer of information is now being compared to the fast-moving conveyance of people and goods via the highway system. In analogy to this system, we refer to the electronic communication system by means of the double compound *information highway*.

Such compounds are easily analyzable on the basis of three facts: We understand the composing elements *information* and *highway*, we "see" that they are composed using familiar word classes (adjective plus noun in *highway*); we interpret the metaphorical meaning of *highway* by blending elements from the traffic frame as the source domain with elements from the information frame as the target domain; and as native speakers of a language and members of a cultural community we know the cultural background to which the complex word refers. That is, we draw upon the building rules in word formation, upon general cognitive strategies such as knowledge of conceptual frames, command of conceptual blending, and metaphor, and upon our cultural knowledge of our material and non-material environment.

## 3.3 Derivation

In this section, after looking at the two different types of affixes that may occur, we will see how affixes may develop from words. Then we will look at the related senses some morphemes may have and the "generalization" function affixes may have. Finally we will look at the subtypes of affixes.

### 3.3.1 Derivational versus inflectional affixes

Whereas a compound in its simplest form consists of two free morphemes, a derivation consists of a free morpheme and one or more bound morphemes, called affixes. In order to distinguish between affixes in derivations and in grammar, we speak — as already said before — of **derivational affixes**, used in order to form derived words, and of **inflectional affixes**, used to form grammatical constructions. An affix is added to what is called a **word stem** or free morpheme. The notion of "word stem" is especially clear in languages with declensions like Latin. Here we find two forms for *heart*, i.e. the nominative form *cor* and the inflected forms *cordis, corde, corda*. So the stem cannot be *cor*, but rather *cord-*, to which a suffix can be added, as is still visible in the English loan-word *cordial*. In a derivation, then, a stem is combined with an affix to form a composite word.

The important difference between derivational affixes and inflectional affixes is that the former are always restricted in their application to a certain group of word stems, whereas inflectional affixes can be applied to all the members of a given linguistic category. Whereas all countable nouns can have a plural affix, not all nouns take the adjective suffix *-ful*, and certainly not *-less*. We can say *beautiful*, but not *\*beautiless*. One of the main reasons why we often do not form a derivation is that there is no conceptual need to do so. If we already have the word *ugly* there is no need to form words such as *beautiless*; or if we already have *hormone-free,* we do not normally form *hormoneless.*

### 3.3.2 Where do affixes come from? Grammaticalization

Where do derivational affixes like *-ful, -less, -ship,* and *-ly* come from? Affixes like these have come from full words (free morphemes) and gradually changed into affixes (bound morphemes). This process is called grammaticalization. **Grammaticalization** is a process whereby a once free morpheme acquires the function of an affix or grammatical morpheme, either in the lexicon or in syntax (i.e. grammar), e.g. the verb *go* has developed a use with future meaning in *It is going to rain.*

Similarly, in *careful, beautiful,* or *wonderful* the suffix *-ful* originates from the adjective *full,* which was first used in compounds such as *mouthful, spoonful,* etc. As a suffix, the form *-ful* has gradually acquired the more generalized and abstract meaning of "possessing some value to a very high degree". This explains why derivations with the suffix *-ful* now tend to be restricted to abstract stems and produce adjectives such as *careful, hopeful, trustful, beautiful, aweful, hateful,* and *regretful.* The affix *-ful* is the opposite of *-less,* which goes back to Old English *leas* 'without'. Compare *careful/careless, hopeful/hopeless, merciful/merciless.*

Affixes such as *-ful* and *-less* are still transparent, but in most cases affixes have grammaticized to such an extent that their origin is no longer understandable with the result that most affixes are no longer transparent. Thus, for instance, the suffix *-ship* in *hardship, craftmanship, friendship* is related to an old Germanic form *skap* 'to create' (which is related to modern English *shape* and German *schöpfen* 'create') and denotes "the state or condition of being so and so"; added to nouns, *-ship* denotes the state, quality or condition of what the noun denotes, i.e. being a craftsman or a friend.

A similarly complicated grammaticalization process occurred with the English adverb suffix *-ly* in *beautifully.* This suffix derives from ME *-lich,* OE *-lic,* which means "body" as in present-day Dutch *lichaam* or in German *Leichnam* 'body'. As a suffix *-lic* meant something like "in a manner characteristic of some person or thing" and was later generalized to mean 'manner' in general.

### 3.3.3  Meaning and productivity of affixes

If we take a prefix like *un-* and a random number of adjectives, we would get the following theoretically possible words with *un-*: *unfair, unred, unripe, unselfish, unempty*, etc. The question is: What is the difference between all these composite forms and the negations *not red, not ripe, not selfish*, etc.? In order to explain why the over two thousand derivations with *un-* have become accepted, and why others have not and probably never will, we must take into account the general meaning of the affix *un-*; only then can we explain where it is productive and where it is not. We can formulate the meaning of *un-* as in (9), in which A stands for adjective.

(9)  [*un-* + A] — "lacking the property of A, even implying its opposite"

This means that a composite form like *unfair* not only means 'not fair', but at a more general level also 'not giving a fair or equal opportunity' as in *an unfair advantage* (DCE) and even 'illegal' as in *an unfair dismissal*. As a general principle of the acceptability of derivations, we can state the following rule: An affix will only be applied to a particular word form if its abstract, generalized sense is compatible with any of the senses of the word stem. This principle explains the use of *unfair, unripe* and *unselfish*: They all denote the lack of the properties in question.

The same argument holds for adjectives in *-able*. In contrast with *drinkable* or *realizable*, a lot of theoretically possible forms with *-able* are unusual or strange: *buyable, cuttable, paintable, sayable, writable, stealable*. The meaning of the suffix *-able* is not only "something that can be V-ed", but it is again more general as the following paraphrase may suggest:

(10)  [V + *-able*] — "having the inherent capacity of being V-ed"

Since most things do not have inherent properties that make it possible to *buy* or to *cut* or to *paint* them, their derived forms with *-able* are not likely to occur. But in combination with the generalizing prefix *un-*, this construal becomes much more possible e.g. *unbuyable paintings* or *uncuttable meat*. Here again we are dealing with time-stable, salient properties, since the permanent absence of a given property is denoted.

It is also the general characterization of "having the inherent capacity" that makes less prototypical derivations without a passive meaning possible, e.g. *knowledgeable* 'knowing a lot, and hence being able to give information'.

In the same way that word stems have prototypical or more central senses, affixes also have senses or uses that are more prototypical and others that are more peripheral. This typically applies to the highly productive agentive suffix *-er* as in *killer*, which has various meanings. Historically, it means, if attached to a noun, a relation of a human person to a certain locality as in *Londoner, villager, southerner, prisoner, foreigner, stranger*. When the *-er* suffix is attached to verb stems it becomes extremely productive and denotes a human agent as in *singer, teacher, learner, hairdresser, worker*, etc. Here *-er* does not mean 'someone who happens to be singing, teaching or learning', but rather something like (11), in which $V_{human}$ means a verb with a human subject.

(11)    $[V_{human} + \textit{-er}]$ — "someone who regularly or by profession V-es"

Thus *a speaker* is not just "someone who engages upon talking" but someone who in a given process of interaction regularly assumes the role of a speaker or someone who speaks on behalf of a group, etc. It evokes a wider scene in human interaction so that words like *buyer* assume a more general meaning than someone who buys one item at one particular moment.

The agentive meaning of *-er* can also be extended to non-human forces and we then have an instrumental meaning as in *an eraser, a sharpener, an opener* or instrumental appliances using electric force such as *a cooker, a burner, a dish washer*. This can be paraphrased as in (12), where $V_{object}$ is a verb with a non-human subject.

(12)    $[V_{object} + \textit{-er}]$ — "something having the capacity or force to V"

This paraphrase is wide enough to account for more metonymical or metaphorical extensions of *-er* as in a *best-seller* or an *eye-opener*.

The different senses of the suffix *-er* may be seen in two different ways: Either as the meanings of different morphemes or else as being so closely interrelated that they form senses of one morpheme and can be represented in a radial network as in Table 4.

We can even go a step further and subsume the various meanings of the English suffix *-er* in its productive use under one very abstract characterization as in (13).

(13)    $[V + \textit{-er}]$ — "a human being or other force that is functionally linked to the event of V"

Such a general abstract characterization of all the meanings of a morpheme in (13) is called a **schema**. A schema is so abstract that it can subsume all the single meanings of a morpheme. The schematic characterization in (13) may also

**Table 4.** Radial network of the *-er* suffix

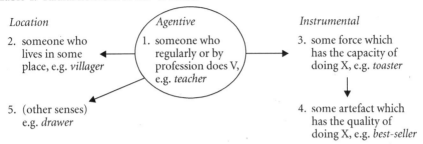

| Location | Agentive | Instrumental |
|---|---|---|
| 2. someone who lives in some place, e.g. *villager* | 1. someone who regularly or by profession does V, e.g. *teacher* | 3. some force which has the capacity of doing X, e.g. *toaster* |
| 5. (other senses) e.g. *drawer* | | 4. some artefact which has the quality of doing X, e.g. *best-seller* |

explain why we have no regular derivations like *hammerer* in the sense of 'someone who is hammering a box' nor *joiner* in the sense of 'someone who joins a group', nor *ice-cream eater*, since all these derivations do not denote functional performers of the actions or states denoted by the verb.

### 3.3.4 Subtypes of affixes and new affix-like forms

The two main types of affixes in English are suffixes and prefixes whereas infixes and even circumfixes occasionally occur. English is not an infix-using language in the same way as, for instance, Latin, which exploits the infix *-n-* for oppositions between present tenses as in *vincit* 'he conquers' vs. perfect *vicit* 'he has conquered'. However, in recent years English has also developed a kind of form with infix-like character, i.e. *-o-* in *speedometer*. In words like *thermodynamics* the stress is on the first syllable of *thermo*, but in *thermómeter*, the main stress of the composite word is on the second syllable so that the *-o-* is very salient. This stressed *-o-* has now been "reanalyzed" as part of the second element, i.e. *-ometer* so that *-o-* can now be seen as a kind of infix in words that originally had no *-o-* as in *speedómeter*, *mileómeter* (BrE), *odómeter* (AmE). Recently in the context of breeding live stock for producing meat with pigs and animals other than cattle, *beefómeter* has also occurred. However, the infix *-o-* cannot be associated with any particular meaning and, hence, may not claim to be seen as a morpheme.

   In line with this new tendency for creating infix-like elements we also see slang words like *blood(y)*, or *fucking* assume infix-like functions as in *fan-bloody-tastic*, *a-bloody-mazing*, *hoo-bloody-ray* or *kanga-fucking-roo*. The tendency to create new forms from existing forms in the use of new affixes also shows up in such words as *laundromat* from *automat* or *washeteria* from *cafeteria*, *irangate* or *chinagate* from *watergate*. Here *Watergate* first was the place of criminal action by the Nixon presidential team in the USA. The ending

*-gate* has now become a kind of new suffix indicating 'criminal political action' and can now be attached to the name of any suspect political affair as in the Clinton accusations of *zippergate.*

A **circumfix** is an affix that envelopes a word at both ends. It is typically found in German and Dutch past participles of verbs, e.g. *kaufen* 'to buy' has the past participle *ge-kauf-t* 'bought'. English has occasional examples in the older form *aworking.*

### 3.4 Other word-formation processes

Compounding and derivation are the two main word-formation processes in English. More restricted processes of word formation are conversion (*clean* ⟹ *to clean*), back derivation (*television* ⟹ to *televize*), lexical blending (<u>br</u>eakfast + lunch ⟹ *br*<u>unch</u>), clipping (*advertizement* ⟹ *ad*) and acronym (*United Kingdom* ⟹ *UK*). All these processes have in common that they do not create longer forms but predominantly reduce existing forms into shorter ones.

A **conversion** is a special case of derivational morphology: Instead of adding an affix to a stem, the stem takes a **zero form,** i.e. one that is present, but not perceptible as in a *bank* (noun), which by adding the verb class status to it becomes *to bank.*

Conceptually, each conversion process implies a metonymical extension from one element in an event to the whole event: Thus in *to bank* the place where the transaction takes place, i.e. the bank, comes to stand for the whole of the transaction. In an example such as *to nail the carpet* the conversion process picks one essential element in the event, i.e. the nails, and names the whole event of fixing the carpet by highlighting the instruments used for it. The same instrumental metonymy occurs in *to shampoo one's hair.* In such instrumental verbs the exact relation between the action, the instrument and the object is not named, but only implied: From our cultural knowledge we know that we "hammer" or "shoot" nails into surfaces and "rub" the shampoo on our hair to wash it.

In a conversion we therefore usually, though not always, find a specialization process. In *to author* the meaning in AmE is limited to "writing movie scripts"; a *carpool* is a group of people who agree to drive everyone in the group to work or school etc., but *to carpool* (AmE) only denotes the driving to work together; *to onion* is a manner verb and transfers the way we cut onions into slices to other items so that we can *onion* a hamburger or sausages.

**Backderivation** is another derivation process; as the name might wrongly suggest, it does not mean that we just go back to an earlier form but it means that we derive a new word from an earlier more complex form: Thus from *stage-manager* [noun + (composite noun (verb + suffix))], we derive a simpler form *to stage-manage*, which looks like a compound, but which is in fact a conversion from a more complex noun to a less complex verb. The meaning of a backderivation is often far more general than that of its source: Whereas a *stage-manager* is someone who is in charge of a theatre stage during a performance, *to stage-manage* means "to organize any public event, such as a press-conference", e.g. *The press-conference was cleverly stage-managed.* Similarly we have backderivation from the noun *intuition* to the verb *to intuit (Somehow a baby must intuit the correct meaning of a word)*, from *burglar* to *burgle (My house has been burgled)*, from *intermission* (AmE for 'a short break between the parts of a play or a concert') to the verb *to intermit*, and from *opinion, television,* and *typewriter* to the verbs *to opine, to televize,* and *to typewrite.*

**Clippings** are forms from which a part has been cut off. They are not always semantic innovations, but often purely formal phenomena. Many are as old as 16th century English, when many words were borrowed from Latin. Who would guess that *sport* was originally *disport* meaning 'to amuse, recreate (oneself)?' Similarly, many other words in English no longer feel like clippings, but as the normal word form. Thus *fridge* is derived from *refrigerator* and *pram* from *perambulator*. A more transparent form is *telly* from *television*. Whereas in *television* the last part has been clipped, in *telephone* the first part has gone, so that we have *the phone* and *to phone*. A big modern city is, with a Greek loan word, also called *a metropolis*; the underground railway or tramway system in a metropolis is metonymically either called *the metro* or the *underground*: The first is the clipping of a word, the second is the clipping of a whole phrase, i.e. the *underground railway system.*

**Lexical blending** is a special case of conceptual blending. In the process of lexical blending, not only various elements from two conceptual frames are blended, but also elements from the phonological strings symbolizing those concepts, e.g., from *breakfast* and *lunch*, yielding the phonological blend as a new form, i.e. *brunch*. That this process is not just a process of formal blending, but one of conceptual blending is typically shown by the German blending *Jein,* which blends *ja* 'yes' and *nein* 'no' into an answer which in other languages is expressed by the phrase *yes and no* and suggests that the question is to be answered both affirmatively and negatively. Similarly, *brunch* is 'a meal eaten in the late morning, combining elements from the breakfast frame and the lunch frame.

Similar conceptual and formal blendings are found in *workaholic*, for someone addicted to his work in the same way an alcoholic is addicted to alcohol. The conceptual blending is one between the notion of being addicted (*-aholic*) and the target area of the addiction, i.e. *work*. Another example is *chocaholic*, 'someone addicted to chocolate' or *sexaholic*. Other examples are *motel* (hotel for the motorcar driver), *infotainment* or *edutainment* (television programmes halfway between information or education and entertainment), *Chunnel* (tunnel under the Channel), *sexploitation* (exploitation of sex instincts), *swimathon* (the marathon length of this activity) and *screenager* (teenager addicted to television or film screens).

**Acronyms** like *USA* are "letter words", i.e. words composed of the first letter(s) or syllable(s) of a series of words. In a highly structured type of society such as the one we are living in, we create ever new gadgets and numerous political, military, scientific, social, and cultural networks or services. We cannot continuously use their full names and need to be able to refer to them, to memorize them, and to retrieve them in a short and easy-to-process form. Traditional examples are nouns for political entities such as *USA* for the United States of America, *UK* for the United Kingdom (of England and Scotland), *EU* for the European Union, *UN* for the United Nations and *UNESCO* for the United Nations Educational, Scientific, and Cultural Organization.

Acronyms abound in every possible domain of life, e.g. *AIDS* is an acronym for *Acquired Immune Deficiency Syndrome*, i.e. 'a disease caused by a virus, passed from person to person, that stops the body defending itself against infections, i.e. the immune system'. Due to its acronym form, technical terms like *AIDS* have become every day words and thus the awareness factor has been both activated and internationalized. After a certain time however acronyms may no longer be recognizable as such and become entrenched as normal words. A typical example is *radar*, which originally was an acronym meaning 'ra(dio) d(etecting) a(nd) r(anging)', but is no longer marked as such in most dictionaries. It is now described as 'a method of finding the position of things such as planes or missiles by sending out radio waves' (DCE).

## 3.5  Inflection and function words

Earlier in this chapter, in Section 3.3, we looked at derivational morphology. Now we will take a closer look at inflectional morphology, which looks quite similar at first sight. But the differences are fundamental. A first difference

a. *He is waiting*     *vs.*     b. *He is waiting upon customers = a waiter*

**Figure 1.** Inflectional vs. derivational morphemes

between derivational and inflectional morphology is that the former usually changes the word class status of forms (*book – bookish*), but the latter does not (*book – books*). A second difference is that derivational morphemes are added before grammatical morphemes e.g. from the adjective *dark* we may derive the verb to *darken* and this can take the tense morpheme as in *darkens*. A third fundamental distinction ist that in derivations such as *waiter* an affix is attached to a stem in only one of its meanings, thus strongly limiting the range of application. *A waiter* is not someone waiting for a bus, but someone serving customers in a restaurant. In inflectional morphology the affix can always be applied to all the members of a category without any exception. As Figure 1 shows, we can equally well say: *Someone is waiting at the busstop* as *Someone is waiting upon the customers*, but *a waiter* only denotes the profession.

Grammatical morphemes, as already presented in Table 2 of this chapter, are either free morphemes, also called **function words** such as articles as in *the book* or particles as in *to read,* or bound inflectional morphemes affixed to nouns such as the plural morpheme in *books*, the tense morpheme in *reads* or the comparative morpheme in *stronger*. In English, only the three major word classes take inflectional morphemes.

A noun phrase like *the house* consists of two free morphemes, a grammatical one and a lexical one. But the status of a so-called free grammatical morpheme or function word like *the* is not as "free" as that of a really free morpheme such as *house*. Whereas the noun *house* is a very central or prototypical member of the category "free morpheme", a determiner like *the* is rather a peripheral member and cannot stand by itself. In some languages the article is even tied to the noun like an affix, as in Norwegian *huset* 'house + the'.

In English, nouns can be combined with four kinds of grammatical morphemes: two sets of function words (determiner, preposition) and two sets of inflectional morphemes (plural, genitive) as shown in (14).

(14)  *One of    the   cars  of    the   boy's* father (got damaged)
      Det.  Prep.  Det.  Plural Prep. Det.  Genitive

The two inflectional morphemes surrounding the noun (plural *-s* and genitive *'s*) are completely different in meaning, but they have the same set of allomorphs. An **allomorph** is a variant of the same basic form, especially in pronunciation. Thus the plural or genitive morpheme is phonologically realized as /z/ in *cars* or in *boy's*, as /s/ in *books* or *Rick's*, and as /iz/ in *buses* or *Charles's*. Alongside these three allomorphs of the plural morpheme, there are also allomorphs in *-en* (*oxen*), umlaut (*mouse – mice*) and the zero morpheme (*sheep – sheep*).

The function words in (14) are the various determiners *the, one,* and the preposition *of.* The plural morpheme as in *children* and the genitive morpheme can also be combined with one another as in *the children's mother.*

The English verb has function words in the form of auxiliaries and inflectional morphemes for tense and aspect. English can also combine tense with the progressive aspect as in *she is working/she was working* or with the perfective aspect as in *she has worked/she had worked.* The progressive and the perfective are composed of two morphemes each, which function like a kind of circumfix in that they surround one another and the verb form *work.* If the progressive and the perfective are combined, the two morphemes of the perfective, *have* and past participle, "circumfix" tense and the first part (*be*) of the progressive, and the two morphemes of the progressive, *be* and present participle, "circumfix" the past participle of the perfective and the verb *work* as in (15).

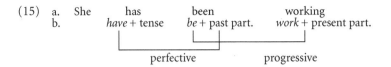

Compared with the morphemes of the noun and the verb, the other word classes have relatively little morphological structure.

Adjectives have bound morphemes for the degrees of comparison (*stronger*, *strongest*), but free morphemes if the word has more than two syllables (***more*** beautiful, ***most*** beautiful).

Adverbs take the adjective stem plus the bound morpheme *-ly*, e.g. *strongly*, *beautifully*. Since inflectional morphemes do not change word class status, the adverb ending *-ly* is a derivational rather than an inflectional morpheme. It is rather a borderline category, which is also supported by the fact that a number of adverbs do not take the adverb morpheme *-ly*, but just have the same form as the adjective. Thus there is no difference between the adjective in *Iron is hard* and the adverb in *He works hard*. Even their degrees of comparison look the same, e.g. *Iron is harder than stone* or *He works harder than his brother*.

There is still a major difference amongst these three word classes. It is in fact only nouns and verbs and not adjectives that are rich in inflection. Inflectional morphemes usually express highly abstract conceptualizations, e.g. the function of tense and aspect is to help indicate how the speaker assesses reality.

## 3.6  Conclusion: Morphology, lexicology and syntax

In Chapter 2 we looked at lexicology, in this chapter we have looked at morphology and in the next chapter we will look at syntax. The fact that lexicology, morphology, and syntax are covered in three different chapters might give the impression that these areas of language and of linguistic analysis are all neatly separated units which are completely independent of each other. In fact, this view has dominated the thinking about language in modern linguistics from its very outset with de Saussure (1916).

However, this view cannot be quite correct. As we saw in this chapter and the previous one, similar form/meaning principles apply to both lexicology and morphology. If we assume a basic identity between the conceptual world and the meanings we use, we must remain consistent and accept a basic conceptual identity for all linguistic forms, including syntactic ones. As Table 5 shows, the distinctions between these form/meaning pairs are not at all absolute, but they can be said to form a continuum.

We can see gradually differing types of conceptualizations at the two ends of the continuum: Highly individualized ones at the lexicon end and fairly abstract ones at the grammar (or syntax) end. At the same time we see that there is a gradual move from the individualized concept via the specialized concept in a compound and the generalized or abstract element in a derivation, to the highly abstract type of concept found in syntax. But in spite of these differences, all morphemes are basically of the same nature since all concepts are by nature abstractions of human perceptions and experiences. Although there are degrees in the level of abstraction, they form a continuum. This means that they are basically more similar than different. Each of the types of morphemes are areas in this continuum and reflect different degrees of abstraction.

Table 5. The continuum of language areas and types of concepts

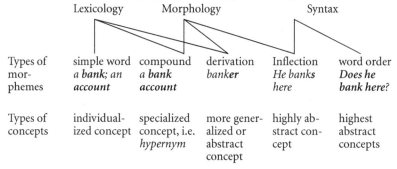

| | Lexicology | Morphology | | Syntax | |
|---|---|---|---|---|---|
| Types of mor- phemes | simple word *a bank; an account* | compound *a bank account* | derivation *banker* | Inflection *He banks here* | word order *Does he bank here?* |
| Types of concepts | individual- ized concept | specialized concept, i.e. *hypernym* | more gener- alized or abstract concept | highly ab- stract con- cept | highest abstract concepts |

### 3.7 Summary

Morphology is the study of building elements used to form composite words or grammatical units. The smallest meaningful elements in a language, whether they are simple words, i.e. **lexemes**, or affixes, are all called **morphemes**. They can be **free morphemes** (e.g. *fruit*), occurring independently, or **bound morphemes** (e.g. *-less*), which are attached to free morphemes (e.g. *fruitless*). Morphology as related to **word formation** takes care of a number of **word-formation processes**, i.e. operations by means of which composite words are formed. A morpheme may have many different senses. A general abstract characterization of all the meanings of a morpheme or any other unit is called a **schema**.

The two main word-formation processes are compounding and derivation. Compounding is a case of **conceptual blending** in which elements from a **frame** and a domain are blended. At the linguistic level, two free morphemes are combined to form a compound. A **compound** usually expresses a specialization, i.e. a subcategory of a basic level category. According to the word form of the **head** in a compound, compounds appear as **noun compounds** (e.g. *kitchen chair*), **verb compounds** (e.g. *sleep-walk*) or **adjective compounds** (e.g. *dark blue*). A compound differs from a **syntactic group** by a different stress pattern and a different conceptualization: that of a subcategory (e.g. ´*blackbird*) in a compound vs. a non-specified subset of the category in question (e.g. *a* `*black* ´*bird*) in a syntactic group, which is a **noun phrase** here. Some compounds are no longer transparent or analyzable as compounds and are therefore called **darkened compounds** (e.g. *daisy* from *day's eye*).

In contrast to a compound, a **derivation** consists of a free morpheme and a bound morpheme (*fruitless*). Bound morphemes which are used to build derivations are called **derivational morphemes**. This branch of morphology is known as **derivational morphology**.

Bound morphemes are added or affixed to words or rather stems and are thus subsumed under the cover term **affix**. There are four kinds of affixes: prefixes, suffixes, infixes and circumfixes. A **prefix** appears at the beginning of the **word stem** from which the new word is derived (*unfair*), a **suffix** is attached to it (*drinkable*), an **infix** is inserted into the middle (*speedómeter*), and a **circumfix** is wrapped around it (*a-singing*). A derivation tends to express a generalization or even a highly abstract category. Most affixes were originally free morphemes which have lost their lexical meaning and taken on ever more abstract meanings. Their form has also usually been reduced. This historical process is called **grammaticalization**.

Other word-formation processes are less **productive**, i.e. they apply to smaller sets of words. **Conversion** changes a word in its word class status and often involves a process of metonymy (*bank* vs. *to bank*). **Backderivation** derives a simpler word from a complex word (*to stage-manage* from *stage-manager*). A **clipping** is a reduction from an original compound or derivation, part of which has been cut off (*telly* from *television*). A **lexical blend** is a compound or derivation only consisting of some elements of the combined morphemes (*breakfast* + *lunch* = *brunch*). An **acronym** is formed from some letters (usually the initial letters) of the lexical morphemes in a syntactic group or compound (*EU* for *European Union*).

**Grammatical morphemes** can occur as free morphemes or bound morphemes and occur with the three main word classes: nouns, verbs, and adjectives. Free grammatical morphemes are **function words** whereas lexical morphemes are **content words**. Function words for nouns are determiners and prepositions like *of*. **Inflection** or **inflectional morphemes** occur especially with nouns, verbs and adjectives. **Inflectional affixes** for nouns are the **plural morpheme** and the genitive morpheme, which have the same phonological allomorphs.

## 3.8 Further reading

The traditional standard work which surveys all cases of English word formation is Marchand (1969). For a cognitive and typological perspective on morphology, see Bybee (1985). Classical theoretical introductions to the study of morphological phenomena are Matthews (1991) and Bauer (1988). For a survey of the more technical work within the generative approach, see Spencer (1991). More recent cognitive approaches are legion: compounding is addressed from a conceptual blending perspective by Fauconnier (1997) and especially by Coulson (2000); -*er*-derivations are discussed in strongly divergent cognitive approaches by Ryder (1991), Panther & Thornburg (2002), and Heyvaert (2003).

## Assignments

1.  Arrange the items below in one of the six categories (as in Table 3): (a) simple words, (b) compounds, (c) derivations, (d) complex types, (e) syntactic groups and (f) others:

    - drilling rig          - spacecraft          - synthetic fibre
    - submarine             - water cannon         - the take-away
    - baptism of fire       - artificial light       restaurant

2.  Which process or processes of word formation can you identify in the examples below?

|   |   |   |   |
|---|---|---|---|
| a. | Franglais | g. | to shop |
| b. | espresso (instead of espresso coffee) | h. | vicarage |
|   |  | i. | unselfishness |
| c. | docudrama | j. | boy-crazy |
| d. | CD player | k. | pillar-box red |
| e. | euro (i.e. new currency) | l. | best-sellers |
| f. | radar | m. | bit (from 'binary digit') |

3.  Read the following paragraph and then answer the questions below:

For all his boasting in that 1906 song, Jelly Roll Morton was right. Folks then and now, it seems, can't get enough of his music. Half a century after his death, U. S. audiences are flocking to see two red-hot musicals about the smooth-talking jazz player; and for those who can't make it, a four-volume CD set of Morton's historic 1938 taping of words and music for the Library of Congress has been released (*Jelly Roll Morton: The Library of Congress Recordings*; Rounder Records; $15.98) and is selling nicely. Morton was not the creator of jazz he claimed to be, but such was his originality as a composer and pianist that his influence has persisted down the years, vindicating what he said back in 1938: "Whatever these guys play today, they're playing Jelly Roll" (from: *Time*, January 16, 1995)

a.  List the plural nouns which occur in this extract, and arrange them according to their respective plural allomorphs: /s/, /z/, /ɪz/

b.  List those nouns in the extract which have the meaning 'one who performs an action' and state which of these are formed according to a productive morphological rule.

c.  Which types of inflectional morphemes do you find in the extract? Give one example of each type, i.e. two nominal inflections, and four verbal inflections.

4.  Here are the names of the inhabitants of 14 European countries. (i) Can you describe the compounding or derivational processes used in the labelling of inhabitants? (ii) Can you find out after what type of word -man is used, after what word forms -ian and -ese are used, and in which cases we find conversion?

| | | |
|---|---|---|
| Austrian | Finn | Norwegian |
| Belgian | Frenchman | Portuguese |
| Briton | German | Spaniard |
| Dane | Irishman | Swede |
| Dutchman | Italian | |

5.  English has two noun-building suffixes for qualities: -ness and -ity as in aptness, brightness, calmness, openness, strangeness, and beauty, conformity, cruelty, difficulty, excess-ivity, regularity. These differences are often related to the origin of the word stems.

    a.  Can you see any regular pattern for the cases when -ness is used and when -(i)ty?
    b.  The adjective odd has two derivational nouns, oddness and oddity. Which one do you feel to be the normal derivation? Why? What is the difference in meaning between oddness and oddity? Consult a dictionary to check your answers.

6.  In a training information leaflet, two new composite words to cold call (call potential clients for business) and you-ability are used. Without knowing their intended mea-nings, how can you make sense of them?

    a.  Can you on the basis of existing words that look similar or have some associa-tion in meaning such as to dry-clean and usability or availability make sense of these two new complex words?
    b.  What are the typical patterns for these types of compound or derivation? Which word class has been used instead of the prototype in you-ability?

7.  The following are all compounds with a colour term. Using the notions of specializa-tion, generalization, metaphor and metonymy, say which process applies in each example and try to explain how they are motivated.

    a.  bluebell          e.  redroot          i.  black-eyed pea
    b.  bluebird          f.  redbreast        j.  blackbird
    c.  blue baby         g.  redneck          k.  Black (person)
    d.  blueprint         h.  red carpet       l.  black art

8.  What are the words the following blends are composed of: Boatel, hurricoon, wintertainment, bomphlet, stagflation?

9.  For each of the following items, say

    a.  which word-formation process is involved,
    b.  which meaning of the -er suffix is used,
    c.  why BrE and AmE may use different words for the same object in this domain.

    1.  burner (AmE), (electric) ring (BrE)
    2.  counter (AmE), work top (BrE)
    3.  food processor
    4.  tin opener (BrE), can opener (AmE)
    5.  toaster
    6.  fire extinguisher
    7.  drawer

# 4   Putting concepts together

## Syntax

## 4.0 Overview

In the previous chapters on lexicology and morphology we analyzed links between concepts and morphemes. We will now tackle the question of how to put concepts together and express an event. (The notion of event is used here in its widest sense, as both an action or a state). We express events by means of a sentence. A sentence, in writing usually marked with a full stop or other punctuation marks and in speaking with certain intonation contours, is a complex construction consisting of the following components: an event schema, a sentence pattern and grounding elements.

When describing an event as a whole, we can pick out one, two or at the most, three main participants which we relate to each other in one way or another. Even though each event is unique in its own way, our language shows that we tend to group events according to a limited number of types, called "event schemas".

Each of these general event types is matched to a typical sentence pattern with a particular kind of word order, which reflects the way the participants in an event are related to each other. There are other elements to help us "place" the event relative to ourselves and the time we are speaking. By means of certain grammatical morphemes, called grounding elements, we express when and where the event occurs or occurred, and — in the case of hypothetical events — whether an event may occur, may have occurred or will occur.

## 4.1  Introduction: Syntax and grammar

*The Shorter Oxford English Dictionary (SOED)* defines the **sentence** as "the grammatically complete expression of a single thought". This definition reflects traditional thinking about the interrelationship of language and thought. From a cognitive point of view, the sentence is also understood to combine conceptual and linguistic completeness. Conceptually, a sentence expresses a complete event as seen by a speaker. Linguistically, a typical sentence names at least one participant and the action or state it is involved in. By means of verb morphemes, it indicates how this action or state is related to the speaker's here and now in time and space.

To express such an event, a typical sentence consists of various interrelated meaningful units. The preceding chapters surveyed the main categories that form such building blocks of language: lexical items and grammatical morphemes. In a sentence, these units occur together in a systematic order. The field of study that is concerned with such systematic order is traditionally known as **syntax.** The term *syntax* derives from two Greek word forms: the prefix *syn* 'with' and the word *tassein* 'arrange'. Syntax "arranges together" the elements of a sentence by means of regular patterns.

Our ability to recognize these general sentence patterns in a language allows us to understand the thoughts expressed in sentences. We might even detect more than one pattern or more than one possible order of participants in the same string of words and then such a string has more than one meaning. For example, in writing, a sentence like (1a) can be interpreted in two different ways and paraphrased as in (1b) and (1c), respectively:

(1) a. Entertaining students can be fun.
    b. Students who entertain (people) can be fun.
    c. It can be fun (for people) to entertain students.

In speaking, it might be clear which sense the phrase *entertaining students* conveys by means of differences in intonation and stress, but in writing such a sentence is ambiguous. This ambiguity can be explained as follows. Conceptually, a verb such as *entertain* has two participants: One participant who does the entertaining and one who is being entertained. In simple sentences like *They entertained the students* or *The students entertained them* the same pattern and the different word order clearly indicate who is doing the entertaining. The one before the verb, **the subject,** names the person doing the entertaining and the one after the verb, the **direct object,** the one being entertained.

However, in (1a), the expression *entertaining students* is not a complete sentence but a phrase in which we may recognize two distinct word orders, one in which *students* can be interpreted as subject and one in which *students* is direct object. Paraphrase (1b) illustrates *students* with the subject function and (1c) with the object function.

Our knowledge of the linguistic categories of a language combined with our knowledge of the patterns in which they may occur is known as the **grammar** of a language (see Table 1). This wider understanding of the notion of grammar thus includes all the components of linguistic structure: lexicology, morphology, syntax as well as phonetics and phonology, discussed in the next chapter.

Table 1. Grammar and its components

| Linguistic fields | Linguistic categories | Composition processes |
| --- | --- | --- |
| lexicology | lexemes (*words*) | lexical extension patterns (e.g. *metaphor, metonymy*) |
| morphology | morphemes (e.g. *affixes*) | morphological processes (e.g. *compounding*) |
| syntax | grammatical categories (e.g. *word classes*) | grammatical patterns (e.g. *word order*) |
| phonetics/phonology | phonemes (e.g. *consonants; vowels*) | phonemic patterns (e.g. *assimilation*) |

In this chapter, we will limit ourselves to three main areas. First, in Section 4.2 we will look more closely at how we conceive of types of events in event schemas. In Section 4.3 we will look at sentence patterns with which event schemas are described. Section 4.4 will deal with the way we relate events to our own situation at the moment of speaking.

## 4.2  Event schemas and participant roles

When we describe an event, it is not necessary to name all the possible persons, things and minor details involved. Instead we "pick out" only those elements that are the most salient to us at that moment. The relationship between a whole event and the sentence we use to describe it is a way of filtering out all the minor elements and focusing on one, two or three participants only.

As our anthropocentric perspective of the world (see Chapter 1.2.1) would predict, the things that catch our eye most are quite often most like us. They are usually persons, animals or things with which we, as humans, would most often associate.

This is typically shown by the various construals we can use to describe the following situation. While the teacher is absent, two children in class have an enormous fight. Things get so tense that Kim takes a baseball bat, walks over to Bruce and tries to hit him. However, Kim misses and accidentally hits the window, which shatters. When the teacher comes in, this event may be described in many different ways, with different focus, and more or less detail:

(2)   a.   Kim is the one who did it.
      b.   The window broke.
      c.   Kim broke the window.
      d.   Kim felt very angry and tried to hit Bruce.
      e.   Kim had a baseball bat in his hand.
      f.   The baseball bat went through the window.
      g.   Bruce had given Kim a nasty picture of himself.

Each of these sentences evokes the event, but each shows that the speaker has focused on different aspects of the event. These typical English sentences in (2) show how we consider events in a very schematic way, according to certain conceptual schemas.

A conceptual schema of an event, i.e. an **event schema,** combines a type of action or state with its most salient participants, which may have different "roles" in the action or state. These roles may range from very active ones in which an animate being performs an intentional action or a rather passive one where an entity is involved in a state or undergoes an action. For example, in an event schema such as "A hit B", the action of hitting typically takes an **Agent**, a human instigator who performs the act, and a **Patient**, the participant undergoing the action.

As we will see below, there are different types of **event schemas**, involving participants with different **semantic roles**. Some events we describe involve participants such as an Agent who exert a great deal of energy. Others involve participants such as a Patient who undergo energy. Others do not involve any energy and are therefore called states. This flow of energy or its absence is typically expressed by different types of verbs.

Therefore, event schemas can be indicated by the most prototypical verbs that are used to ask questions about the events taking place. Interestingly enough, as Chapter 6 will show, these verbs are not only used in English, but their equivalents are present in all the languages of the world. These verbs are *be, happen, do, feel, see,* etc. and are consequently appropriate labels for the main event schema they specify, as shown in the list below:

1. *"Being" schema:*           Who or what is some entity (like)?
2. *"Happening" schema:*       What is happening?
3. *"Doing" schema:*           What is someone doing? What does he or she do?
4. *"Experiencing" schema:*    What does someone feel, see, etc.?
5. *"Having" schema:*          What does an entity have?
6. *"Moving" schema:*          Where is an entity moving?
                               Where does an entity move?
7. *"Transferring" schema:*    To whom is an entity transferred?

Each of these schemas is discussed in more detail below and in Section 4.3 we
will discuss the typical sentence patterns and word orders with which they are
described.

### 4.2.1 The "being" schema

The main function of the **"being" schema** is to relate a characteristic or any
other conceptual category to a given entity which does not really play a dominant role in the relationship. The role of the main participant is described as a
**Patient**, whereby the role of Patient is defined as that role which is least involved in any type of relationship. The Patient in a "being" schema can be
related with different ways of "being": It can be linked to an identifying element
(3a), to a category or class (3b), to a characteristic (3c), to a given place (3d), or
to the notion of mere existence (3e):

(3)  a.  This place on the map here is *the Sahara.*              (*Identifier*)
     b.  The Sahara is *a desert.*                          (*Class membership*)
     c.  The Sahara is *dangerous (territory).*                 (*Attribution*)
     d.  This desert is *in Northern Africa.*                      (*Location*)
     e.  *There is* a desert *(in Northern Africa).*              (*Existential*)

These semantic relations can be subsumed under the cover term Essive (from
the Latin verb *esse* 'to be'). An **Essive** is any role that is related to a patient via a
"being" link. In (3a), the speaker identifies a given place on a map by using a
proper name, *the Sahara.* A typical test applicable in any identifying construction is that one can turn the two definite noun phrases round without changing
the meaning. Thus the difference between (3a) and a sentence like *The Sahara is
this place on the map here* is only a question of which element the speaker wants to
identify. Both can serve as Identifier. In (3b) we find an act of categorization,
namely, that the Sahara is a member of the class or category "desert". In (3c) the

speaker attributes a property to the Sahara. In (3d) the Patient *Sahara* is linked not to a property, but to an Essive location. Similarly, the existential use of *there is* or *there are* in (3e) is a peripheral member of this category of Essives. The category of Essives has in common that they all denote a state of being.

## 4.2.2 The "happening" schema

Whereas the "being" schema denotes a state, the **"happening" schema** emphasizes a process that is taking place and the participating entity involved in it. However, the participating entity itself need not really be actively involved in the process and is therefore also a Patient. There is a gradual increase in autonomy between the Patient and the process, as suggested by the following series of examples: The series begins with an atmospheric situation as Patient in (4a) and ranges from lifeless objects in (4b,c) to living and even human (4d,e) entities:

(4)   a.   The weather is clearing up.
      b.   The stone is rolling down.
      c.   The kettle is boiling.
      d.   The dog is whining.
      e.   The boy is getting better.

In each of these processes, we find an entity which does not contribute to the energy developed in the ongoing process, but rather undergoes it and therefore this entity in the "happening" schema is a more prototypical Patient than the one in a "being" schema. Even the whining of the dog can be seen and explained as the result of some inherent stimulus-reflex energy which is stronger than the dog itself. But of course the dog is self-acting, and hence more autonomous than the water in the kettle (4c) or the rolling stone (4b), which cannot be stopped by a new stimulus, but only by some counterforce. Such instinctive energy of a dog whining is also stronger than the physical and/or psychological processes of becoming ill or getting better. Human beings may undergo these processes rather than control them. The Patient character of all the subjects in (4) thus emerges as an answer to the question "What is happening to an entity?". Even the question "What is happening to the dog?" does not sound funny in the context of a whining dog or even the dog's wild continued bout of barking without any noticeable explanation. But in a different context, the dog's barking might rather belong to the next schema, and it is therefore a peripheral member of each of the two schemas.

### 4.2.3 The "doing" schema

In instances of the "happening" schema as in (4) it is usually not possible to ask "What is X doing?" or "What does X do?" Of course, in the case of animals like a barking dog we can say "What is the dog doing?" or "What did the dog do when you told him to shut up?", and then we interpret the dog's behaviour as somehow controllable. In a "**doing**" schema one entity is seen as the source of the energy that is developed, and consequently as instigating the action. We can see the dog's barking as "doing something", namely as a controllable action rather than as simply undergoing an instinctive process. This distinction also helps to explain why the "doing" schema is almost exclusively linked to human Agents, whereby an **Agent** is defined as the entity that deliberately instigates the action expressed by the verb. The main difference between the "happening" schema and the "doing" schema is in the role of an Agent as the source of the energy, that is, the wilful instigator of the action. The energy he or she generates can often be seen to flow to a Patient. These two extremes of the "doing" schema, i.e. energy produced in oneself (5a) or energy transmitted to some other object (5e) and all the variations in between are illustrated in (5).

(5)  a.   John got up early.                    (*No object possible*)
     b.   He painted all morning.               (*Object not relevant*)
     c.   He painted the dining-room.           (*Object affected*)
     d.   He also painted a picture.            (*Object effected*)
     e.   Later he destroyed the picture.       (*Object affected*)

In (5b) there is no Object, since the speaker focuses on the action itself and the time it takes. In (5c) the same verb *paint* is used with an Object that was already in existence and which is affected by the energy of the Subject. In (5d) the Subject produces a new entity, i.e. the picture he painted: This is the result or effect of his painting.

### 4.2.4 The "experiencing" schema

Most conceptual categorization is based on the experiences humans have in their environmental and cultural world. Experiences may be understood in the most general way, including bodily experiences, social and cultural experiences. But here, in the context of conceptual schemas, we use the term *experience* in a somewhat narrower technical sense; by "**experiencing**" **schema** we mean the mental processing of the contact with the world. This is expressed by mental verbs such as *to see, to feel, to know, to think, to want* etc. Unlike the "doing" schema, which requires an Agent, the entity involved in an "experiencing" schema is neither passive like a Patient, nor active like an Agent, but it is the "registration centre" of these perceptions, emotions, thought processes and wants. This role is therefore called the **Experiencer**, the role of the entity that has a mental experience.

(6)  a.  Little Bernice *sees* a snake.
     b.  He *knows* that it is a dangerous one.
     c.  Even so, he *wants* to pick it up.
     d.  He *thinks* that he can do so if he's quick.
     e.  When he does, he *feels* a sharp pain.

The second participant of the sentences in this "experiencing" schema can either denote a concrete object like *snake* in (6a), or a second event schema as in (6b–d), which is expressed in a subclause with *that* or *to*-infinitive. All these types of second participants in the experiencing schema are Patients. The main difference with the Patient in a "doing" schema is that the Patient in an "experiencing" schema is not affected and cannot become the subject of a passive sentence (*\*A snake is seen by him*).

### 4.2.5 The "having" schema

The "having" schema subsumes several subtypes. In the most prototypical case, the **"having" schema** relates a human Possessor to the object possessed, but it may also relate an affected entity to its cause of affection, a whole to its parts, or one family member to another.

(7)  a.  Doreen has a nice penthouse.            (*Material possession*)
     b.  Maureen often has brilliant ideas.       (*Mental possession*)
     c.  John has very bad flu.              (*Affected – affection*)
     d.  This table has three legs.            (*Whole – part*)
     e.  She has one sister.                (*Kinship relation*)

In the prototypical realization of the "having" schema (7a), a (human) **Possessor** is linked with an object which is material, movable and transferable in that it can be passed into someone else's possession. This type of the "having" schema is known as ownership. Less central are mental objects (7b), and quite peripheral on the continuum of the "having" schema are affections (7c), part-whole relations (7d) or kinship relations (7e).

Just as with an "experiencing" schema there is no real energy flow between the two participants as the first one does not wilfully act, but undergoes a state; therefore, the Possessor is very much like a Patient. In many languages the patient is even expressed as a direct object, i.e. something like "A very bad flu has John" instead of English (7c).

It might look as if the "being" schema and the "having" schema are somehow related, but in English *have* and *be* are quite different. Unlike the "being" schema, the "having" schema can be paraphrased by means of *with*: *The woman with a nice penthouse/The girls with brilliant ideas/The man with very bad flu/The table with three legs/The woman with one sister.* The fact that each of these is somewhat different again shows up when we paraphrase them either with *of* (the *three legs of the table*) or with the genitive *'s* in *John's flu, Doreen's penthouse, Maureen's brilliant ideas* and *the woman's sister.* Here English takes a very strong anthropocentric perspective: "Human" possessors can always be paraphrased with the *'s*-genitive, but a non-human relation such as a part-whole is usually rendered with an *of*-phrase.

## 4.2.6 The "moving" schema

The **"moving" schema** is a combination of either a "happening" schema or a "doing" schema with the places where the process or action starts (**Source**), where it passes by (**Path**), and where it goes to (**Goal**). These three places are synthesized in a "source-path-goal" schema. The **"source-path-goal" schema** can be understood in a literal, spatial sense as in (8a,b), in a temporal sense as in (8c,d) and in an abstract, metaphorical sense as in (8e,f).

(8) a. The apple fell from the tree into the grass.
      *"happening" schema + Source – Goal*
   b. I climbed from my room up the ladder onto the roof.
      *"doing" schema + Source – Path – Goal*
   c. It went on from ten all night long till two.
      *"happening" schema + Start – Duration – End*
   d. The police searched the house from noon till midnight.
      *"doing" schema + Start – End*
   e. The weather changed from cloudy to bright in one hour.
      *"happening" schema + Initial State – Resultant State*
   f. She changed from an admirer into his adversary.
      *"happening" schema + Initial State – Resultant State*

As these examples show, a concrete event schema can very easily change into a more abstract one, with some elements changing quite radically.

Thus the notion of "path" in the concrete spatial sense (8b) changes into a "duration" concept in a temporal context (8c,d) and into two successive "states of being" in a process context (8e,f).

a. Apple falling from tree          b. Apple falling into grass

**Figure 1.** Equal salience of source and goal in the "moving" schema.

In combination with a "moving" schema, the elements of the **"source-path-goal" schema** — as shown in Figure 1 — are equally salient and can all occur independently as in *The apple fell from the tree* (source) or *It fell into the grass* (goal) or *It fell down the roof* (path) or in any combination of these. But a "doing schema" by nature involves human volition, and we tend to be far more interested in the goal of the action than in the source of the action, at least if this is a mere starting-point with *from*. Therefore, when human action is involved, goal is far more salient than such a starting-point. Thus it is strange to say *\*I climbed from my room*, but much more natural is *I climbed onto the roof* or *I climbed up the ladder*.

In temporal contexts we find a similar principle at play. Combined with a "happening" schema, the source, path or goal elements can occur with a slight difference in saliency as in *It went on from ten* (start) — which is somewhat less acceptable vs. *It went on till two* (end point). But with a "doing" schema involving a human action we would tend to include the end point rather than naming only the start. For example, *They searched from noon till midnight* or *They searched till midnight* sounds more natural than *They searched from noon*.

More generally, we may conclude that there is a strong hierarchy in the every-day experience of the "source-path-goal" schema: For human actions, the goal is usually more important than the source and the source and goal are usually more important than the path. This principle has been called the "**goal-over-source**" **principle**. This applies to abstract changes too. For example, while pointing to the barometer, we could say *The weather has changed to bright*, or *The weather has got brighter* but not *\*The weather has changed from cloudy*.

### 4.2.7 The "transferring" schema

Like the "moving" schema, the "transferring" schema is a combination of different schemas: the "having" schema, the "happening" or "doing" schema, and the "moving" schema. The "**transferring**" **schema** implies two states. There is an initial state where one participant has something and passes it on to another participant. The resultant state indicates that the second participant has the thing passed on. These processes of transfer are illustrated in (9):

(9)  a.  Janice gave Lynn a birthday cake.
     b.  Janice gave a birthday cake to Lynn.
     c.  Janice gave the door a coat of paint.
     d.  *Janice gave a coat of paint to the door.

In both (9a and b), *Janice* has a *birthday cake*. She gives it to *Lynn* and the result is that Lynn now has the thing. Both sentence patterns in (9a,b) reflect the "transferring" schema, but there is a clear meaning difference between them. The pattern in (9a) without *to* expresses that the second participant becomes the real possessor of the third entity or she is the **Receiver**. In (9b) Lynn is not necessarily the new possessor; Janice may just have too much to carry or to do and may want Lynn to hold the cake for a little while. So *to Lynn* denotes a Goal, not necessarily a Receiver. In the case of abstract possession like (9c) we use the same type of construction and since the paint is to become part of the door, this cannot become a "temporary" possessor so that sentence (9d) is ungrammatical.

In summary, these types of event schemas are presented in Table 2.

**Table 2.** Configuration of "roles" in event schemas

|  | Participants | | |
|---|---|---|---|
|  | First | Second | Third |
| 1. "Being" schema | Patient | Essive | |
| 2. "Happening" schema | Patient | (Patient) | |
| 3. "Doing" schema | Agent | (Patient) | |
| 4. "Experiencing" schema | Experiencer | Patient | |
| 5. "Having" schema | Possessor | Patient | |
| 6. "Moving" schema | (Agent) | Patient | Goal |
| 7. "Transferring" schema | Agent | Receiver | Patient |

## 4.3  Hierarchical and linear structure of the sentence

As has been said before, the word order in the sentence reflects the way in which participants are related to each other. Word order constitutes the **linear structure** of the sentence. But this is only one aspect of the complex structure of the sentence. The other aspect is the **hierarchical structure** governing within a sentence. This means that some parts or constituents of the sentence belong together more than others. Thus verb (V) and object (O) belong together, forming the **verb phrase**, and are in contrast with the subject (S). Now we will look into more complex aspects of all the hierarchical levels within a sentence.

### 4.3.1  Hierarchical structure of the sentence constituents

The tremendous achievement of language is to map the levels of thought onto the linear order of spoken or written language. Before resuming the question of how the event schemas presented above are mapped onto language structure, it is necessary to first look into the way linearization takes shape. The way people conceive of events may already be language-specific to some extent — as we will see in Chapter 6 — but the order in which constituents of a sentence are linearized may take radically different forms in the languages of the world. Even in closely related languages such as English, French and German we find major differences with respect to linearization. Compare:

(10)  a.  He has given <u>them to his sister</u>.
     b.  *Il <u>les</u> a donnés <u>à sa soeur</u>.*
     c.  *Er hat <u>sie seiner Schwester</u> gegeben.*

Theoretically, there are eight slots available into which the constituents of a sentence may be put, and each of the three languages makes different use of the slots, as represented in Table 3.

In these languages, the most volatile constituent to be placed in the linear structure of the sentence is the direct object (O) in pronoun-form. The most fixed constituent in the linear structure is, apart from the subject, the auxiliary. In English and French, the participle cannot be split from its auxiliary by a (pronoun) object, while German has a two-pronged construction for the auxiliary and the participle. The slot between them can actually contain any number of constituents as in (11).

(11)   *Gestern hat er Jane nach einem heftigen Streit, ohne auch nur ein einziges Wort zu sagen, alle ihre Briefe zurückgegeben.*
Yesterday he has Jane after a heavy fight, without a word to say, all her letters, back-given.
'Yesterday, after a heavy fight, he gave Jane all her letters back without saying a word.'

However, there is far more to language structure than the filling in of slots. Once a speaker of German has heard the auxiliary *hat* 'has' in the sentence above, his grammatical knowledge of the "two-pronged rule" tells him that somewhere there must be a verb in the form of a participle such as *gegeben* 'given' with which the auxiliary forms a composite unit.

**Table 3.** The various slots in the structure of a sentence

|          | Subject | Pronoun | Auxiliary | Pronoun | IO   | Participle | Pronoun | Complement |
|----------|---------|---------|-----------|---------|------|------------|---------|------------|
| English  | *He*    |         | *has*     |         |      | *given*    | *them*  | *to Jane*  |
| French   | *Il*    | *les*   | *a*       |         |      | *donnés*   |         | *à Jane*   |
| German   | *Er*    |         | *hat*     | *sie*   | *Jane* | *gegeben* |         |            |

More generally, as was also shown for the two senses of the sentence in (1) *Entertaining students can be fun,* in processing a sentence the hearer has to extract the compositional structure of a sentence. Sentences are composed in a hierarchical way, and there are different grammatical levels at which lower constituents are composed into higher constituents. The combined linear and

Table 4. Tree diagram of a sentence

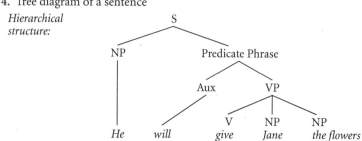

(S = sentence, NP = noun phrase, VP = verb phrase, S = subject, Aux = auxiliary, IO = indirect object, O = direct object)

compositional structure of the sentence *He will give Jane the flowers* might be represented by means of a tree diagram as in Table 4.

The diagram reflects a three-level hierarchical structure of this sentence; at the lowest level, the verb phrase (VP) unites the verb *give* with the NP *Jane* and the NP *the flowers*; at the next higher level, the **predicate phrase** unites the verb phrase with the AUX(iliary) elements, and at the highest level of the sentence, the predicate phrase and the subject NP are united. This hierarchical structure of the sentence, as represented in Table 4, makes two things clear: (1) that the pronouns (*them, les, sie*) in Table 3 can be put into various slots between the major constituents: Subject–Auxiliary–Verb Phrase; and (2) that Aux is an independent constituent, which in English expresses the difference between a statement and a question. Compare: *she will come/will she come?* Or *she comes/ does she come?* The linear structure in Table 4, i.e. S–AUX–V–IO–O represents just one of the various sentence patterns available.

### 4.3.2 Linear sequence in the sentence: Sentence patterns

The grammar of English, as well as any other natural language, only provides a limited set of basic sentence patterns. **Sentence patterns** are the structural frames of the basic types of sentence in a language, i.e., the grammatical structure of simple sentences which consists of obligatory elements only. English has six main types of sentence pattern, which are listed in Table 5. They are characterized by different combinations of five basic functional constituents, i.e., subject, verb, direct object, indirect object and complement. All sentence patterns have a subject and a verb. The **subject** is the constituent, with which the verb agrees and about which something is said or predicated in the predicate phrase. Or in reverse, the **predicate phrase** can be defined as all that is said or predicated of the subject of the sentence. The **direct object** is the second most important noun phrase and, by a somewhat circular definition, occurs in transitive sentences. The **indirect object** is the third most important constituent and occurs in ditransitive sentences. **Complements** are essential constituents of the structure of a sentence other than the subject and the direct or indirect object. This term is also used to characterize verb-like structures after a verb such as a *to*-infinitive in *He is trying to cross the street* or *He sees that he can cross the street now.*

**Table 5.** Basic sentence patterns of English

| | | | | | |
|---|---|---|---|---|---|
| a. | Doreen | is | such a nice person. | | *copulative pattern* |
| | S | V-cop | C | | |
| b. | Doreen | smiled. | | | *intransitive pattern* |
| | S | V | | | |
| c. | Doreen | invited | all of us. | | *transitive pattern* |
| | S | V | O | | |
| d. | We | gave | Doreen | roses. | *ditransitive pattern* |
| | S | V | IO | O | |
| e. | The flat | belongs | to her mother | | *complement pattern* |
| | S | V | C | | |
| f. | We | took | the bus | back home. | *transitive complement pattern* |
| | S | V | O | C | |

S = subject, V = verb, V-cop = copulative verb, O = direct object, IO = indirect object, and C = complement

a. The **copulative pattern** stands out from the other patterns in that its copulative verb, *to be*, merely serves to "link" a complement to a subject.
b. The **intransitive pattern** consists only of a subject and a verb.
c. The **transitive pattern** requires a direct object, which may become the subject of a passive sentence as in *All of us were invited.*
d. The **ditransitive pattern** is characterized by two objects. In English, both the direct object and the indirect object may become the subject of a passive sentence: *A bunch of roses was given to Doreen* and *Doreen was given a bunch of roses.*
e. The **complement pattern** usually takes a prepositional phrase as its obligatory complement. In English, complements may also become the subject of a passive sentence as in *She was laughed at.*

f.   The **transitive-complement pattern** fuses the transitive pattern and the
complement pattern. It often provides a structural alternative to the
ditransitive pattern. Thus, the sentence *We gave Doreen roses* with a ditransitive pattern may also be phrased as a transitive-complement pattern *We
gave roses to Doreen.*

Each of the sentence patterns is associated with an abstract meaning of its own.
When we want to describe a certain event, we will use the pattern whose
meaning most appropriately fits our idea of the event. For example, if we want
to express the idea that we intend to go somewhere, we are most likely to select
the complement pattern as in (12a); if, however, we understand this to be a
special mountaineering feat, the transitive pattern as in (12b) is better suited:

(12)  a.   Tomorrow, I will be climbing on Mount Snowdon.
           *(complement pattern)*
      b.   Tomorrow, I will be climbing Mount Snowdon.
           *(transitive pattern)*

The sentence patterns of a language may be said to form the mould for the basic
event schemas. The number of conceivable individual events is, of course,
enormous, but in communicating an event, we are forced to express it in one of
the six available sentence patterns. There is, however, a systematic link between
certain event schemas and certain sentence patterns. The Essive role can only
occur in a copulative pattern (*She is my best friend*) or in a transitive pattern (*I
consider her my best friend*). The happening schema and the doing schema can
occur both in a transitive pattern or in an intransitive pattern. This depends on
the question whether the energy flow is directed towards another entity or not.
In the first case the transitive pattern is used (*The tennis racket hit the window* or
*The man painted the door*). Here, the window and the door are objects towards
which energy is directed. In the second case the intransitive pattern is used (*The
dog is whining* or *The boy is walking*). Here, there is no particular object toward
which the energy generated by the dog or the boy is directed. The experiencing
schema and the having schema as a rule require two entities: a Processor or a
Possessor and the entity that is experienced or possessed. Consequently the
transitive pattern is required here in most cases (*He felt a sharp pain* or *She has
a nice penthouse*). The moving schema and the transferring schema may require
the Source, Path or Goal to be expressed, which is done by the complement
pattern (*I climbed onto the roof*) or by the transitive complement pattern (*We
sent a bunch of flowers to her*). If, as a result of an object's motion, the object

comes into possession of a human, the ditransitive pattern is used. (*We gave her a bunch of roses; He gave the door a new coat of paint*). The instances presented here constitute the regular cases in the matching of event schemas and sentence patterns. There are hundreds of special cases, which, however, we will not go into here.

## 4.4  The grounding elements of a sentence

In the previous sections we saw that different types of events may be described by means of a few basic sentence patterns. But when we describe events it is — according to the specific culture we live in — also very important to know where the participants are located and when the event took place. Relating an event to the speaker's experience of the world is technically called **grounding**. The participants of an event and the event as a whole need to be anchored, or grounded in order to ensure successful communication. Usually we take the person speaking as the reference point in space and the moment the person is speaking as the reference point in time (see Ch. 1.2.1).

For example, words like *this* and *these* point to things close to the speaker, and *that* and *those* to those further removed. Other ways in which we can make things accessible to a hearer is by using proper names, the personal pronouns (*I, you, we*), or definite noun phrases to refer to the things spoken about as in *Mum is talking to me on the phone*. This process of pointing to things in the world by means of language is known as **reference** and will be discussed more fully in Chapter 8.

Not only do people need to "ground" things, but they also need to indicate different factors concerning the events they talk about. For one thing, they need to indicate whether their utterance is a statement, a question, or an order. Secondly, they need to indicate whether they understand their statement to be a reflection of the real world or not. They also indicate the time that the event occurs, how this event might relate to others, and whether the event is seen as ongoing or not. Most of these factors can be expressed with grammatical morphemes, also called grounding elements.

We will now look at these grounding elements that relate an event to the speaker's experience of reality. We may think of them as layers enveloping an event. We will consider the overall picture starting from the outer layer, going gradually to the centre, i.e. the event itself (see Figure 2 at the end of this section on p. 96).

### 4.4.1 Communicative function: Mood

First of all, a sentence contains a **communicative function**. The speaker performing a **speech act** utters a sentence to realize his or her communicative intention. He or she wants to assert something, obtain some information or persuade someone else to do something as illustrated in (13).

(13)   a.   Dylan is riding his motorbike to school today.
　　　 b.   Is Dylan riding his motorbike to school?
　　　 c.   Turn that engine off! (will you?)

Even though the three sentences in (13) are basically about the same event, they have different **moods**, which express different communicative intentions: A statement of fact in (13a), an information question in (13b), and an order in (13c). Very often these different moods are signalled by means of differences in the word order, especially the word order of the subject and the auxiliary.

The normal, most common word order is that of affirmative sentences, i.e. S-V-O as in (13a), used to express statements of facts. This is called the **declarative mood**. An information question is usually expressed in the **interrogative**; in interrogative sentences, subject and auxiliary change places (13b). To express an order, the **imperative mood** can be used. In such a sentence, the subject and auxiliary verb are not expressed, but may be added as a tag at the end of the sentence (13c).

As will be shown in Chapter 7.5, these are the prototypical word order patterns for these functions, but this correspondence between sentence mood and communicative function is not absolute, and many other combinations may occur in actual language use.

### 4.4.2 Speaker's attitude: Modality

The next layer represents the speaker's attitude about the event described. As speakers, we either commit ourselves to the truth of what we say or we regard the events as potential ones. One of the grammatical means by which we can express a speaker's attitude towards the status of an event is **modality**.

Normally, people talk about events that have actually taken place or are taking place. Such cases are not specially marked and are commonly known as the **default** case, i.e. the case that most generally pertains and need not be specially marked. It is also called the **unmarked** case. But, a speaker may also want to talk about an event which carries an air of uncertainty. For example, a speaker may indicate that something may have happened in the past, or that something may or should happen in the future, or that perhaps something is happening at the moment of speaking, which he or she cannot be sure about. What such events have in common is that they are potential events.

To mark such potential events, English — as well as other languages — has a range of **modal auxiliaries**, e.g. *will, would, may, might, shall, should, can, could,* and *must,* each one showing a slightly different attitude towards a potential event as in (14a,b) or a possible situation taking place at the moment of speaking as in (14c,d).

(14)  a.  Chris, you may go now.                                    (*permission*)
        b.  Chris, you must go now.                                   (*obligation*)
        c.  Chris may be at the car dealer's.                     (*possibility*)
        d.  Chris must be at the car dealer's.                    (*inference*)

As the examples show, modal auxiliaries such as *may* or *must* can express two different kinds of attitude. The speaker shows what he wants to happen in (14a) and (14b). In the case of *may* the "wanting" is weaker than in the case of *must*. In (14c) and (14d) the speaker expresses a degree of certainty about the potential occurrence of an event, and again in the case of *may* the degree of certainty is much weaker than in the case of *must*. The modality indicating volition towards an event is called **deontic modality** (14a,b) and modality indicating judgement is called **epistemic modality** (14c,d).

### 4.4.3 Speech act time: Tense

**Tense** is the grammatical category reflecting concepts of time. It relates an event in time with respect to the moment of speaking, called **speech act time**. Speech act time is the most obvious point in time to choose because it is evident to both speaker and hearer. Events may take place at speech act time itself, before it in the past, or possibly after it in the future. In general, present and past events are understood to have reality status, while (most) future events have only the status of potential reality. This distinction is reflected in the tense system of many languages, including English, which have two tenses, **present tense** and **past tense**, which are directly marked on a verb, for example, *go/goes* versus *went*. To indicate future time, English uses modal auxiliaries or other helping verbs that indicate potentiality.

(15)  a.   Helen *goes* to work by bike.                         (*present tense*)
      b.   Helen *went* to work by bike.                        (*past tense*)
      c.   Helen *will/is going* to drive to work tomorrow.     (*future time*)

### 4.4.4 Relating events to each other: Perfective aspect

The next grounding element represents how the speaker relates an event to what is happening at speech act time or at another specified time. The relationship whereby one event is situated before another event or before speech act time is expressed by the **perfective aspect**. For example, the event of "buying a new car" can be expressed as in (16a) or (16b).

(16)  a.   Chris bought a new car.
      b.   Chris has bought a new car.
      c.   Chris had just bought a new car, when he had an accident.
      d.   By the time he passes his driving test, Chris will have bought a new car.

The difference in meaning between these sentences lies in how the speaker regards the events. In (16a) the past tense expresses the event as finished and completed with no real connection to the moment of speaking. The focus is more on the past act of buying. In (16b) the speaker emphasizes what the event means to the moment of speaking: "I have a car now". The perfective aspect can also highlight a relevant connection between two past events as in (16c) or two future events as in (16d). In such cases the perfective aspect is used to express the notion of "anteriority": In (16c) the buying of the new car takes place before the accident; in (16d) the buying of the car will take place before taking the driving test.

### 4.4.5 Internal phases in an event: Progressive aspect

By means of the progressive aspect the speaker describes the internal phases in events; by means of the non-progressive he takes an external perspective. With the progressive aspect, which consists of *be V+ing*, the speaker construes the event as ongoing. The non-progressive form is the unmarked, default case. The **progressive aspect** focuses on the ongoing progression of an event, the non-progressive aspect views the event as a whole as illustrated in the examples of (17):

(17)  a.   Mum is talking on the phone now.
      b.   Mum answers the phone now.

In using the progressive aspect in (17a), the speaker mentally zooms onto the event as it progresses and, as a result, does not have the beginning and end of the action in his scope of vision. Although people's talking does not go on indefinitely, the speaker ignores the event's boundaries and perceives it as if it were unbounded. In using the non-progressive aspect in (17b), on the other hand, the speaker takes an external perspective of "the mother's answering the phone" and views it as a whole. Now the event's boundaries at the beginning and at the end are in view. Sentence (17b) would only be used in a holistic context such as a movie picture or stage directions or for habitual or repetitive action, but not for the description of an event taking place at speech act time.

### 4.4.6 Synthesis: Grounding of events

We have looked at the grounding elements that relate an event to the speaker's experience of reality. Events as a whole involve different layers of grounding. We may think of the sentence as an onion-like configuration with the event at its core and the various grounding elements as its leaves layering and enveloping the others as represented in Figure 2.

The grounding elements of a sentence include mood, modality, tense, perfective aspect and progressive aspect. The outermost layer of the sentence represents the level of the speech act, the communicative function for which a sentence is used. In the structure of the sentence, it is realized as sentence *mood*. The next layer represents the speaker's attitude about the event described: The speaker either commits himself to the truth of what he says — this *default* situation is not marked in English —, or he regards the event as a potential one and expresses this by using forms of *modality*. The next layer pertains to the moment when the speech act is uttered: This speech act time determines the use of *tense*. The next layer represents the time at which the event described is situated in relation to speech act time or to other events: This relationship is expressed by the *perfective* aspect. The innermost layer concerns the internal progression of the event, which is expressed by the *progressive* aspect. To summarize, it can be stated that the layers are ordered around the event according to the principle of distance or proximity (see Chapter 1.2.2), i.e. according to how distantly or how closely the layers are conceptually related to the event.

All these sentential elements are shown in Figure 2, which may be called "the sentence onion", aptly suggesting the image of a hard core (the event) and the many "grounding" layers around it.

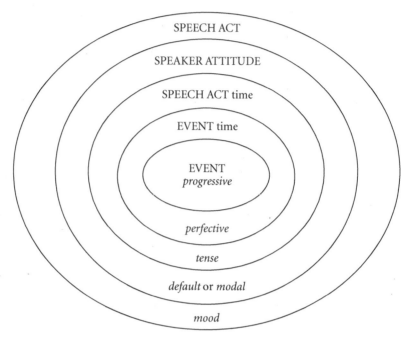

**Figure 2.** The sentence onion

## 4.5  Summary

**Syntax** is concerned with the **sentence** as the unit of language, combining our description of events with our communicative intentions, and 'grounding' all this into the reality of our here and now. This composite whole is put together in the **linear structure** or the word order of the sentence.

The events to be described are reduced to a small set of types of event and expressed, together with the participants in the event, as **event schemas**. These event schemas are based on the **semantic role** of the participants and the presence or absence of an energy flow from one participant to the other. The typical energy flow goes from an **Agent** or wilfully acting participant to a **Patient,** who receives the energy. This energy flow is typically found in the **doing schema**, the **moving schema** and the **transferring schema**. Although the **happening schema** may involve some energy flow, there is usually no autonomous instigator. The complete absence of energy marks a state, which may be described as a **being schema**, a **having schema**, or an **experiencing schema**. Semantic roles can be found as follows: In a being schema, an **Essive** role is linked to a **Patient,** in a having schema a Patient is linked to a **Possessor,** and in an experiencing schema a Patient is linked to a (human) **Experiencer.** A transferring schema combines an Agent, a **Receiver** and a Patient. A moving schema combines a happening or doing schema with a **Source, Path,** and/or **Goal.** In the **Source-Path-Goal schema** we often find the **Goal-over-Source principle.**

These conceptual event schemas and their participants are "linguistically framed" into the linear and **hierarchical structure** of a sentence. The centre of this unit is the predicate or verb, which together with a (direct) object or complement forms the **verb phrase.** This is the lower level, which combines with the **Aux(iliary)** elements to form the **predicate phrase,** and this second level combines with the subject to form the sentence. Based on this hierarchical structure, English and many other languages, give rise to a small set of **sentence patterns,** which, in various combinations, combine a **subject** via the verb, with a **direct object,** an **indirect object** or a **complement.** These five constituents and the type of verb lead to the main **sentence patterns:** The **copulative** pattern with the verb *be* and a subject plus complement, the **intransitive** pattern with a subject only, the **transitive** pattern with a subject and direct object, the **ditransitive** pattern with a subject and two objects (a direct and an indirect one), the **complement** pattern with a subject and a (prepositional) complement and the **transitive complement** pattern with a subject, direct object and complement. These syntactic slots take into account all the possible participants at the conceptual level of the event schemas.

Events are grounded. The grounding of all these elements is also centered around the verb — or if there is one — the auxiliary. These help to constitute the three **moods,** i.e. **declarative, interrogative,** and **imperative** moods, which reflect the **communicative functions** of asserting, questioning, requesting and ordering. In the **unmarked** or **default** case, the speaker assesses the truth of the event he evokes, but in the **marked** case he or she only sees the event as potential and expresses this by means of **modality.** With a **modal auxiliary** like *may* or *must,* the speaker may express **deontic modality** (to indicate what he/she wants to happen) or **epistemic modality** (to indicate how certain he/she is about an event).

The ultimate point of reference is the speaker's own position in time and space at the time the **speech act** takes place, known as **speech act time.** By the choice of **tense,** which may be **present** or **past,** a speaker relates the time of the events as simultaneous with speech act time or anterior to it. If a speaker wants to locate events in relation to other events he or she chooses the **perfective aspect,** if a speaker wants to focus on the internal progression of an event he or she chooses the **progressive aspect**. All these grounding elements are layered around the event schema like the layers of an onion around its core according to the principle of conceptual distance or proximity, and together form the sentence (onion).

## 4.6  Further reading

The introduction to (English) grammar closest to this presentation and developing its elements in further detail is Radden and Dirven (2005). Other introductions to syntax, from a cognitive-functional viewpoint are Givón (1993) and Haiman ed. (1985). The theoretical foundation of the present approach is offered by Langacker (1987, 1991a, 1991b, 1999). A detailed analysis of one particular event schema and the predicate "give" is Newman (1996). An analysis of grammatical morphemes such as the Dative or the Instrumental is Janda (1993). A construction approach to ditransitives is Goldberg (1995, 2002). The Goal-over-Source principle has been described by Ikegami (1987). A thorough and many-faceted analysis of 'grounding' is offered in Brisard, ed. (2002). An overall semantic approach to grammar is Wierzbicka (1988).

## Assignments

1. Analyze the described events as follows: (i) Is there an energy flow? If so, from where to where? (ii) What are the semantic roles of the participants? (iii) Which event schema is used?
    a. Dad must fix the telephone.
    b. It fell down last night.
    c. My brother is a doctor.
    d. He goes to Great Britain.
    e. He has given me all his books.
    f. He will take a few books to Britain.
    g. He watches a lot of television.

2. Which type of Essive relation do you find in each of the following sentences?
    a. She is a year older than her brother.
    b. She is my niece.
    c. A mule is not a horse and not a donkey.

d. This puppet is my favourite one.

e. My friend is not at home.

f. There are many problems left.

3. Characterize the subtype of "doing" schema in the following examples. Or is it not really a "doing" schema?

a. He was tickling his brother.

b. The brother was laughing.

c. He was drawing a train on the blackboard.

d. Then he wiped off the train.

e. He put water on the blackboard.

f. Then he dried it.

4. Characterize the subtypes of possession in the following examples.

a. Have you any good red wine left?

b. I haven't the slightest idea.

c. That wine bottle has a pretty label.

d. Would you like to have a glass of wine?

e. No, I have got a terrible headache.

f. Well, if you want one, I have got an aspirin here.

5. Analyze the following sentences as in assigment 1. Then comment on the (subtle) meaning differences between each pair.

a. He will read from the Bible.

b. He will read the Bible.

c. The children washed in the bath.

d. The children washed the bath.

6. Below the sentences from example (8) are repeated. Which of the elements indicated in parentheses can occur alone and which cannot? Is there evidence for any general principle(s) like Goal over Source, Source over Goal, or Path over Goal.

a. The apple fell from the tree into the grass.
   (Source + Goal)

b. I climbed from my room up the ladder onto the roof.
   (Source + Path + Goal)

c. It went on from ten all night long till two.
   (Start + Duration + End)

d. The police searched the house from noon till midnight.
   (Start + End)

e. The weather changed from cloudy to bright in one hour.
   (Initial State + Resultant State + Duration)

    f.   She changed from an admirer into his adversary.
       (*Initial State + Resultant State*)

7. What are (i) the event schemas, and (ii) the sentence patterns of the sentences below (repeated from examples (2))?

    a. Kim is the one who did it.
    b. The window broke.
    c. Kim broke the window.
    d. Kim felt very angry and tried to hit Bruce.
    e. Kim had a baseball bat in his hand.
    f. The baseball bat went through the window.
    g. Bruce had given Kim a nasty picture of himself.

8. The following pairs of phrases and sentences have different grounding elements. For each pair indicate (i) which grammatical verb morphemes are grounding elements, (ii) which one of the phrases or sentences is an unmarked case (if there is one), (iii) which one(s) is/are marked. (iv) Explain the semantic difference between each pair.

    a. Mum, answer the phone now!/Mum answers the phone often.
    b. Mum must answer/may answer the phone now.
    c. Mum answered/has answered the phone.
    d. Mum has answered/had answered the phone.
    e. Mum is answering/answers the phone.

# 5  The sounds of language
## Phonetics and Phonology

## 5.0 Overview

In the preceding chapters we have talked about meaningful units in language: syntactic groups consist of words, which in turn consist of morphemes. Each is meaningful at its own level. In this chapter, we will look at the parts that make up morphemes: speech sounds. A separate speech sound on its own does not have meaning, but when combined with other sounds, a small distinction such as *it* vs. *fit* may make a meaningful difference.

This chapter describes speech sounds in their general, physical appearance and in their functioning in one specific language, i.e. English. This difference constitutes the basis of the two sciences of speech sounds, i.e. phonetics and phonology.

First the speech organs and the main types of speech sounds are analyzed and the ways to describe them are discussed. These speech sounds are the consonants, vowels and diphthongs. In the sound system of a particular language, things may be different from another language: what counts as two different sounds in one language, may just be two variants of one element in the sound system of the other language. Therefore a distinction between a sound and a phoneme is introduced as well as a distinction between a phonetic description and a phonemic one.

Groupings of sounds form a syllable and such groupings are again subject to highly language-specific combination patterns. Syllables form words, which are characterized by their own stress patterns. Words are combined in a sentence, which carries one of the various intonation patterns possible in a language. In the longer units of word groups or sentences, the sounds of single words undergo massive changes such as linking, elision, assimilation etc. All these processes enable a quick and efficient delivery of speech production and transmission.

## 5.1 Introduction: Phonetics and phonology

Human beings can make an infinite number of speech sounds. If you say the same word several times, or ask different people to say the same word, there will be differences between the pronunciations. In spite of these differences, we would still want to say that the pronunciations are in some important respects "the same".

The same holds with the written language. The following symbols all have a different shape. Nevertheless, we are able to regard the different shapes as examples of the "same" entity, i.e. the "first letter of the alphabet".

$$A \quad a \quad \text{A} \quad a \quad a \quad A \quad a$$

A very general cognitive ability is involved here: *categorization*, i.e. the ability to perceive different things as examples of the same category. One aspect of knowing a language is the ability to categorize the great variety of speech sounds heard in that language. The sound categories that a speaker of one language recognizes will not necessarily coincide with those that a speaker of another language will "hear". Speakers of Thai hear the two "p"-sounds in *pie* and *spy* as different; conversely, for the Japanese, the "s" and "sh" sounds in *sushi* are the same.

Here we have the basis of the distinction between phonetics and phonology. **Phonetics** studies speech sounds as sounds, in all their complexity and diversity, independent of their role in a given language. **Phonology** studies speech sounds as these are categorized by speakers of a given language. In standard British English, there are about 45 different categories of speech sounds, called **phonemes**. As the languages of the world go, English is about average. Some languages have fewer phonemes (Japanese has about 20). Others, e.g. !Xóõ, one of the Bushman ("Khoisan") languages of Southern Africa, have over a hundred, amongst which a very intricate system of click sounds [!].

### 5.1.1 Spelling and pronunciation

Some languages (e.g. Spanish) have a writing system that is (almost) a phonemic one, i.e. each phoneme is always represented by the same letter, and vice versa. But in English the relationship between pronunciation and spelling is, as we all know, far from perfect. There are various reasons for this. First there are more phonemes (about 45) than there are letters of the alphabet (26). Next, there are historical reasons: when English spelling was standardized, many centuries ago, it was broadly phonemic in character. Spelling has remained virtually the same, while pronunciation has changed considerably over the centuries, and continues to do so. The vowels of English have been especially "unstable". Moreover, English has borrowed from other languages. Words of foreign origin may be spelt according to the rules of the donor language, thereby introducing numerous "irregularities" into English spelling. Examples include French borrowings like *rouge, chateau, champaign, quiche*. Furthermore, spellings have sometimes been influenced by speakers' beliefs about etymology (**etymological spelling**). *Debt* is a borrowing from Old French *dette*. The "b" was never pronounced, but was inserted to show the supposed relation of the word to Latin *debitum*. Finally, there is a very marked tendency for a given morpheme always to be spelled the same way, even though its pronunciation may vary from context to context. *The* is spelled the same way in *the man* and *the apple*, although it is pronounced differently. You can recognize the invariant spelling of the root morphemes in *photograph* and *photographer, clean* and *cleanse, sign* and *signature, family* and *familiar*, even though the morphemes are pronounced differently in each case.

Speakers sometimes attempt to re-establish the link between spelling and pronunciation, not by changing the spelling, but by modifying the pronunciation. At the beginning of this century, *waistcoat* was pronounced /ˈweskɪt/ or /ˈweskət/, to rhyme with *biscuit*. The current pronunciation /ˈweistˌkəut/ is a **spelling pronunciation**; the pronunciation is based on the conventional spelling. Speakers who pronounce the "t" in *often* are likewise being influenced by the spelling.

### 5.1.2 Phonetic symbols

Because spelling is not a faithful representation of pronunciation, it is useful to have a set of special symbols whose values are generally agreed upon. This is the function of the **phonetic symbols** of the **International Phonetic Alphabet** (IPA). These symbols are in general use amongst linguists and are employed in this book. Most modern dictionaries now give pronunciations of words using these symbols.

### 5.2 Production of speech sounds

We can distinguish two main stages in the production of speech sounds: phonation and articulation.

- **Phonation** stands for the airstream becoming voiced or voiceless as explained further on (Figure 1). As air is expelled from the lungs, it passes through the glottis (located behind the "Adam's apple"). Located in the glottis are the vocal folds — two flaps of flesh that can be brought together or held apart. Phonation refers to the modulation of the airstream in the glottis. If the vocal folds are brought together, they may vibrate, to produce **voice**. If air passes freely through the glottis, the air stream is minimally affected (this is the state of **voicelessness**).

- **Articulation** refers to the creation of a special resonance space for each sound (Figure 2). This involves the shaping of the vocal tract (i.e. the tubular structure above the larynx), by adjustment, in the oral cavity, of the tongue, jaw, velum (soft palate), lips, etc. The great variety of speech sounds that we are able to make depends very largely on the manner in which we shape the vocal tract.

Phonation and articulation will be discussed in more detail below.


### 5.2.1 Phonation

If you clasp your hand tightly over your larynx while saying the word *zoo*, you should be able to feel a certain vibration. The vibration is that of the vocal folds, technically known as **voice**. Both [z] and [u] are **voiced** sounds.

If you repeat this exercise while saying a prolonged [s], you should feel no vibration in the larynx. [s] is a **voiceless** sound.

For the production of voice, the vocal folds are brought together. When air is pushed out from the lungs, it encounters the vocal folds as an obstacle. Air pressure builds up under the folds until the folds are literally blown apart, and air escapes through the glottis. The folds then return to their original position. Air pressure builds up again, and the cycle is repeated. This repeated cycle makes the folds vibrate. Each opening and closing cycle is very brief. In men, the frequency ranges from about 80 to 150 cps (cycles per second), in women, from about 120 up to 300 cps. For children, the rate may be even higher.

The frequency of the opening and closing cycle determines the **pitch** of the sound; the higher the frequency, the higher the perceived pitch. The auditory sensation of pitch is produced by the pattern of regular bursts of air passing through the glottis.

Voicelessness ensues when the vocal folds are completely brought apart. When air from the lungs reaches the larynx, it encounters no obstacle, and flows

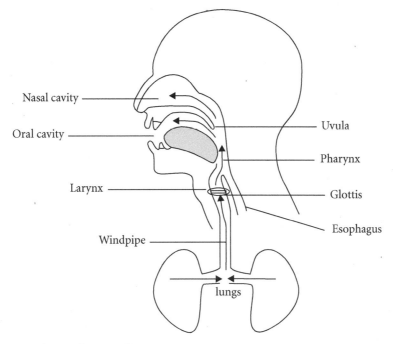

**Figure 1.** The vocal tract airflow

freely though the glottis. Whisper is characterized by voicelessness throughout. For obvious reasons, it is not possible to produce a voiceless sound with pitch, or with pitch variations.

When the airstream, in passing through the oral cavity, is "obstructed" to a marked degree, the sounds thus formed are collectively known as **obstruents**. Many obstruents come in pairs of voiced and voiceless sounds. Here is a list of the English obstruents, in their voiced/voiceless pairings.

| Voiced | | Voiceless | |
|---|---|---|---|
| [b] | "big" | [p] | "pig" |
| [d] | "do" | [t] | "too" |
| [g] | "gum" | [k] | "come" |
| [v] | "vine" | [f] | "fine" |
| [ð] | "them" | [θ] | "thin" |
| [z] | "zoo" | [s] | "Sue" |
| [ʒ] | "measure" | [ʃ] | "mesh" |
| [dʒ] | "jeer" | [tʃ] | "cheer" |

The other main class of consonants, the **sonorants**, are typically voiced. (We can think of sonorants as the "hummable" consonants.) These include the nasals [m], [n] and [ŋ], the liquids [l] and [r], and the glides [j] and [w].

| | |
|---|---|
| [m] | "me" |
| [n] | "knee" |
| [ŋ] | "sing" |
| [l] | "love" |
| [r] | "ray" |
| [j] | "yes" |
| [w] | "when" |

### 5.2.2 Articulation

The second major component of speech production is articulation, i.e. the shaping of the vocal tract as air passes through it. Aspects of articulation will be studied in the next sections, which deal with the characterization of consonants and vowels.

### 5.3 Consonants

Consonants and vowels are distinguished mainly in terms of the degree of constriction in the vocal tract. **Consonants** involve some major constriction, which obstructs the airflow at some point. **Vowels** on the other hand merely involve a distinctive shaping of the oral cavity, with relatively little impedance of the air flow.

Consonants can be described in terms of two major parameters: the place in the vocal tract at which constriction occurs (**place of articulation**), and the nature of the constriction (**manner of articulation**).

### 5.3.1 Places of articulation

In the articulation of a consonant, a movable articulator (usually some part of the tongue, or the lips) is moved towards a more stable articulator (e.g. the upper teeth, or some part of the palate). The following terms describe the more common places of articulation.

– *bilabial* [p, b, m]. The lower lip articulates with the upper lip

- *labiodental* [f, v]. The lower lip articulates with the upper teeth
- *dental* [θ, ð]. The tongue tip articulates with the top teeth
- *alveolar* [t, d, n, l, s, z]. The tongue tip articulates with the alveolar ridge. Also many articulations of "r".
- *alveopalatal* [ʃ, ʒ]. The tongue front (excluding the tip) articulates with the back part of the alveolar ridge.
- *palatal* [j]. The tongue blade articulates with the back part of the alveolar ridge.
- *velar* [k, g]. The tongue back articulates with the velum (soft palate). [k, g] before back vowels, as in *core, gore.*

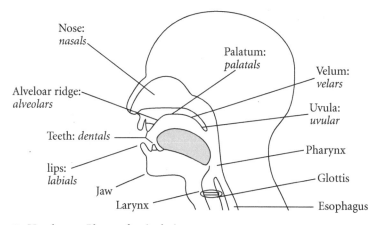

**Figure 2.** Vocal tract: Places of articulation

## 5.3.2 Manner of articulation

Manner of articulation describes the kind of constriction that is made. The following are the major categories (see Table 1):

- *stops (plosives)* [p, t, k, b, d, g, ʔ]. Stops are made by completely blocking the airstream at some point in the oral cavity.
- *fricatives* [f, v, θ, ð, s, z, ʃ, ʒ]. They are made with a very narrow gap between the articulators. The airstream passes through this gap under high pressure, causing **friction**.
- *affricates* [tʃ, dʒ]. They are complex sounds, consisting of a stop followed immediately by a fricative *at the same place of articulation*. Here, the stop is gradually released so as to form a narrow constricted gap for the air to flow through; this is the fricative part of the affricate.

– *approximants* [r, l, j, w]. They are articulated with only minimal constriction; consequently, there is virtually no friction. In most varieties of English, word initial "r" is an approximant. It is articulated by moving the tip of the tongue towards the alveolar ridge, deflecting the air over the tongue without causing friction.

It is useful to distinguish several subcategories of approximants:

- *laterals* [l]. In laterals the air flows along the sides (or along one side) of the tongue. For [l], the tip of the tongue forms a complete closure centrally against the alveolar ridge (as in a stop), but the side(s) of the tongue is/are lowered, and air is deflected between the side(s) and the gums.
- *glides* [j, w]. They are very short unstable versions of vowels, functioning in syllable structure as consonants. The initial [j] of *yes* is actually a kind of [i], whilst the [w] of *we* is a short version of [u]. Notice that [w] has a prominent bilabial ("lip-rounding") component also.
- *trills*. Here, one articulator is let to vibrate in the outflowing air stream. Scottish pronunciation of "r" is often an alveolar trill, with the tongue tip vibrating under the alveolar ridge. The "r" in some varieties of French and German is typically an uvular trill [R], with the uvula in vibration.
- *flaps* are produced when the tongue strikes agains the alveolar ridge once in passing. American speakers often articulate "t" and "d" as flaps, especially when "t" and "d" occur intervocalically (between vowels), e.g. *matter, city, medal.* Phonetic symbol: [ɾ]

– A difficult sound to classify is [h]. It is a kind of fricative, and essentially involves a slight friction at the not completely opened vocal folds, and no further significant modification of the airstream.

– *nasals* [m, n, ŋ]. They involve a blocking of the oral airstream, by lowering of the velum. Thus, the air is allowed to escape through the nasal cavities.

## 5.4 Vowels

As will be remembered from the previous section, consonants involve some major obstruction of the airflow at some point of the vocal tract. Vowels differ from consonants in that there is relatively little impedance of the air flow, but the oral cavity is shaped in many different ways and this gives rise to the different vowels and diphthongs. Vowels are more difficult to describe than consonants. There are three reasons for this:

Table 1. Consonants of British English

| Manner of articulation | Place of articulation | | | | | | | |
|---|---|---|---|---|---|---|---|---|
| | *bilabial* | *labio-dental* | *dental* | *alveolar* | *alveo-palatal* | *palatal* | *velar* | *glottal* |
| *o*  stops | p, b | | | t, d | | | k, g | ʔ |
| *r*  fricatives | | f, v | θ, ð | s, z | ʃ, ʒ | | | h |
| *a*  affricates | | | | | tʃ, dʒ | | | |
| *l*  approximants | w | | | l, r, ɾ | | j | | |
|      nasals | m | | | n | | | ŋ | |

a. Because there is no constriction of the vocal tract, it is often difficult to describe precisely the posture adopted by the oral cavity;
b. Vowel categories tend to "overlap" and "merge into" each other, much more than consonant categories;
c. Vowels tend to vary from accent to accent. **Accent,** in this sense, means the regional or social differences in pronunciation. What makes the different varieties of English sound so different, is mainly the vowels.

Since the tongue is the instrument par excellence to determine the posture adapted by the oral cavity, vowel sounds are described primarily in terms of the position of the tongue. Two parameters are important.

a. **front** vs. **back.** The highest part of the tongue may be towards the front of the mouth, or towards the back;
b. **high** vs. **low** (also called **close** vs. **open**). The degree to which the tongue is raised.

Independent of these two aspects are the following:

a. *lip position.* The lips may be rounded, or spread;
b. *duration.* A vowel can be long or short;
c. *nasalization.* A vowel can be oral or nasal.

In the next sections, we will first look at "ideal" vowels and then more particularly at standard British vowels and diphthongs, which are sequences of vowels within one syllable.

### 5.4.1 Cardinal vowels

Because of the inherent difficulties of defining tongue positions, phoneticians appeal to a set of reference point vowels. These are called **cardinal vowels**. The cardinal vowels define "fixed points" in articulatory "vowel space". Any vowel under consideration can then be "placed" with reference to a cardinal vowel.

First, we define the four extreme points on the dimensions front/back, high/low. These are:

[i]:   high and front
[u]:   high and back
[a]:   low and front
[ɒ]:   low and back

These can be displayed in the vowel quadrilateral. Conventionally, the quadrilateral is shorter at the bottom. This represents the fact that with your mouth wide open, there is less manoeuvre space for the tongue to go from front to back. The front vowel space is then divided up by placing [e] and [ɛ] at equidistant intervals between [i] and [a], while the back space is divided up with [o] and [ɔ]. This gives the eight **primary cardinal vowels** (Table 2).

**Table 2.** Primary cardinal vowels

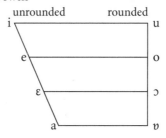

Of the eight primary cardinal vowels, the four back vowels are rounded, the four front vowels are unrounded. This is the "normal", or unmarked state of affairs, in the sense that front vowels in the world's languages are predominantly unrounded, while back vowels are predominantly rounded. We can, however, make rounded back vowels unrounded, and unrounded front vowels rounded. In this way, we get the eight **secondary cardinal vowels** (Table 3). Some of these vowels are found in languages other than English, such as French, German, Dutch, and Turkish.

**Table 3.** Secondary cardinal vowels

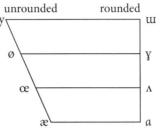

## 5.4.2 The vowels of (standard) British English

It is important to remember that cardinal vowels are reference points. When describing the vowels of a language (e.g. English), we "place" each vowel with respect to these reference points. The symbols that we use are largely a matter of convention. Although the vowel in *see* does not coincide with cardinal [i], we may nevertheless use the symbol [i], provided that we do not forget that we characterize English [i] with respect to cardinal [i].

Since the same convention is applied in other languages, we will have differences in the realizations of [i] in English and in the other languages. That is, [i] is pronounced quite differently in English, German or French, but by convention we use the same symbol.

Because of the large number of vowels in English, it is necessary to employ several symbols over and above the cardinal vowel symbols.

Here are the vowels of standard British English (also see Table 4).

| beat | i | the | ə | boot | u |
|------|---|-----|---|------|---|
| bit | ɪ | bird | ɜ | put | ʊ |
| bet | e | but | ʌ | bored | ɔ |
| bat | æ | bard | ɑ | pot | ɒ |

The schwa vowel /ə/ is used exclusively in unstressed syllables, e.g. *a sofa*, *a banana*. Some of these vowels are noticeably longer than the others. The "long" vowels are the vowels in *beat, bird, boot, bored, bard*. Some dictionaries include the length symbol [ː] in their transcription of the vowels.

The approximate location of the vowels in the vowel quadrilateral is shown in Table 4.

**Table 4.** Approximate location of English vowels

### 5.4.3 The diphthongs of (standard) British English

English has several diphthongs. A **diphthong** is a sequence of two vowels within a single syllable. One component of the diphthong is more prominent than the other. In the English diphthongs, it is usually the first component which is more prominent, but in other languages, e.g. French this may be different.

When the tongue moves during a diphthong, the diphthong obviously comprises a whole series of vowel qualities. The transitional qualities however are of no perceptual significance. What is important is only the starting and end point of the diphthong.

Even so, the precise quality of the less prominent component is also often unimportant. In *boy*, it is important only that the diphthong ends up somewhere in the general area of "high, front, unrounded". In such a situation, it is acceptable to use the symbol [i] as a cover symbol for "highish, frontish, unrounded", and [u] for "highish, backish, rounded". Thus, *boy* may be transcribed as [bɔi], and *so* as [səu]. Since the second element of these diphthongs is a high vowel, they are called *rising diphthongs*; if the second element is a schwa, we have *centring diphthongs*.

There are two broad categories of diphthongs in English, which differ according to the direction of vowel movement. The rising diphthongs, where the movement is towards a high vowel, and the centering diphthongs, where the movement is towards schwa. Rising diphthongs are in turn divided into those which have movement towards /i/, and those which have movement towards /u/. The different types are listed below, with suggestions for their transcription.

|  | *rising* |  |  | *centring* |  |
|---|---|---|---|---|---|
| say | ei | how | au | hair | eə |
| sigh | ai | so | əu | here | iə |
| soy | ɔi |  |  | poor | uə |

Some speakers have triphthongs, i.e. sequences of three vowel sounds within a syllable. Here are some examples, with suggestions for their transcription:

| | |
|---|---|
| shower, flower | auə |
| fire, hire | aiə |
| lawyer | ɔiə |

## 5.5   Phonemes and allophones; phonemic transcription

Just as one word may have many different senses and the exact sense of the word does not become really clear until it is used in a context, sounds may have many variations, too, dependent on the sounds surrounding them. In the next sections we will look at the terms used for a "family of sounds" and where the different "family members" may occur.

### 5.5.1   Definitions

The "p" sound in *pin* is different from the "p" sound in *spin*; the former is aspirated [pʰ], the latter unaspirated [p]. Yet, in an important sense, we want to say that the two "p" sounds of English, in spite of their phonetic difference, are variants of the same sound. The term **phoneme** designates the more abstract unit, of which [pʰ] and [p] are examples. [pʰ] and [p] are **allophones** of the same phoneme, /p/. (See Figure 3.)

By convention, phonemes are written between slashes / /, while allophones (or, more generally, sounds considered in their phonetic aspects) are written between square brackets [ ].

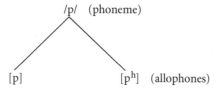

**Figure 3.**  A phoneme and its allophones

Two languages may classify their sounds in different ways. English and Spanish both have [d] and [ð]. For English speakers, the sounds are different (they are categorized as different phonemes), and they serve to distinguish word meanings (*den* vs. *then*). For the Spanish speaker, the two sounds are merely variants of the same phoneme. Thus, [d] occurs word-initially, while [ð] occurs intervocalically. Compare *donde* "where" [donde] and *lado* "side" [laðo]. If you pronounce *lado* with a [d], you get a variant pronunciation of *lado*, but you do not get a different word.

Whereas English speakers regard aspirated and unaspirated voiceless stops as variants of the same sound, Thai speakers do not. Compare Thai /pʰaa/ "split" and /paa/ "forest".

As this example shows, a simple way of deciding whether two sounds in a language belong to one phoneme or to two different phonemes is to look for **minimal pairs**. A minimal pair is a pair of words that are identical in all respects except for the sounds in question. The minimal pair *pat, bat* confirms that /p/ and /b/ constitute separate phonemes in English. On the other hand the impossibility of a contrast between [spʰai] and [spai], or between [pʰai] and [pai] confirms that [pʰ] and [p] do not belong to different phonemes in English.

### 5.5.2 Free variation and complementary distribution

The precise amount of aspiration in English stops (as in the initial stops in *pat, cat, tat*) is not linguistically relevant. Stops with different degrees of aspiration are in **free variation**. When sounds are in free variation, it basically doesn't matter which sound you select, and the meaning of an utterance is not affected.

Another situation is where one allophone occurs exclusively in one environment (context), another allophone occurs exclusively in another environment. The sounds are then said to be in **complementary distribution**. Here are some examples of sounds that are in complementary distribution in English.

a. Aspirated and unaspirated voiceless stops. The former occur in syllable-initial position before a stressed vowel, e.g. *top*; the latter occur after syllable-initial [s], e.g. *stop*.

b. Allophones of English /h/ can be regarded as voiceless versions of the following vowel. The "h" sounds in *hen, heart, hat, who* are phonetically very different. Yet the choice of one variant over the other is fully determined by the following vowel. The different varieties of "h" are therefore in complementary distribution.

c. A dental stop [t̪] occurs in the word *eighth* /eit̪θ/. But dental stops do not contrast with alveolar stops in English. Dental stops occur only before a dental fricative. Dental stops are therefore in complementary distribution with alveolar stops.

d. The vowel in *leave* is longer than the vowel in *leaf*. The length difference is a consequence of the voicing of the following consonant. In general, a vowel is shorter before a voiceless consonant than before a voiced consonant. The length difference is therefore not phonemic. The longer and shorter varieties of the vowel are in complementary distribution.

e. In English, vowels before a nasal consonant are often nasalized, e.g. *can't* [kãnt]. Whereas in French, oral and nasal vowels contrast in minimal pairs, this is not so in English. In English, oral and nasal vowels are in complementary distribution.

Native speakers are usually quite unaware of the extent of allophonic variation in their language. English speakers think of the /p/ in *pie* and the /p/ in *spy* as "the same sound"; it is only after studying phonetics that one realizes that they are in fact very different sounds! Speakers' intuitions thus reflect a knowledge of the phonemic structure of their language, rather than its phonetic reality.

### 5.5.3 Principles of transcription

What is usually called "phonetic transcription", e.g. in dictionaries for foreign language students, is in actual fact a phonemic transcription. A **phonetic transcription** aims to represent phonetic variation in all its detail. The ability to produce a good phonetic transcription is a skill which requires many years of training.

Fortunately, for many purposes of linguistic analysis, a **phonemic transcription** is sufficient. A phonemic transcription represents each sound segment by the phoneme which it instantiates. For any given language, the inventory of phonemes is quite limited (between 30 and 50 in most cases). A phonemic transcription can then be supplemented by a set of statements which give details of the possible **realizations** of each phoneme in its different environments.

It is therefore quite legitimate to transcribe the words *pie* and *spy* as /pai/, /spai/, with the understanding that syllable-initial /p/ before a stressed vowel is realized with aspiration [pʰ].

You can think of a phonemic transcription as an "ideal" alphabetic spelling system. English spelling does not represent aspiration, because aspiration is not phonemic. Spanish spelling does not represent the difference between [d] and [ð] because the difference in not phonemic. The same difference in English *is* phonemic, however, and *is* represented in spelling.

### 5.6  Beyond the phoneme

In describing the sound system of a language, it is not enough to list the phonemes and their allophones. We also need to state the ways in which sounds are combined. To do this, it is often necessary to refer to units "above" the individual sounds. One such unit, of fundamental importance in all languages, is the **syllable**. Other units are stress, tone and intonation.

### 5.6.1  Syllables

i.  *What is a (phonological) syllable?*
It is actually rather difficult to give a precise definition of "**syllable**". One way to think of syllables is as units determined by "peaks of sonority" (i.e. vowels), flanked by elements of lower sonority (i.e. consonants). The stream of speech consists, therefore, of alternations of sonorous and less sonorous elements.

Languages differ considerably with respect to the kinds of syllables which they allow. On the one hand there are languages like Maori, which tolerate only syllables of the form (C)V. A syllable, that is, consists of an obligatory vowel, preceded by an optional consonant. In such languages, it is not possible for two consonants to occur adjacent to each other; in addition, every syllable (and hence, every word and every utterance) must end in a vowel.

English, on the other hand, permits syllables of considerable complexity, with **consonant clusters** (i.e. groups of more than one consonant) allowed in both syllable-initial and syllable-final position, e.g. *spray* /sprei/, *sixths* /sɪkstθs/. Even so, it is not the case that *any* combination of consonants can occur. A syllable-initial cluster of three consonants can only consist of /s/ + voiceless stop + one of /l, r, j, w/, as in *string, scream, splice, spew, skew, squat.*

Some languages permit consonant clusters which are quite alien to English. Russian allows syllable-initial clusters consisting of two voiced stops, as in *gd'e* "where", two voiceless stops, as in *ptit'a* "bird", two nasals, as in *mn'e* "to me", or a stop plus nasal, as in *kniga* "book". (Note: in transliterating Russian words, it is normal to indicate palatalization, i.e. the articulation of a consonant with a high front tongue position, by means of the apostrophe, as in *mn'e.*)

The **distribution** of a phoneme is the position in a syllable where a given phoneme can occur. The velar nasal /ŋ/ can only occur in syllable-final position, and then only after the "short" vowels /ɪ, e, æ, ɒ, ʌ, ə/; there are, for example, no native English words beginning with /ŋ/. These facts about English cannot be stated without reference to syllables. It would be false to claim, for example, that

/ŋ/ cannot occur before vowels; it obviously can, as in *singing* /sɪŋɪŋ/.

Syllable boundaries can be represented in a transcription by means of [.]. The syllabification of *singing* could be represented as /sɪŋ.ɪŋ/.

## ii. *Long and short vowels*

Some monosyllabic words lack a postvocalic consonant, e.g. *he, car, saw, sow.* Only a subset of the English vowels occur in such words. There are no English words */bɪ/, */bæ/, */bʊ/, etc. The so-called "short" vowels /ɪ, e, æ, ɒ, ʊ, ʌ/ *must* be followed by a consonant: /bɪt/, /bæt/, /bʊk/. On the other hand, the so-called "long" vowels (i.e. all the remaining vowels, and the diphthongs) can readily occur without a following consonant in a monosyllabic word.

## iii. *The case of "h" and "r"*

We need to refer to syllables in order to describe the distribution of /h/ and /r/. Concerning /h/, we need to say that the sound can only occur in syllable-initial position; it would not be enough to say that /h/ cannot occur after a vowel.

The case of /r/ is especially interesting. We can make a broad distinction between two groups of English accents according to the pronunciation of words like *car, part, nurse, source.* Most North American speakers (as well as speakers of Scottish and Irish English) pronounce the "r" in these words. Speakers of standard British English (as well as speakers of "Southern hemisphere English", i.e. New Zealanders, Australians, South Africans) generally do not pronounce the "r". For speakers who do not pronounce the "r", the words *sauce* and *source* are **homophones** (they are pronounced identically); Americans, however, pronounce the words differently.

How can we describe the difference between the two dialect groups? It is not sufficient to say that in British English (etc.) the "r" does not occur post-vocalically. In *The car runs well* the "r" of *runs* occurs after the vowel in *car.* It would be more accurate to say that "r" occurs only in syllable-initial position than to say it may not occur after a vowel within the same syllable.

## iv. *The linking "r"*

Although British (etc.) speakers pronounce *car* without the final "r", the "r" often does emerge if the following word begins with a vowel. Compare

the car was mine/the car (r)is mine

In the second example, the "r" is pronounced, and gets attached to the following syllable. This is the linking "r".

Sometimes, an "r" is inserted even if there is no "r" in the spelling: *Asia (r)and Africa, the idea (r)of it.* This is often called the "intrusive r". You some-times get an "intrusive r" within a word, as in *withdraw(r)ing, saw(r)ing.*

### 5.6.2 Stress, tone, intonation

**Stress** is a property of syllables. A stressed syllable is produced with more energy than an unstressed syllable. Stressed syllables, therefore, are more "prominent" than unstressed syllables. They are typically longer and louder than unstressed syllables, and are produced with greater clarity. Unstressed syllables tend to be short, and are often pronounced rather indistinctly.

Each word in English has a distinctive **word stress** pattern. Some words are, amongst others, distinguished by stress location: *SUBject* vs. *subJECT*. The phonetic symbol for stress is ['] placed before the stressed syllable: ['sʌbdʒekt], [səb'dʒekt].

Within an utterance, stress can highlight the important words, often by suggesting a contrast. Compare: *HE didn't do that, He DIDN'T do that, He didn't DO that, He didn't do THAT.* It is not difficult to construct contexts in which each of these variants would be appropriate.

**Tone** is also a property of syllables. In a tone language like Chinese, most syllables are associated with a characteristic pitch melody. This means that the same syllable spoken with a different tone each time has a different meaning. The pitch melody assigned to the syllable is just as much a part of the word as is the phonemic structure of the syllable.

**Intonation** is the melody superimposed on an utterance. Intonation is of importance in English for signalling the function of an utterance (e.g. as a statement or question), and for expressing speaker attitudes (see Chapter 4.4.1 and 4.4.2). It may be very interesting to compare the many intonations that can be associated with *really.*

### 5.7   Sounds in context

It is not sufficient to study sounds in isolation since sounds may change under the influence of other sounds when words are combined with other words. In the longer units of word groups or sentences, the sounds of single words undergo massive changes such as linking, elision, assimilation etc.

### 5.7.1 "Linking"

One kind of change involves adding **linking elements** at the boundaries of words. Examples from English are the linking and "intrusive r", discussed in the preceding section.

### 5.7.2 Elision

Sounds are often omitted in the stream of speech, especially in informal speaking styles. This is known as **elision**. Elisions should not be thought of as "careless", or "lazy". On the contrary, not to use elided pronunciations in relaxed, informal speech could be perceived as pedantic.

In careful speech, *library* would have three syllables. In informal speech, it could have only two [laibri]. Likewise, *ordinary* has four syllables only in very careful speech.

Consonant clusters are often the target of elision, i.e. one or more consonants in a cluster are elided. The elided consonants are nearly always alveolar or dental.

*Clothes* in careful speech is [kləuðz]. In informal speech it is [kləuz]. This pronunciation is especially likely if the next word begins with a consonant, as in *clothes cupboard*.

*And* typically loses the final stop, especially if the following word begins with a consonant: *you and me* [ju ən mi].

*Next and last* generally lose their final /t/ before a word beginning with a consonant: *last night* [las nait].

/h/ is generally elided in unstressed syllables. In *I saw HIM* (with stress on *him*), the /h/ is pronounced. If *him* is unstressed, the /h/ is elided: *I SAW him* [ai 'sɔ ɪm] or [ai 'sɔ əm]. It is even possible for an "intrusive r" to appear in the phrase: [ai sɔ rɪm].

### 5.7.3 Assimilation

**Assimilation** is a process whereby one sound causes an adjacent sound to be "more similar" to itself. Assimilation can be progressive (a sound influences the following sound), or retrogressive (a sound influences a preceding sound).

**Progressive assimilation** is illustrated by the alternative pronunciations of the plural morpheme. After a voiceless consonant, plural "s" is voiceless: *cats* [kæts]. After a voiced sound (either consonant or vowel), plural "s" is voiced:

*dogs* [dɔgz], *bees* [biz]. Further examples of progressive assimilation are the devoicing of the normally voiced [l, r] when these sounds occur after a voiceless consonant in a syllable-initial cluster: *please, pray* [pl̥iz, pr̥ei].

**Retrogressive assimilations** are frequent in English. *News* has a final voiced [z]. Yet in *newspaper* voiceless [p] causes preceding [z] to become [s]: [njuspeipə].

The above examples illustrate **voicing assimilation**, i.e. the voice/voicelessness of a segment "spreads" into a neighbouring segment.

**Place assimilation** is when the place of articulation of a consonant spreads into a neighbouring consonant. Retrogressive place assimilation is frequent in English. Thus, *good boy* may be spoken as [gʊb bɔi], *good girl* as [gʊg gɜl]. The nasal in the negative prefixes *un-* and *in-* often assimilates to the place of articulation of a following consonant. In *unbelievable* the negative prefix is followed by a bilabial, and may be pronounced [əm], while in *unconscious* it is followed by a velar, and may be pronounced [əŋ]. In *unfavourable* one might get the labiodental nasal [ɱ].

**Nasal assimilation** occurs when one segment takes on the nasality of a neighbouring segment. Vowels often nasalize before a nasal consonant: *can't* [kãnt].

Assimilation can be total, i.e. a sound can become identical to its neighbour. By retrogressive voicing assimilation, *is Sam* [ɪz sæm] becomes [ɪs sæm].

Some assimilations (e.g. the devoicing of /z/ in *newspaper*) are obligatory within word boundaries, often, however, they are optional, and tend to be more frequent the more informal and relaxed the speaking style.

Assimilation can sometimes appear to change the phonemic structure of a word. In the example *good boy*, the final [d] of *good* is changed to [b], i.e. an allophone of the /d/ phoneme has been replaced by an allophone of a different phoneme, i.e. /b/. In other cases, assimilation replaces one allophone of a phoneme by another allophone of the same phoneme, as when the [l] of *play* becomes voiceless. Although we cannot pursue this matter here, facts of this nature have led some linguists to question the theoretical status of the phoneme, as traditionally defined. For example, given that *comfort* is pronounced [kʌɱfət], and that the use of [ɱ] represents place assimilation to the following [f], to which phoneme should [ɱ] be assigned, to /m/ or to /n/?

### 5.7.4 Palatalization

**Palatalization** is a rather common process in which the palatal glide [j] causes a preceding obstruent to be articulated in the palatal region.

Palatalization has the following effects, and may occur across word boundaries or within a word:

| | | | | | |
|---|---|---|---|---|---|
| [d] + [j] | → | [dʒ] | did you | [dɪdju] | → | [dɪdʒu] |
| [t] + [j] | → | [tʃ] | hit you | [hɪtju] | → | [hɪtʃu] |
| [z] + [j] | → | [ʒ] | please you | [plizju] | → | [pliʒu] |
| [s] + [j] | → | [ʃ] | issue | [ɪsju] | → | [ɪʃu] |
| | | | | (conservative British) | (progressive) |

Strictly speaking, this is an example of retrogressive assimilation. Its effects however, merit separate treatment. Some of the oddities of English spelling reflect palatalizations that occurred in the past. The fact that orthographic "s" in *sure*, *sugar* is pronounced [ʃ] is a consequence of the sound change [sju] → [ʃu].

### 5.7.5 Vowel reduction

**Vowel reduction** is the process in which unstressed vowels in English typically lose their distinctive quality and take on the quality of the schwa vowel. Compare the [æ] vowel that occurs in stressed *and*, with the schwa vowel that occurs in unstressed *and*.

Vowel reduction can be clearly observed in sets of words like the following. Note how the vowels change according to whether they are stressed or not.

| | |
|---|---|
| PHOtograph | /ˈfəutəgraf/ |
| phoTOgrapher | /fəˈtɒgrəfə/ |
| photoGRAphic | /fəutəˈgræfɪk/ |

### 5.7.6 "Weak" and "strong" forms

Many of the shorter **function words** of English, i.e. free grammatical morphemes such as prepositions, articles, parts of the verbs *be* and *have*, etc., have two pronunciations, according to whether they are stressed or unstressed, called "strong" and "weak" forms respectively. The **strong forms** occur in sentences such as "He *should* do it". The **weak forms** (pronunciations used when the words are unstressed) exhibit a mixture of vowel reductions and elisions.

*You should have done it* [jə ʃʊdəv dʌnət]

### 5.7.7 Complex processes

Sometimes it is possible to display the series of processes whereby careful and relaxed pronunciations can be related.

|  | boys and girls | girls and boys |
|---|---|---|
|  | [bɔiz ænd gɜlz] | [gɜlz ænd bɔiz] |
| (vowel reduction) | [bɔiz ənd gɜlz] | [gɜlz ənd bɔiz] |
| (elision) | [bɔiz ən gɜlz] | [gɜlz ən bɔiz] |
| (place assimilation) | [bɔiz əŋ gɜlz] | [gɜlz əm bɔiz] |

|  | does she |
|---|---|
|  | dʌz ʃi |
| (place assimilation) | dʌʒ ʃi |
| (voice assimilation) | dʌʃ ʃi |
| (elision) | dʌ ʃi |

### 5.8 Summary

**Phonetics** is the study of the physical aspects of speech sounds which may occur in any language, whereas **phonology** is the study of the sound system of a given language. Spelling and pronunciation may differ very strongly. Sometimes an **etymological spelling** as in *debt* /det/ is introduced to mark the etymology of a word. **Spelling pronunciation** is the opposite: a letter that is written such as *t* in *often* is pronounced by some people because they "see" it. Because the spelling and the pronunciation may differ so strongly the **International Phonetic Association** has developed a set of **phonetic symbols**. We characterize speech sounds from the point of view of **phonation**, which determines the difference between **voiced** and **unvoiced** (or **voiceless**) sounds, and **articulation**, which determines the shape of the vocal tract and thus creates the space for each individual sound. **Consonants** are determined by both the **place of articulation** and the **manner of articulation**, such as full occlusion, strong restriction or almost no impediment of the airstream. **Vowels** and diphthongs have no impediment whatsoever and are far more difficult to localize. Therefore some reference points, known as **cardinal vowels**, are chosen in the oral cavity and with the help of the parameters, **high** vs. **low** and **front** vs. **back**, all the vowels may be characterized. The pronunciation of vowels may greatly differ because of **accent**, i.e. the regional or social differences in pronunciation. **Diphthongs** are combinations of two vowels in one syllable. Since different sounds may be variants of one and the same **phoneme**, this category is of a psychological rather than physical nature. It is what in a given language is considered to be meaning-discriminating. Two different sounds are two different phonemes if they cause a difference in meaning as in a **minimal pair** like *pear* and *bear*. Different sounds that do not create a difference in meaning like the [tʰ] in *top* and the [t] in *stop* are **allophones**, which in this case occur in **complementary distribution**. This means that they are bound to a given position: [*tʰ*] can only occur in initial position, [*t*] in non-initial position. If the context does not play a role, allophones are in **free variation**. We must also distinguish between a **phonetic transcription**, describing all the allophones of a phoneme, and a **phonemic transcription**, only taking care of the phonemes.

In addition to speech sounds, also larger entities such as the syllable, stress, tone and intonation are important. A phonological **syllable** consists of a vowel(-like) sonorant core, i.e. a vowel or diphthong, represented as V and optionally a consonant (C). Languages differ very strongly in their patterns of syllable structure. The position which a phoneme can have in a syllable is known as its **distribution**. In English many consonants can be combined into **consonant clusters**. If a phoneme is not pronounced in a given position, e.g. /r/ *source* in British English, we may have **homophones** as with *source* and *sauce*. Also **stress** and **tone** are properties of syllables, whereas **intonation** is the melody superimposed on an utterance. Syllables are grouped into words and therefore **word stress** is needed to mark the main syllable. The flow of sentences causes the individual words to be adapted in various ways. **Linking elements** may have to be added between words ending and beginning with a vowel, **elision** may be needed, and especially consonants may have to be adapted to each other, which is known as **assimilation**. We distinguish between two types of **voice assimilation**: **progressive assimilation** as in *dogs* /dɒgz/ and **retrogressive assimilation** as in *hotdog* /hɒdɒg/. **Place assimilation** occurs in *good boy* /gʊbɔi/. Other processes of adaptation to the speech stream are **palatalization, vowel reduction** and the use of **weak forms** in unaccented syllables and **strong forms** in accented ones.

## 5.9 Further reading

Good introductions on phonetics are Ladefoged (1993) and Catford (1990) and on phonology Katamba (1982) and Lass (1991). Specific treatments of British English are Gimson (1989) and Giegerich (1992). Cognitive approaches are Nathan (1994, 1996, 1999) and Taylor (2002).

## Assignments

1. The underlined segments in the following words represent different pronunciations. Group the segments accordingly and find the appropriate terms to characterize the differences.

    a. thin – then – mother – cloth – clothes
    b. sees – seize – cease – seizes – ceases – house – houses

2. Compare the written forms and the pronunciations of the following words and (i) say whether they rhyme or not, (ii) write the words in phonemic transcription

    a. horse – worse
    b. heart – heard – beard
    c. lumber – plumber
    d. tough – bough – dough – hiccough
    e. broom – brook – brooch
    f. tomb – bomb – womb
    g. roll – doll
    h. golf – wolf
    i. seize – sieve
    j. kind – kindle

3. a. Do you think it would be good idea if English spelling more closely represented pronunciation?
    b. Can you see any disadvantages if English spelling were 100% phonemic?
    c. Comment on Mark Twain's plans for the improvement of English spelling:

    For example, in Year 1 that useless letter "c" would be dropped to be replased either by "k" or "s", and likewise, "x" would no longer be part of the alphabet. The only kase in which "c" would be retained would be the "ch" formation, which will be dealt with later. Year 2 might reform "w" spelling, so that "which" and "one" would take the same konsonant, wile Year 3 might well abolish "y" replasing it with "i" and lear 4 might fiks the "g/j" anomali wonse and for all.

Jenerally, then, the improvement would kontinue iear bai iear with lear 5 doing awai with useless double konsonants, and lears 6–12 or so modifaiing vowlz and rimeining voist and unvoist konsonants. Bai lear 15 or sou, it wud fainali bi posibl tu meik ius ov thi ridandant letez "c", "y" and "x" — bai now jast a memori in the maindz ov ould doderez — tu riplais "ch", "sh", and "th" rispektivli.

Fainali, xen, aafte sam 20 iers ov orxogrefkl riform, wi wud hev a lojikl, kohirnt speling in ius xrewawt xe Ingliy-spiking werld.

4. Voicing

   a. It is not possible to produce voiced sounds while whispering. Why not? Consequently, a whispered utterance of the word *hand* ought to be virtually indistinguishable from a whispered utterance of the word *and*. Why? Try it, and see!

   b. Is it possible to distinguish the words *Sue* and *zoo*, *cease* and *seize*, *do* and *too*, in whisper? If you find that it is possible (which you should!), what explanation can you offer?
      (Hint: [d] and [t], [z] and [s], are not only distinguished by presence vs. absence of voice, but by other features as well. What are these?)

5. Consonants

   a. The first sound of *yes* is very similar, phonetically, to the final sound of *say*. Yet you would probably want to say that the first sound of *yes* is a consonant, and the final sound of *say* is a vowel. Why?

   b. Try to isolate the "k" sound in *keen* and the "k" sound in *cool*. How do they differ? Say the sounds independently of the words in which they occur.

6. Phonemes and allophones

   If you consider the environments in which they occur, you will discover that "h"-sounds and [ŋ] are in complementary distribution in English. State the environments in which these sounds occur as precisely as possible. Would you want to say that "h"-sounds and the velar nasal are allophones of one and the same phoneme? Why not? What additional criteria, over and above the fact of complementary distribution, need to be invoked in identifying the phonemes of a language?

7. Vowels

   a. Make a pure (i.e. unvarying) "i"-type vowel, as in *see*. Make the vowel as front as possible, and as high as possible. Now make a pure "u"-type vowel, as in *too*. The [u] vowel should be as back as possible, and as high as possible, and with prominent lip rounding.

Alternate between the two vowels: [i – u – i – u]. You should feel your tongue moving from the front to the back of your mouth. At the same time, your lips will round with [u] and unround with [i].

b. Now go from [i] to the "a"-like sound in *cat*. The "a"-sound should be as front as possible, and as low as possible. Alternate between them: [i – a – i – a]. You should feel your tongue going up and down, but still remaining front.

Now go from [u] to a back "a"-like vowel [ɑ], as in *car*. You should feel the up-down movement of the tongue at the back of your mouth as you alternate between [u] and [ɑ].

c. Go from the front [a] sound to back [ɑ]. Alternate between them [a – ɑ – a – ɑ – a].

8. Syllables

Is "intrusive r" possible in the following phrases?

| | |
|---|---|
| the idea of it | low and high |
| Africa and Asia | high and low |
| Pa and Ma | you and me |
| law and order | me and you |
| so and so | |

Make a list of those vowels after which the "intrusive r" can occur.
List those vowels after which the "intrusive r" may not occur.
Is it possible to characterize the two groups of vowels?

# 6  Language, culture and meaning
## Cross-cultural semantics

## 6.0 Overview

The previous chapters have shown repeatedly that linguistic conceptualization may be radically different in various, even closely related languages. This applies to concepts expressed through all aspects of linguistic structure, i.e. the lexicon, morphology, syntax, and even in phonology, at the level of tone and intonation.

This chapter will look into cross-linguistic semantic differences in a systematic way. We will present a method for pinpointing semantic distinctions and for exploring their cultural relevance. A key question is whether differences in linguistic conceptualization play a central role in language and thought or whether they are rather marginal. Both positions have been advocated. The first is known as linguistic relativity, in its extreme form as linguistic determinism. The second is known as universalism and holds that all people all over the world basically think in the same way. This chapter proposes a compromise between the extremes: Most linguistic concepts are indeed language-specific, but there is also a small number of universal linguistic concepts which occur in all languages. These universal concepts can be used as a "neutral" basis for paraphrasing the huge variety of language-specific and culture-specific concepts in the languages of the world. This is illustrated firstly for lexical concepts, then for grammatical concepts, and finally for the cultural norms of behaviour which underlie people's behaviour in different cultures.

## 6.1  Introduction: Linguistic relativity and universalism

A key question is whether language influences thought or thought influences language. Both positions have been advocated. The first is known as **linguistic** relativity. The rival position is known as **universalism**. It assumes that human thought is significantly similar across all cultures — that humankind shares a certain "psychic unity" — and that since language is a reflection of human thought, all languages are significantly similar as far as their conceptual categories are concerned. In its extreme version, this position asserts that linguistic conceptualization is essentially the same in all languages. Though incompatible in their extreme versions, this section will show that it is possible to see some truth in both linguistic relativity and universalism.

### 6.1.1 Linguistic and cultural relativity

How much does our language influence the way we think? How deeply do language and culture interpenetrate and influence one another? Few questions about language have fascinated thinkers more throughout the ages.

In 1690 the English philosopher John Locke observed that in any language there is a "great store of words … which have not any that answer them in another [language]". Such language-specific words, he said, represent certain "complex ideas" which have grown out of "the customs and manner of life" of the people (1976:226). This same insight recurred throughout the German Romantic tradition, especially in the writings of Johann Gottfried Herder and Wilhelm von Humboldt, who regarded language as a prisma or grid spread over things in the world so that each language reflects a different **worldview** (*Weltsicht*). It was eventually taken to America in the person of Franz Boas, the founder of cultural and linguistic anthropology in that country.

In America Boas and his students encountered languages and cultures which differed enormously from those of Europe. So great were differences in the area of vocabulary alone that, as Edward Sapir (1949:27) observed: "Distinctions which seem inevitable to us may be utterly ignored in languages which reflect an entirely different type of culture, while these in turn insist on distinctions which are all but unintelligible to us."

Similar observations were made in the thirties by Russian researchers such as Luria and Vygotsky (1992), who found that indigenous Sami (Lapp) societies in the north of Norway had huge vocabularies, but often lacked a more abstract general category or hypernym:

> One of the Northern primitive peoples, for example, has a host of terms for the different species of reindeer. There is a special word for reindeer aged 1, 2, 3, 4, 5, 6 and 7 years, twenty words for ice, eleven for the cold; forty-one for snow

in its various forms, and twenty-six verbs for freezing and thawing. It is for this reason that they oppose the attempt to make them change from their own language to Norwegian, which they find too poor in this regard. (1992:63)

The grammatical systems of the languages of the New World also came as a shock to European sensibilities. There were languages lacking familiar categories like countable and uncountable, adjective and verb (only an affix), tense and case, but prolifically endowed with "exotic" distinctions, such as whether an event or action was reiterated in space or in time; whether it took place to the north, south, east or west; whether the speaker knew of it from personal observation, from deduction, or from hearsay; or whether a thing was visible or not.

Sapir (1958:157–159) himself gives the example of what in English is described in terms of a "happening" schema, i.e. "The stone falls". Kwakiutl (a native American language of British Columbia) specifies whether the stone is visible or invisible to the speaker at the moment of speaking and whether it is nearest the speaker, the hearer or a third person. But Kwakiutl does not specify whether it is one stone or several stones. Neither does it specify the time of the fall. In the immediately neighbouring language of the Nootka, the comparable expression does not contain any noun equivalent to "stone", but only a verb form consisting of two elements, one for the movement or position of a stone or stone-like object, and a second for the downward direction, so that the scene would be more faithfully expressed in English as "It stones down". In Nootka, according to Sapir, the English view of "a stone" as a time-stable entity is not present; rather, the "thing status" of "stone" is implied in the verbal element which designates the nature of the motion involved.

In view of examples like this one, it is hard to avoid the conclusion that the different grammatical categories of different languages invite, or even compel, their speakers to see the world in distinctive ways. This view is referred to as the "**Sapir-Whorf hypothesis**". Benjamin Lee Whorf, who coined the term *linguistic relativity*, explained it as follows:

> We dissect nature along lines laid down by our native languages... We cut nature up, organize it into concepts, and ascribe significances as we do, largely because we are parties to an agreement to organize it in this way — an agreement that holds throughout our speech community and is codified in the patterns of our language. The agreement is, of course, an implicit and unstated one, BUT ITS TERMS ARE ABSOLUTELY OBLIGATORY; we cannot talk at all except by subscribing to the organization and classification of data which agreement decrees. (Whorf 1956:213–214)

Admittedly, Whorf may have exaggerated the degree to which the agreement that holds throughout a speech community is "absolutely obligatory". We can always find a way around the canonical "terms of agreement" by using paraphrases and circumlocutions of one kind or another. But this can only be done at a cost — by using longer, more complex, more cumbersome expressions than those offered to us by the ordinary habitual patterns of our native language. We can only try to avoid linguistic conventions of which we are conscious. However, the grip of people's native language on their perceptual and thinking habits is usually so strong that they are no more aware of such linguistic conventions than they are of the air they breathe.

Whorf has been criticized and attacked as no linguist before or after him for claiming that language influences thought, but lately it has been argued quite convincingly that very few of his former critics have really read and understood what Whorf was trying to say.

One of the most potent objections was that no one has given independent evidence that linguistic patterns really do influence people's patterns of attention and categorization. Recently, however, evidence of this kind has come to light. For example, the child language researchers Choi and Bowerman (1991) and Bowerman (1996) have shown that English and Korean-speaking children at 20 months of age, which is the age when children begin to speak, respond quite differently in experiments which require them to compare and group together actions such as (a) placing pieces in a puzzle, (b) putting toys into a bag, or (c) putting a cap on a pen, and (d) putting a hat on a doll's head. The English children classify the relations between the pieces of a puzzle and their "fixed" position in the puzzle as an *in* relation just like the "loose" relation of toys in a box. That is, they assign (a) and (b) to one group (Table 1).

Similarly, they make a different group for the "fixed" relation of a cap on a pen or the "loose" relation of a hat on a head, and consequently assign (c) and (d) to the other group. Note that this classification is entirely forced on these children by the contrast between the English prepositions *in* and *on*. But the Korean children have learned different words, i.e. *kkita* for something that has a "firmly fixed" or "tight fit" position, and different other verbs for things that are loosely put in or on other entities. Consequently, the Korean children group the equivalent of (a) "tight *in*" and (c) "tight *on*" together as a first group, and (b) "loose *in*" and (d) "loose *on*" as a second group. In other words, these children construe the relations between objects in the world on the basis of their language-specific categories, and not on the basis of some universal, conceptual categories, which extreme universalists claim to exist for all linguistic categories.

**Table 1.**  Cross-cutting classification of acts of "putting on/joining" and "taking off/separating" by young English-speaking and Korean-speaking children

| | | | English-speaking children | |
| --- | --- | --- | --- | --- |
| | | | **In**<br><br>*put in/take out*<br>'containment' | **On**<br><br>*put on/take off*<br>'surface contact, support' |
| **Korean-speaking children** | **Tight fit** | *kkita*<br>'tight fit and attachment'<br>*ppayta*<br>'remove from tight fit' | a.<br>piece/puzzle<br>picture/wallet<br>hand/glove<br>book/fitted case | c.<br>cap/pen<br>lid/jar<br>glove/hand<br><br>magnet/surface<br>tape/surface<br><br>Lego pieces together/apart |
| | **Loose fit** | other verbs<br>'loose fit' | b.<br>toys/bag or box<br>blocks/pan<br><br>getting in/out of tub<br>going in/out of house, room | d.<br>clothing on/off<br>(hat, shoe, coat, etc.)<br><br>getting on/off chair |

In other research, John Lucy (1992b) has found significant differences in the way in which adult speakers of English and Yucatec Maya process information about concrete objects. English speakers show greater attention to number than Yucatec speakers and tend to classify by shape, while Yucatec speakers tend to classify by material composition. These differences correspond to what could be predicted on the basis of linguistic differences (English has number marking, Yucatec has classifiers).

### 6.1.2  Semantic primes as a key to cross-cultural comparisons

The traditional view of human thought is that of **universalism**, i.e. that all people all over the world basically think in the same way. But since languages are so different, how could linguistic concepts in various languages be the same?

Stating differences and similarities between two languages is one thing. Formulating these differences is another. In the past, research into the relationship between language, culture and thought lacked descriptively adequate methods for analyzing the similarities and differences between the meaning systems of different languages. The key to achieving the necessary rigour is basing our method of semantic analysis on universal concepts. Many thinkers through the centuries have believed that a set of universal concepts exists. Philosophers like Pascal, Descartes, Arnauld, and Leibniz called them "simple ideas". Modern linguists generally refer to them as **semantic primes** or semantic primitives.

By means of empirical research, especially by comparison of equivalent words in a large number of languages, so far about 60 semantic primes can be thought of as **universal concepts** or as the basic "atoms" of meaning, in terms of which the thousands upon thousands of complex meanings are composed (Table 2).

Table 2. Universal semantic primes

| | |
|---|---|
| Substantives | I, you, someone, people, something, person, body, word |
| Determining elements | this, the same, other, one, two, some, much, all |
| Experiencing verbs | know, think, want, feel, see, hear |
| Actions and processes | say, do, happen, move |
| Existence and possession | there is, have |
| Life and death | live, die |
| Evaluation and description | good, bad, big, small |
| Spatial concepts | where, here, above, below, near, far, inside, side |
| Temporal concepts | when, now, before, after, a long time, a short time, for some time |
| Relational elements | kind of, part of, very, more, like |
| Logical elements | if, because, not, maybe, can |

However, there are a few complications which should be mentioned. Firstly, a single semantic prime can sometimes be expressed by different words in different contexts, called "**allolexes**" (in analogy to "allophones"). For example, in English *else* and *don't* are allolexes of *other* and *not*, respectively. Secondly, in some languages the equivalents of semantic primes may be affixes or fixed phrases rather than individual words. Thirdly, words usually have more than one meaning, which can confuse the situation. For example, the English word *move* has two different meanings in the sentences *I couldn't move* and *Her words moved me*, but only the first meaning is proposed as a semantic prime.

We can now present an approach for cross-linguistic and cross-cultural semantics. In Chapter 2 we saw that one way of describing the sense of a word is to "paraphrase" it by forming a string of other words which is supposed to "say the same thing". Paraphrasing works effectively only if simpler words are used in the paraphrase. Unfortunately, dictionary definitions often violate this principle, thus falling into the trap of **obscurity**. For example, one dictionary defines the word *remind* as: "Make (person) have recollection of". If a person's knowledge of English does not include the word *remind*, is it likely that he or she would understand *recollection*? Presumably not. Obscure definitions do not serve to make a meaning clear and explicit. They merely replace the job of understanding one unknown term by the job of having to understand another.

Hand in hand with obscurity goes **circularity**. This describes a situation in which word A is defined in terms of word B, then word B is defined in terms of word A, as in the following example (again, from a dictionary): *Fate* "a person's destiny"; *destiny* "that which happens to a person or thing thought of as determined by fate". Sometimes it takes several steps before the circle closes: For example, A is defined via B, B via C, then C via A. Obviously, we get nowhere by "defining" words in a circular fashion.

When we attempt to describe the meanings of words from a language different from our own, there is a third problem. Most words don't have precise equivalents across languages. This applies even to apparently simple and concrete words, for example, *hand* and *break*. Russian is a language which doesn't have an exact equivalent for English *hand*, because the Russian word which refers to a person's hand (*ruka*) applies to the entire arm. Malay is a language which doesn't have a precise equivalent for *break*, because there are distinct words, *putus* and *patah*, depending on whether the break is complete or partial.

Such meaning variation across languages brings with it the danger of **ethnocentrism** (culture bias) in semantics. If we use concepts which are English-specific in describing another language, then our description will inevitably be a distorted one because we will impose our own conceptual categories onto the other language. For example, it would be ethnocentric to explain the meaning of *ruka* as "hand or arm", because the distinction between the hand and the arm is not important to the meaning of the Russian word.

How can these problems be overcome? To avoid obscurity and circularity we have to phrase any description of a word's meaning in simpler terms than the word being described. A description of a word meaning which follows this principle is called a **reductive paraphrase**, because it breaks down (or "reduces") the complex meaning into a combination of simpler meanings. The most complete reductive paraphrase is achieved when we have phrased the entire concept in terms of universal semantic primes.

Phrasing our definitions in terms of semantic primes offers a way of avoiding obscurity and circularity. But what about the third problem, that of ethnocentrism? In fact, there is good reason to think that ethnocentrism can be minimized by relying on semantic primes, because the evidence suggests that the primes are not the "private property" of English, but are found in every human language. The meanings listed in Table 2 could equally well have been presented as a list of words in Russian, or Japanese, or Yankunytjatjara, or any other language. The semantic primes are the vocabulary of a kind of "mini-language" which is an excellent tool for semantic and conceptual analysis

## 6.2 Culture-specific words

The fact that the universal core of semantic primes appears to be so small (almost certainly less than 100 words) highlights the great conceptual differences between languages. The vast majority of words in any language have complex and rather language-specific meanings, and this can often be seen as reflecting and embodying the distinctive historical and cultural experiences of the speech community. In this case, we speak of **culture-specific words.**

We can see some prosaic examples in the domain of food. It is clearly no accident that Polish has special words for cabbage stew (*bigos*), beetroot soup (*barszcz*) and plum jam (*powidla*), which English does not; or that Japanese has a word *sake* for a strong alcoholic drink made from rice, whereas English does not. Customs and social institutions also furnish abundant examples of culture-specific words. For example, it is no accident that English doesn't have a word corresponding to Japanese *miai*, referring to a formal occasion when the prospective bride and her family meet the prospective bridegroom and his family for the first time.

Apart from differing in their inventories of culture-specific words, languages often differ in the number of words they have for speaking about a particular domain of meaning. When a language has a relatively high number of words for a single domain, e.g. the Sami words for reindeer, forms of snow, freezing and thawing, this is known as **lexical elaboration.** Lexical elaboration can often be seen as reflecting cultural facts. It is understandable that many Asian languages have several words for rice; for example, Malay *padi* 'unhusked rice', *beras* 'rice without the husk but uncooked', *nasi* 'cooked rice'. On the other hand, compared with most non-European cultures, European languages have a very large stock of expressions to do with measuring and reckoning time (words such as *clock, calendar, date, second, minute, hour, week, Monday, Tuesday,* etc., *January, February,* etc.).

Sometimes it is possible to nominate certain highly salient and deeply culture-laden words in a language as the **cultural key words** of that culture. For example, one could argue that *work*, *love* and *freedom* are among the key words of mainstream English-speaking culture (Anglo culture). Such words are usually very frequent, at least in their own domains. Often, they stand at the centre of a large cluster of fixed phrases, and occur frequently in proverbs, sayings, popular songs, book titles, and so on.

To illustrate how words in different languages can differ semantically in subtle but culture-related ways we will examine some emotion terms in various European languages. In general, the meanings of emotion terms can be described by linking a feeling (good, bad, or neutral) with a **prototypical scenario** involving action schemas ("do"), or experiencing schemas ("think", "want"). For instance, English *sadness* is, roughly speaking, a bad feeling linked with the thought "something bad happened". Saying this does not imply that every time one feels *sadness*, one necessarily has this particular thought. Rather, it says that to feel *sadness* is to feel like someone would who is having that thought. These scenarios are presented in explications. **Explications** are descriptions composed in semantic primes; they can be transposed between languages without altering the meaning. Unlike technical formulations, they can also be understood by ordinary people.

To see this approach in action, let us home in on a fairly subtle difference in meaning — between the English words *happy* and *joyful* (or *joy*). Two differences are the greater immediacy and intensity of *joy*, and the more personal or self-oriented character of *happy*. There is also a third difference, which is that *happy* (unlike *joy*) suggests a meaning component akin to "contentedness"; for example, in response to a question such as (1a) one can answer (1b):

(1)  a.  Are you thinking of applying for a transfer?
     b.  No, I am quite happy where I am.

(It would be impossible to substitute *joyful* in place of *happy* in this context.) This idea is further supported by the contrast between the sentences in (2):

(2)  a.  The children were playing happily
     b.  The children were playing joyfully

Here, (2a) implies not only that the children were enjoying themselves, but also that they were fully satisfied with what they were doing. (2b) suggests a great deal more activity. These differences suggest the explications below.

(A)  Explication of "X feels *happy*"
    sometimes a person thinks something like this:
        something good happened to me
        I wanted this
        I don't want anything else
    because of this, this person feels something good
    X feels like this

(B)  Explication of "X feels *joy*"
    sometimes a person thinks something like this:
        something very good is happening now
        I want this
    because of this, this person feels something very good
    X feels like this

The difference between the components "something good" (in *happy*) and "something very good" (in *joy*) helps account for the greater intensity of *joy*. The difference between "something is happening" (in *joy*) and "something happened TO ME" (in *happy*) reflects the more personal and self-oriented character of *happy*. The difference between the components "I want this" (in *joy*) and "I wantED this" (in *happy*) accounts for the greater immediacy of *joy*, as well as contributing to its greater intensity. The differences in the phrasing of the explications reflect particular differences in meaning, manifested in the overlapping but different ranges of use of the two words.

It is interesting to note that *happy* is a common and every-day word in modern English, and belongs, according to DCE to the class of the 1,000 most frequent words, whereas *joy* belongs to the 3,000 class and is more literary and stylistically marked. In many other European languages, words closer in meaning to *joy* are more common in every-day language. For example, in German the verb *sich freuen* and the corresponding noun *Freude* (roughly, "joy") are used very frequently, on a daily basis, unlike the adjective *glücklich* (roughly, "happy") and the noun *Glück*. But this difference in frequency aside, it is important to see that there is only a rough meaning correspondence between *glücklich* and *happy* (or between French *heureux* and *happy*).

Essentially, English *happy* conveys a "weaker", less intense emotion than *glücklich* and *heureux*. Speaking metaphorically, emotions such as *Glück* and *bonheur* fill a person to overflowing, leaving no room for any further desires or wishes and so *glücklich* and *heureux* are closer to English *overjoyed* than to *happy*. The more limited character of *happy* also shows itself in a syntactic contrast. For example, one can say in English *I am happy with his answer* (where the complement *with his answer* specifies the limited domain or focus of one's happiness). In German or French one could not use the words *glücklich* and *heureux* in this way: one would have to use semantically weaker, less intense words such as *zufrieden* or *satisfait/content* (roughly, "pleased") instead.

The meaning of *glücklich* and *heureux* can be captured in the following explication:

(C)  Explication of "X feels *glücklich* (*heureux*)"
    sometimes a person thinks something like this:
        something very good happened to me
        I wanted this
        everything is very good now
        I can't want anything more
    because of this, this person feels something very good
    X feels like this

This explication contains the new component "everything is very good now" (implying a "total" experience). It includes the intensifier *very* (like *joy* but unlike *happy*). Furthermore, its final "thinking" component is phrased as "I can't want anything more" (rather than "I don't want anything else", as with *happy*). These differences imply an intense, but generalized and almost euphoric, view of one's current existence.

If we look across other languages of Europe, we can see that many of them have words which are similar (if not identical) in meaning to that of *glücklich/ heureux* stated above. For example, there is *felice* in Italian, *shtshastliv* in Russian, *szczesliwy* in Polish. The English language seems to be the "odd one out" with its relatively bland word *happy*. This fact is probably not unconnected with the traditional Anglo-Saxon distaste for extreme emotions. True, the English language does possess more exuberant words (such as *joy*, *bliss*, and *ecstasy*), but their comparative rarity only reinforces the point that emotional discourse in English has a distinctly muted quality when compared with many of the other languages of Europe.

## 6.3  Culture-specific grammar

In any language there will be aspects of grammar which are strongly linked with culture. Proponents of linguistic relativity such as Sapir and Whorf concentrated on pervasive grammatical patterns such as whether or not a language insists on marking the distinction between singular and plural referents, or the relative time reference (tense) of an event, or the source of one's evidence for making a statement, etc. A language continually forces its speakers to attend to such distinctions (or others like them), inescapably imposing a particular subjective experience of the world and ourselves. A celebrated example of this comes from Whorf (1956: 139), who contrasted the way in which "time" is conceptualized in English and in Hopi (a native American language of north-eastern Arizona). In English and other European languages, time is very often spoken of in the same way as we speak of material, countable objects. Just as we say *one stone/five stones*, we say *one day/five days*, extending the use of cardinal numbers and plural marking from material entities to immaterial entities. This implies that we have conceptualized our experience of time in terms of our experience of material objects which may be present before our eyes. We are "objectifying" time. Units of time are, however, fundamentally different from objects. Five days are not "seen" simultaneously but can only be experienced sequentially. In the Hopi speaker's non-objectified view of time, the concept "five days" does not make sense. If the speaker wants to express this notion, he or she will make use of ordinal numbers, i.e. something like "the fifth day". According to Whorf, their primary conceptualization is in terms of the succession of cycles of day and night. The cycles are not lumped together as material objects.

We will now illustrate an aspect of **culture-specific grammar** from Italian. Although the constructions under analysis are not so all-pervasive and fundamental as those envisaged by Whorf, they are still very frequent and dominant in the Italian way of life and are certainly an important aspect of the Italian experience of things. Our focus will be on two grammatical constructions which serve an expressive function fully congruent with the general expressiveness of Italian culture: syntactic reduplication and absolute superlative. **Syntactic reduplication** refers to the repetition, without any intervening pause, of adjectives, adverbs, and even nouns, as in expressions like *bella bella, adagio adagio, subito subito* (*bella* 'beautiful', *adagio* 'slowly', *subito* 'at once'). It is a distinct grammatical construction of Italian, different from the repetition of full utterances as in English *Come in, come in!* or *Quickly, quickly!*, but rather resembles expressions of the type *bye-bye*.

The Italian expressions just mentioned are usually described as indicating "intensity". Thus one could suggest equivalences such as *bella bella* 'very beautiful' or *adagio adagio* 'very slowly'. But there are two problems with this. Firstly, the range of the Italian construction is broader than that of *very*; for example, one could hardly translate *subito subito* as 'very at once'. Secondly, the true Italian equivalent to *very* is *molto*, and there is a twofold difference between *molto bella* 'very beautiful' and *bella bella*.

Syntactic reduplication in Italian expresses, firstly, an insistence that the word in question is well-chosen. In saying *bella bella* the speaker is emphasizing that he or she regards the word *bella* as being used responsibly, strictly, or accurately (notice that repetition of the word draws attention to it). Thus, *bella bella* is more accurately rendered in English as 'truly beautiful' (and *caffè caffè* as 'true coffee').

There is, however, a second component also, an emotive one. A sentence like *Venga subito subito* 'Come at once at once' virtually demands a highly expressive, emotional tone. Even when a purely descriptive adjective such as *duro* 'hard' or *leggera* 'soft' is reduplicated, it is usually easy to detect clues to the emotional undertones in the context. For instance, in one novel the hero experiences a great spiritual crisis. As he tosses and turns at night, it seems to him that his bed has become *duro duro* 'hard hard'. Later in the same novel, the hero wants to cross a river in a fisherman's boat without being noticed by anyone because he is trying to escape from the police. He addresses the fisherman in a voice which is *leggera leggera* 'soft soft'.

The meaning expressed by the reduplication construction can be stated as follows:

(D) Explication of Italian reduplication of adjectives/adverbs:
when I say this word (e.g. *bella*, *duro*, *bianca*) two times
I want you to know that I want to say this word, not any other
when I think about this, I feel something

A second characteristically Italian grammatical device is the **absolute superlative**, formed from adjectives with *-issimo* (in the appropriate gender/number variant). For instance, *bellissimo* 'most beautiful', *velocissimo* 'most fast', *bianchissimo* 'very white'. This construction is conceptually related to expressions with *molto* 'very' (*molto bella* 'very beautiful', and so on). Both are restricted to qualities, and more specifically to qualities which can be "graded" and compared. One cannot say *\*subitissimo*, for example. There are affinities between the absolute superlative and the ordinary superlative formed with *più* (for instance, *più bello* 'the most beautiful').

There is also a certain similarity with syntactic reduplication — some Italian grammars even describe the two constructions as equivalents. But unlike syntactic reduplication, the absolute superlative is not meant to convey accuracy.

On the contrary, it normally involves an obvious exaggeration. The function of this exaggeration, however, does share something with syntactic reduplication, it serves to express the speaker's emotional attitude. We can capture these ideas in the explication below:

> (E)  Explication of Italian absolute superlative "it is X-*issimo*"
>       it is very X
>       I want to say more than this
>       because of this, I say: it could not be more X
>       when I think about this, I feel something

The similarity with expressions with *molto* 'very' is made obvious by the presence of *very* in the first line. The similarity with the ordinary superlative is in the third component: Implicitly there is a comparison of sorts being made with the highest degree ("it could not be more X"). The similarity with syntactic reduplication is shown in the final component ("when I think about this, I feel something"). All in all, the absolute superlative enables speakers of Italian to perform a kind of "expressive overstatement".

Constructions like syntactic reduplication and the absolute superlative are surely linked with what has been called the "theatrical quality" of Italian life (Barzini 1964: 73), the "importance of spectacle", "the extraordinary animation, … the expressive faces, the revealing gesticulation … which are among everybody's first impressions in Italy, anywhere in Italy". This animation and this love of loudness and display go a long way to explaining the relevance of expressive grammatical devices like syntactic reduplication and the absolute superlative in Italian culture.

## 6.4  Cultural scripts

In different societies people not only speak different languages, they also use them in different ways, following different cultural norms. Cultural norms of communication are usually described using vague and impressionistic labels such as "directness", "formality", and "politeness". Though useful up to a point, such labels are really quite vague, and are used with different meanings by different authors. They can also lead to ethnocentrism because they are usually not translatable into the language of the people whose culture is being described. These problems can be largely overcome if we use semantic primes to formulate our descriptions of cultural norms of communication. When cultural norms are described in this way, they are referred to as **cultural scripts.**

In this section we will focus on cultural scripts for saying "what you want". To begin with, let's take a brief look at a culture far removed from Europe. Japanese culture is well-known for its verbal reticence. This applies in particular to the expression of personal desires, a fact linked with the Japanese ideal of *enryo* 'restraint, reserve'. One finds that Japanese people are reluctant to express their preferences directly. When asked what arrangements would suit them, they will often decline to say, using expressions like 'Any time will do' or 'Any place will be all right with me'. Direct questioning about a person's wishes is far from normal. With the exception of family and close friends it is impolite in Japanese to say such things as 'What do you want to eat?' and 'What do you like?' Nor is a guest in Japan constantly offered choices by an attentive host. Rather, it is the responsibility of the host to anticipate what will please the guest and simply to present items of food and drink, urging that they be consumed, in the standard phrase, 'without *enryo*'.

Overall, one may say that Japanese culture strongly discourages people from saying clearly what they want. The culturally approved strategy is to send an "implicit message" of some kind, in the expectation that the addressee will respond. These cultural attitudes can be captured in a script like this:

(F)  Japanese script for "communicating what you want"
 when I want something
 it is not good to say to other people: 'I want this'
 I can say something else
 if I say something else, other people can know what I want

Anglo-American attitudes are of course quite different in this respect. In line with Anglo ideals of individual freedom and personal autonomy, it is considered desirable if people "feel free" to express their preferences:

(G)  Anglo-American script for "saying what you want"
 everyone can say things like this to other people:
  'I want this', 'I don't want this'

On the other hand, the same ideal of personal autonomy inhibits speakers of mainstream English from using the bare imperative and saying *Do this!*, and encourages them instead to apply polite strategies (as later discussed in Chapter 7.4). Therefore they will use more elaborate locutions such as *Could you do this?*, *Would you mind doing this?* and the like. The message that "I want you to do something" is embedded into a more complex configuration which acknowledges the addressee's autonomy by inviting them to say whether or not they will comply. These norms can be captured in the following pair of scripts:

(H)   Anglo-American script blocking "imperative directives"
if I want someone to do something, I can't say to this person something like this:
'I want you to do this; because of this, you have to do it'

(I)   Anglo-American script for "interrogative directives"
if I want to say to someone something like this:
'I want you to do this'
it is good to say something like this at the same time:
'I don't know if you will do it'

It would be wrong, however, to think that the cultural scripts of mainstream English are "typically European". There is considerable diversity among the languages and cultures of Europe in this regard (as in many others). In most of them, bare imperatives are used more often than in English, and the use of interrogative structures in directives is more limited.

According to Béal (1994), French people expect that routine instructions given in a workplace situation will take a more forthright form than would be appropriate in English. As one French executive explained (Béal 1994:51), his English-speaking (Australian) employees used *précaution oratoire* 'oratory precautions', which French people would not normally use:

> *A la limite, le Français s'il l'emploie, il le fera, il prendra cette précaution oratoire si c'est justement en dehors des tâches normales et régulières de la personne à qui il s'adresse. Mais autrement, non, ça sera, bon, 'Faites-moi ci', 'Allez me chercher ça, s'il vous plaît', mais 'Would you mind?' euh…non. A la limite si on fait ça en France, on remet en cause son autorité.*

> [Actually, if a French person does use such precaution, it will be because he is requesting a favour outside the normal job definition of the person he is asking. Otherwise, he will simply say 'Do this, fetch that, please', but 'Would you mind?' … certainly not. Actually, to do that in France is like undermining one's own authority.]

It is also well-known that there are considerable differences in the norms governing requests in German and in English. John Phillips (1989:88–89), a lecturer in English as a Foreign Language at Bayreuth University, comments as follows:

A bank clerk may say "Sie müssen hier unterschreiben" (You have to (must) sign here) and not "Würden Sie bitte hier unterschreiben?" (Would you please sign here?). At best he will say "Unterschreiben Sie bitte" (Sign here please). Although the imperative is used it is not meant as a command. The word *müssen* (must) is very much part of the language and keeps cropping up in situations where it would not do so in English.

Of course the remarks just quoted belong to the genre of "folk comments", and do not represent precise generalizations. But "folk comments" provide evidence of the perceptions of people living in multi-ethnic societies, and of the problems involved in cross-cultural communication. They cannot be ignored, but must be interpreted within a coherent and independently justified framework, such as that provided by cultural scripts written in semantic primes. The method enables us to state hypotheses about cultural norms without resorting to technical or language-specific terms, and in a way which is clear and accessible. Finally, it should be noted that cultural scripts can be used for describing variation and change, as well as continuity in cultural norms, for cultures are, of course, heterogeneous and changeable. However, to study diversity and change we also need a rigorous and illuminating analytical framework.

## 6.5  Conclusion: Language, culture and thought

In a well-known passage, Whorf (1956:212) explained his view of the relation of language to thinking as follows:

> the background linguistic system (in other words, the grammar) of each language is not merely a reproducing instrument for voicing ideas but rather is itself the shaper of ideas, the program and the guide for the individual's mental activity, for his analysis of impressions.

Whorf's views on linguistic relativity have often been misunderstood. He did not claim that all thinking is dependent on language. In fact, he believed there are various mental processes, such as attention and visual perception, which are independent of language and which therefore escape the "shaping" influence of language. But as far as "linguistic thinking" is concerned, Whorf insisted that the patterns of our native language inevitably impose patterns of habitual thinking. As mentioned earlier, recent research indicates that the conceptual categories of one's native language guide categorization at a very young age. As early as 20 months of age, Korean and English children make use of the conceptual patterns of their native languages.

The culture-specific words and grammatical constructions of a language are conceptual tools which reflect a society's past experience of doing and thinking about things in certain ways. As a society changes, these tools may be gradually modified and discarded. In that sense the outlook of a society is never wholly "determined" by its stock of conceptual tools, but it is clearly influenced by them. Similarly, the outlook of an individual is never fully "determined" by his or her native language, because there are always alternative ways of expressing oneself, but one's conceptual perspective on life is clearly influenced by his or her native language.

Much the same can be said about communicative style. An individual's communicative style is not rigidly determined by the cultural scripts which he or she internalizes while growing up in that culture. There is always room for individual and social variation, and for innovation. But the communicative style of both society and individual cannot escape the influence of the "cultural rules" of communication.

In the end, the existence of a common stock of semantic primes in all the world's languages means that all human cognition rests on the same conceptual bedrock. Theoretically, any culture-specific concept can be made accessible to cultural outsiders by being decomposed into a translatable configuration of universal semantic primes, and indeed, this technique can be an important practical aide to cross-cultural communication. Even so, since every language functions as an integrated whole (of enormous complexity), there will never be a better way to understand the inner workings of a culture than to learn, to speak, and to live life through the language of its people.

## 6.6 Summary

The relation between language and culture has fascinated philosophers, poets and linguists for centuries. In German Romanticism, this led to the idea of each language containing its own **worldview** (**Weltsicht**). In America, exposure to the radically different conceptual categories of native American languages further elaborated this idea into the hypothesis of **linguistic relativity**, also known, after its originators as the **Sapir-Whorf hypothesis**.

An opposing philosophical view is that of **universalism**, which holds that human thought is essentially the same all over the world and that this is reflected in language. But in a more modest approach, universalism only claims that there are certain fundamental elements of linguistic meaning which are common to all languages. In recent times, a set of about 60 basic meaning elements, known as **semantic primes**, has been identified. It is hypothesized that these represent **universal concepts** and this hypothesis is currently being empirically checked in a wide variety of languages. Semantic primes can be used in semantic description, enabling us to overcome two failings of the traditional paraphrase approach to definition: **obscurity** and **circularity**. We can apply the technique of **reductive paraphrase** until all the conceptual components of a linguistic expression are analyzed by means of semantic primes. In this way we can also avoid the danger of **ethnocentrism**, i.e. imposing the categories of our own language upon the description of another language. The method of reductive paraphrase into semantic primes can be used for **culture-specific words**, for **culture-specific grammar** and for **cultural scripts**. As for words, they tend to reflect the historical and environmental experience of a people and in the most relevant domains we tend to find **lexical elaboration**, i.e. a great many specific words for certain phenomena. Instances of culture-specific grammatical constructions are the Italian **syntactic reduplication** and **absolute superlative**. Often a reductive paraphrase will incorporate a **prototypical scenario** consisting of several event schemas, which together lead to a full **explication** of any concept. The conceptual content of grammatical categories, and cultural norms for communication behaviour (cultural scripts), can also be made explicit by paraphrase into universal semantic primes. In Japanese culture one does not say explicitly what one wants but relies instead on implicit messages. In Anglo-American culture one can "feel free" to say what one wants, though preferably without "imposing" (hence the frequent use of "indirect requests" in English). Both contrast with the "forthright instruction" style of the French. Cultures tend to express their main norms and values in a number of **cultural key words**.

In conclusion, while few would now defend the **strong version** of linguistic relativity, known as **linguistic determinism**, i.e. the idea that our forms of thought are strictly determined by linguistic categories, many scholars now accept a more moderate **weaker version** of linguistic relativity, i.e. the idea that language influences thinking.

## 6.7 Further reading

Early works on linguistic relativity include Sapir (1958, edited by Mandelbaum), Luria and Vygotsky (1992), and the writings of Whorf 1956m, editied by Carroll). Recent re-evaluations of linguistic relativity can be found in Gumperz and Levinson (eds. 1996), Lucy (1992a, 1992b), Lee (1996), Choi and Bowerman (1991), Bowerman (1996), and Pütz and Verspoor (2000) and Niemeier and Dirven (2000). An explicit step-by-step introduction to cross-cultural semantics is Goddard (1998). A set of field studies on semantic primes in a large number of languages can be found in Goddard and Wierzbicka (eds. 1994, 1996). Older philosophical approaches to the question of culture-specific concepts and universal concepts can be found in Locke (1976[1690]) and Leibniz (1981-[1765]), respectively; see also Ishiguro (1972). There are cultural trait analyses of various European cultures, e.g. Bally (1920), Barzini (1964) for Italian, Philips (1989) for Germany, and Béal (1994) for French. Wierzbicka (1991) analyzes Italian constructions reflecting the Italian way of life; Wierzbicka (1992) deals with grammatical constructions reflecting Russian "fatalism". The notion of key words as a reflection of a culture's main norms and values is first taken up in Williams (1976) and systematically explored in Wierzbicka (1997).

## Assignments

1.  The following statement by Whorf (1956: 263) is a rather strong version of the linguistic relativity theory and contains some overgeneralizations:

    > Hopi can have verbs without subjects, and this gives to that language power as a logical system for understanding certain aspects of the cosmos. Scientific language, being founded on Western Indo-European and not on Hopi, does as we do, sees sometimes actions and forces where there may be only states.

    a.  Can you think of European languages that just like Hopi have verbs without subjects?
    b.  For English *It flashed* or *A light flashed*, Hopi just says *rehpi* 'flashes' or 'flashed'. Do you agree with Whorf that the English conceptualization includes a force, starting from the subject? (Have a look at Chapter 4.2.2 on the "happening" schema).
    c.  From a cognitive point of view there are no 'empty' words in the language. That is, *it* in *It flashed* does have a meaning. What could this meaning possibly be?
    d.  For English scientific terms such as *electricity*, Hopi uses a verb, not a noun. This

would support Whorf's opinion that English sees a state where there may only be a force. Do you agree with this analysis?

2.  Translate the examples of Table 1 (repeated below) into your mother tongue or a language different from English. If you compare your translations with the English expressions, try to tell whether your language classifies locational relationships according to the English pattern, according to the Korean pattern, or according to a distinctive pattern of its own. If your language tends to follow the English pattern, is the classification exactly the same as in English, or are there also things that remind you of the Korean way of classifying things? If your language system is more like Korean, do you find things that go in the English direction?

    a.  a piece in a puzzle, a picture in a wallet, a hand in a glove
    b.  toys in a bag or a box
    c.  a cap on a pen, a lid on a jar, a glove on a hand, a magnet on a surface, a tape on a surface
    d.  a hat on a head, a glove on the hand, a shoe on the foot

3.  Here are the definitions for *anger, love* and *hate* from the *Longman Dictionary of Contemporary English*. Are these common words defined in an obscure and/or circular fashion? Can you suggest how the definitions can be re-phrased more clearly?

    *anger:* A strong feeling of wanting to harm, hurt or criticize someone because they have done something unfair, cruel, offensive etc.

    *love:* 1. Strong feeling of caring about someone, especially a member of your family or a close friend; 2. A strong feeling of liking and caring about someone, especially combined with sexual attraction.

    *hate:* An angry unpleasant feeling that someone has when they hate someone and want to harm them.

4.  Investigate the English words *job* and *privacy* from the point of view of their frequency (use the *Longman Dictionary of Contemporary English* for this purpose), their role in fixed phrases, and in common sayings and proverbs. Would you agree that *job* and *privacy* deserve to be regarded as examples of cultural key words of English?

5.  Do you think the English word *anxiety* corresponds exactly to the Danish word *angest* used by the Danish philosopher Søren Kierkegaard in the passage whose published English translation is given below? Discuss.

    As far as I know, natural scientists agree that animals do not have anxiety simply because by nature they are not qualified as spirit. They fear the present, tremble, etc., but are not anxious. They have no more anxiety than they can be said to have presentiment.

Note that Danish *angest* may be similar, but not identical, in meaning to German *Angst*. Also note that the word *angst* has been borrowed into English from German, but the English loan word does not have the same meaning as the German original.

6. In English-speaking countries, one often hears people talking about the importance of *freedom of speech*. There can be little doubt that this expression refers to an important Anglo cultural norm. But when people say *freedom of speech* they don't mean freedom to say absolutely anything, to anybody. Discuss when it is — and isn't — acceptable to say what one thinks, according to conventional Anglo cultural norms. Try to pin down precisely the notion behind *freedom of speech*, writing an explication as used in the cultural scripts approach discussed in Section 6.4 of this chapter.

# 7  Doing things with words
## Pragmatics

## 7.0 Overview

So far we have mainly looked at the way we form and express ideas by means of language. This is called the **ideational function** of language. A second, equally important function is the use of language for the sake of interaction. This is the **interpersonal function** of language, which will be focused upon in this and the next chapter.

In Chapter 7 we will be looking at what we "do" with language when we interact with each other. A minor case is that we talk to each other just to show that we have taken notice of one another: It is not what we say that counts, but the fact that we say something at all. In the majority of cases, however, we have very specific intentions while interacting and communicating and achieve something substantial with our use of language. In doing something with language we perform all kinds of speech acts. These speech acts realize communicative intentions, which pertain to two cognitive faculties: Our knowledge and our volition. In the domain of knowledge we exchange and ask for all possible kinds of information. This is done by assertions, statements, descriptions and information questions, all instances of informative speech acts. In the domain of volition we impose obligations on others or on ourselves: We give commands, make requests, promises or offers, all instances of obligative speech acts. There is a third group of speech acts whereby the uttering of the words in the appropriate circumstances, e.g. by the chairperson at the end of a meeting determines the ongoing situation. When the chairman says "I hereby declare the conference closed", then the meeting is over. Since such acts constitute (new) social reality, they are called constitutive speech acts.

In this chapter, we will also look at the conditions that must be fulfilled for felicitous interaction, at the ways people must cooperate in communication to understand each other, and at the strategies people use to avoid offending one another by being too direct.

## 7.1 Introduction: What is pragmatics?

**Pragmatics** is the study of how people interact when using language. **Language-in-use** is hereby defined as a part of human interaction. People live, work and interact with each other in social networks. They get up in the morning, see their family, go out to work or to school, meet their neighbours in the street, take buses, trams or trains, meet other people at work or in school, go to pubs and clubs, etc. In all these social networks of the home, the neighbourhood, the village, town or city, the school or job environment, sports clubs, religious meetings and so on, they interact with each other. One of the main instruments for interaction is talk.

In the next two sections, we will investigate the different intentions people may have for saying something and provide a cognitive classification of speech acts.

### 7.1.1 Communicative intention and speech acts

Not all talk is meant to convey intentions. Quite often we talk just for the sake of talking. Thus a lot of talk is just meant to show one another that we have acknowledged each other's presence. For example, in **small talk**, our main intention is not necessarily to convey information or our beliefs and wants, but to socialize as in (1). This is called the **phatic function** of language (from Greek *phatis* 'talk').

(1) Conversation at a coffee stall between an old newspaper seller and the barman

Man:      You was a bit busier earlier.
Barman:   Ah.
Man:      Round about ten.
Barman:   Ten, was it?
Man:      About then. (Pause) I passed by here about then.
Barman:   Oh yes. (From Harold Pinter: A Slight Ache).

In most other cases, we engage in the type of communicative interaction where we convey what is going on in our minds: What we see, know, think, believe, want, intend, or feel — in other words a mental state.

We can make our fellow humans aware of our mental states by using words. Whatever we are trying to accomplish with our language — informing, requesting, ordering, persuading, encouraging, and so on — can be called our **communicative intention**. For example, when I say to my rather pale-looking uncle, "You look a lot better today" I am just trying to make him feel better or, in other words, I am expressing my intention to comfort him. The actual words we utter to realize a communicative intention is called a **speech act**.

Traditionally, philosophers of language, the main or even sole interest in language use was to ascertain how we make true statements and how it is possible to find out about the truth conditions of what is being said. But the language philosopher Austin, author of *How to do things with words* in 1952, discovered that we do not only perform information acts, i.e. "say" things that can be considered either true or false as in (2a), but that we also "do" a lot of other things with words as in (2b–e):

(2)  a.   My computer is out of order.
     b.   Could you lend me your laptop for a couple of days?
     c.   Yes, I'll bring it tomorrow
     d.   Oh, thank you, you're always so kind.
     (Official person or VIP releases bottle at ship, after saying:)
     e.   I name this ship the Queen Elizabeth.

In (2a) the speaker states what he sees or thinks is happening and informs someone else about this. Although we expect this statement to be true, it can, in fact, be true or false. For instance, the speaker may just have forgotten to plug the computer in. In the other speech acts (2b–e) the speaker is not really concerned with the truth or falsehood of what he says. In (2b) the speaker requests the hearer to do something and in (2c) the latter promises to do so. These are two speech acts in which the volition of the speaker is of paramount importance and an obligation is imposed on the partner (2b) or on the speaker himself (2c). In (2d) the first speaker expresses his feelings of thanks and praises his friend.

In (2e) the speaker is not stating an already existing fact, but creates a new fact by uttering the words to name the ship. Moreover, in order to be able to do so, the situation must be an official event, with officials present. The VIP speaker must release a champagne bottle so that it smashes on the ship's bow, having shortly before uttered the appropriate statement (2e).

At first, Austin called a speech act such as (2e) *a performative act,* but later he came to the conclusion that whenever we say anything we always "perform" a speech act because we "do" something with words: We state a belief, we request something of someone, we promise something to someone, we express thanks and so on. He was the first to realize that making an utterance is not foremost and solely a matter of truth or falsehood, but above all that each utterance is a speech act, i.e. that we "do" something with words, rather than only say something.

We can then pose the question as to how we describe the class of speech acts as in (2e). This point was taken up by Austin's disciple, the philosopher John Searle (1969), who proposed a taxonomy of five types of speech acts: Assertives (3a), directives (3b), commissives (3c), expressives (3d), and declarations (3e).

(3)  a. *assertive*    Sam smokes a lot.
     b. *directive*    Get out. I want you to leave.
     c. *commissive*   I promise to come tomorrow.
     d. *expressive*   Congratulations on your 60th birthday.
     e. *declaration*  I hereby take you as my lawful wedded wife.

The examples in (3) largely correspond with those in (2). By means of **assertive speech acts** as in (3a, 2a) we make an assertion or a statement, give a description or ask an information question. By means of a **directive speech act** we give an order as in (3b) or make a request (2b). By means of a **commissive speech act** we make a promise (3c, 2c) or an offer and by doing so impose an obligation on ourselves. By means of an **expressive speech** act we express congratulations (3d), our feelings of gratitude and our praise (2d). Finally, by means of a declaration or **declarative speech act** the speaker declares a (new) social fact to be the case as in the act of marrying (3e) or of naming a ship (2e). Note that the term *declarative* has been used in a different sense in Chapter 4, where it was used in a syntactic sense as *declarative mood* or *declarative sentence*, in contrast to the interrogative and imperative mood or sentence. In this chapter, the term *declarative* is used in a pragmatic sense as a *declarative speech act* or a declaration, in contrast to assertive, directive, commissive, and expressive speech acts.

### 7.1.2  A cognitive typology of speech acts

Some of the five speech acts in (3) are closer to each other than to others. Speech acts can therefore be grouped according to superordinate categories to which similar principles may apply. Thus alongside assertive speech acts, we also find information questions, e.g. *Does John smoke?* Both can be subsumed under the superordinate category of **informative speech acts**. Likewise, directives and commissives can be grouped together in a superordinate category, because in both cases the speaker imposes an obligation, either on the hearer (directive) or on himself (commissive). We will call the **obligative speech acts**. Finally, expressive speech acts and declarative speech acts also have a fundamental feature in common: Both of them require a kind of ritualized social context in which they can be performed. Thus we can only congratulate someone on a given social occasion, e.g. when it is his or her birthday and by performing the act of congratulation we constitute the social signal that we care about others and haven't forgetten their birthday. Therefore we can subsume both the expressive and the declarative speech act under the superordinate category of **constitutive speech acts**.

We will now briefly illustrate these major types and their subtypes.

Informative speech acts encompass all speech acts that convey information to the hearer, ask information of the hearer or state that someone lacks a piece of information of some sort. The information is about what one knows, thinks, believes, or feels.

(4) a. I don't know this city very well.
    b. Can you tell me the way to the station, please?
    c. Yes, turn left, then turn right again. It's on the left.

Informative acts are not only quite varied, they also involve a large number of background assumptions, e.g. the assumption that the hearer may want to know why the speaker is asking the question or that the hearer does not know the answer. Thus in (4a) the speaker first explains why he is asking the question. And as (4b) illustrates, a speaker need not ask straight away "Where is the station?", but can also check whether such knowledge is present by saying "Can you tell me". Even more typically, the addressee does not just answer the question by saying "yes", but interprets the "yes/no" question as an information question and if he or she has this information, it is passed on. Note that the speaker in the answer (4c) uses the imperative — normally used for orders — to relay this information without obliging the hearer to do anything. This illustrates that there is not a one-to-one relation between the form of a linguistic expression (in this case an 'imperative') and its communicative intention.

In obligative speech acts, the motivation as well as the desired consequence is quite different. Imagine the following situation: Mark and Peter are leaving a party. As Mark has not drunk as much alcohol as Peter he says:

(5)  a.  Mark: Peter, can you give me your car keys — I'll drive.
    b.  Peter (handing over the keys): All right, next time it's my turn — I promise.

Mark's utterance (5a) consists of two obligative acts: A directive and a commissive. First of all, the request in (5a) is quite different from an information question as in (4b): Mark doesn't want Peter to say something, but to do something, i.e. to give him the keys. Secondly, Mark wants to do the driving. His first aim is to oblige Peter to do what he requests and he also gives a reason by offering to drive the car. With this offer Mark obliges himself to do the driving, provided that Peter hands over the keys to him. The same is true for Peter's utterance in (5b). First he complies with the request, not by saying so, but by handing over the keys, and then he promises to do the driving next time, thereby committing himself to a future action. Thus all obligative speech acts such as requesting, making offers, and promising have one thing in common: Speakers commit the hearer or themselves to some future action.

Constitutive speech acts are acts which constitute a social reality. This only pertains if something is uttered by the right person, in the right form, and at the right moment. This obviously holds for declarative speech acts as in (2e) *I name this ship the Queen Elizabeth* and (3e) *I hereby take you as my lawful wedded wife*: Only the VIP can name the ship and only the bridegroom can perform the act of (3e). The conditions that hold for such constitutive speech acts as a declaration equally hold for the expressive speech acts of thanking or congratulating as in (2d) *Oh, thank you. You are always so kind* and (3d) *Congratulations on your 60th birthday*. Only when someone has done something for you or promises he will do so, can you thank him or praise him. And only when it is somebody's birthday, can you congratulate him. Consequently, even though expressive speech acts (2d, 3d) and declarative speech acts (2e, 3e) express different communicative intentions, both types are subject to the same conditions for the success or felicity of the speech act.

The various types and subtypes of speech acts are summarized in Table 1, which also contains some typical verbs used in some of the subtypes.

In the next sections, we will discuss each of these main types of speech acts in more detail and we will show how they interact with felicity conditions, cooperativeness, and politeness. We will first discuss the category of constitutive speech acts.

Table 1. Types and subtypes of speech acts

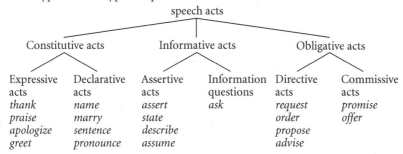

| Constitutive acts | | Informative acts | | Obligative acts | |
|---|---|---|---|---|---|
| Expressive acts | Declarative acts | Assertive acts | Information questions | Directive acts | Commissive acts |
| *thank* | *name* | *assert* | *ask* | *request* | *promise* |
| *praise* | *marry* | *state* | | *order* | *offer* |
| *apologize* | *sentence* | *describe* | | *propose* | |
| *greet* | *pronounce* | *assume* | | *advise* | |

## 7.2 Constitutive speech acts and felicity conditions

When someone expresses how he or she feels by saying "I congratulate you" or when someone performs a declarative act by saying "You are now husband and wife" certain felicity conditions have to be met. These **felicity conditions** are: (1) the act must be performed in the right circumstances, and (2) it is also enough to say the correct formula without doing anything else. Compare these constitutive acts with a commercial transaction like paying back a debt. It is not sufficient to say "I hereby pay you back 1,000 dollars", one must actually hand over the money. In fact, it would even be enough to hand over the money without saying anything. Constitutive speech acts do just the opposite: The mere utterance of a ritual formula in the appropriate circumstances may change the situation. A typical example of this power of a constitutive speech act is (6b), in which the judge, simply by uttering the words, gives an event its legal status. The passive form of the phrase "Objection overruled" is in fact the ritual equivalent of the active sentence "I overrule the objection you have made". But the judge needs only use the short ritual form in the passive at the appropriate moment in a court hearing, and the objection is indeed overruled.

(6)  a.  Attorney:   Objection, Your Honour!
　　 b.  Judge:      Objection overruled.

## 7.2.1 Subcategories of constitutive speech acts

Of the three superordinate categories of speech acts — informative, obligative and constitutive — this last category probably has the most subcategories. This holds for both expressives and declaratives. Cultures have a great many rituals. Many of these relate to the emotional aspects of life, which can be expressed both non-verbally and verbally. For example, in Western culture, people often shake hands to greet people when they meet them. We may also perform such rituals with words, ranging from very informal to institutionalized formal levels.

At the informal end we have the many routinely performed acts of greeting, leave-taking, thanking, comforting, complimenting, congratulating, apologizing, and so on. Even the simplest greeting acts like *Good morning* are to be seen as expressive speech acts. Their original function was to wish good things to other people. The leave-taking formula *goodbye* derives from *God be with you*. This original sense has been so deeply entrenched in the language that it is no longer recognizable and has become a mere greeting ritual. But it still represents an important social reality. It is especially when people refuse to greet each other that we feel the expressive value associated with the ritual. For most expressives we usually have very brief expressions such as *Hello, Hi, (good) bye, bye-bye, bye now, see you later, take care, sleep tight, thanks, cheers, well done, congratulations, I'm sorry, OK,* and so on. One characteristic of such informal ritual acts is that they are often abridged forms as in *bye* (for 'good-bye'), *ta* (for 'thanks'), *ha-ye* (for 'hello'), *g'night* (for 'good night'), reduplicated forms as in *bye-bye, thank you, thank you,* or forms combined with interjections as in *oh, thank you.* It is in such informal situations that we are allowed the most creativity and new forms are quite typical here; for example *hi* instead of *hello, cheers* instead of *goodbye,* and *all right?* instead of *how are you?*

An example of a more formal expressive act can be found in the following fragment spoken by the BBC spokesperson on behalf of a British entertainer who had made fun of the great number of lesbians in the England women's hockey team:

(7)   "That's just his wacky sense of humour and his regular listeners understand that. He's not anti-gay and had no intention of offending anyone. If they have been offended, *we are very sorry and apologise on his behalf.*" (The Daily Telegraph, 8–11–1996)

The fragment as a whole is an expressive act in that its communicative intention is to apologize. But within the fragment we discover sub-intentions. At first the spokesperson informs the audience of the underlying assumption of this apology: You cannot offend people if you do not intend to offend. But the spokesperson is willing to admit that people may feel offended and to those the BBC apologizes "on behalf of" the entertainer. This public apology on someone's behalf shows that the person performing the act must be authorized to make the apology. The use of the *we*-form reiterates that authorization.

This last sentence also makes another distinction clear. The two expressions *we are sorry* and *we apologize* illustrate that there are implicit and explicit speech acts. Both expressions make clear that we feel regret, but the expression *be sorry* is an implicit speech act in itself (by saying it, one expresses a feeling of regret and apologizes). The act being performed is not explicitly named by using *be sorry*. But the verb *apologize* does both. By saying *we apologize* we perform an expressive act simultaneously with the naming of that expressive act. It is for this reason that *apologize* is called a **performative verb**, defined as a verb denoting linguistic action that can both describe a speech act and express it. This explains why we can say that we are sorry, but not that we are sorry on someone else's behalf because *be sorry* only expresses, but does not describe the act of making an apology. If we want to apologize on someone's behalf we can only use *apologize*. Performative verbs can, of course, be found in all of the three major types of speech acts as shown in the list of verbs under Table 1.

At the other extremity of the formal-informal continuum, we have declaratives, which are highly formal and which require an institutional context and institutionally appointed people to perform them, such as refereeing at a football game, baptizing or marrying, leading court hearings, testifying and sentencing, notice-giving, bequeathing, appointing officials, declaring war and many more.

Such declarative acts are usually characterized by a highly "frozen" style. They often mention the one who performs the act, usually in the *I*-form, or use a passive construction as in *Objection overruled*. And, as illustrated in the next examples of marrying and sentencing, they must be in the simple present tense, since in constitutive acts the saying and the doing coincide. Moreover, as illustrated in (8a), they cannot usually be pronounced in isolation, but can only be used at a certain point in a more elaborate ritual. Thus in a marriage ceremony, the priest or official must ask the bride and bridegroom questions such as (8a), to which they have to answer *I do*, or a full sentence like "I hereby take you as my lawful wedded wife" and after that the official confirmation (8b) is given:

(8)  a.  Do you take X to be your lawful wedded husband?
    b.  I now pronounce you man and wife.

(9)  I hereby sentence you to three years' imprisonment for your part in the crime.

(10)  The victim was pronounced dead on arrival.

As illustrated in (9), we may find adverbs like *hereby* indicating the moment and place of the performative act. Such formal, institutionalized expressions often include a performative verb such as *declare, give notice, pronounce,* etc.

The example in (10), however, is not an act of certifying someone's death by a doctor, but it again illustrates that performative verbs like *pronounce* may be used in different ways. In a sentence such as (8b) the performative verb *pronounce* is used to bring about the communicative intention of "constituting a new reality". In sentence (10), *pronounce* is used in a different context, merely to "describe" a situation which is performed as an act of giving information in a very formal context.

### 7.2.2 Felicity conditions

**Felicity conditions** are circumstantial conditions that allow a speaker to make a successful speech act. They relate to all three types of speech act. In an informative speech act like (10) the speaker, e.g. a reporter, must first of all have the correct information himself, and secondly be authorized to pass on the information to the person who asks for it. In a **directive speech act**, e.g. *Get out of here*, the speaker must be in a position to give commands to people lower in rank. For example, in most cultures employees or children would not be able to give such orders to their employer or parents.

But felicity conditions are especially evident in declarative acts. As the question in (8a) illustrates, various conditions may have to be fulfilled in order to make an institutionalized act, such as marrying, **felicitous.** The declarative act can only be effective if all the conditions are satisfied. If one of these conditions is not fulfilled, the act can be legally opposed and eventually be declared not to have been correctly performed and therefore not to have taken place at all. This is precisely the objective of a court case that is taken to a court of appeal. If the proceedings of a court case are found to have been conducted contrary to procedure, the whole act of sentencing has no effect and may be reversed.

Thus if there is no officially authorized person such as a priest, a town official, an ambassador or his attaché, a ship's captain or an aeroplane commander, to pronounce a couple husband and wife, the marriage has no official status. Felicity conditions such as these, however, hold not only for declarations, but also for every-day rituals in expressive acts. Thus, if we want to congratulate people on a birthday, marriage, or promotion, we have not congratulated them if we address the wrong person, if we perform the act at the wrong time, or if the occasion itself has not taken place. In other words, we make an "infelicitous" attempt at congratulating.

(11) a. Husband to wife: Happy birthday, dear.
    b. Wife:           I wonder if you'll ever remember when my birthday is.

In spite of his good communicative intentions, the husband has not congratulated his wife, since the conditions for the congratulating act were not fulfilled. It was an infelicitous congratulation, and consequently no congratulation at all.

Whatever type of constitutive acts we may be engaged in, there is a simple rule of thumb: It must include the right person, the right time, and the right place. Both the saying and the doing can only succeed if all the conditions are fulfilled. If not, there is no "doing", no performing the act, but only the saying of some misplaced ritual words.

Felicity conditions hold for all the three main types of speech acts, not only for constitutive acts. In addition, still other conditions hold for informative and obligative acts, as we shall see in the next sections.

## 7.3 Informative speech acts and cooperative interaction

The exchange of information involves both giving and asking for information. In order to communicate as efficiently as possible, it is important in both cases that the speaker and hearer can reasonably guess what the other already knows, and what can therefore be presupposed and implied by the speaker and what has to be inferred by the hearer. In the next sections, we will look more closely at these presuppositions and implicatures and at the ways that speakers and hearers cooperate with each other to make meaningful interaction possible.

### 7.3.1 Conversational and conventional presuppositions

We would never ask a complete stranger an information question like (12a). On the contrary, such a question presupposes that we already know a lot about each other:

(12) a. Jane: Hello, where are you taking the kids today?
    b. Peter: To the park, I expect. They love going there.

In such an interaction the partners know each other and they have met and spoken to each other before. This is known as **background knowledge**, which is knowledge of things taken for granted. Jane knows that Peter regularly takes out the children and goes to different places with them. Taking such things for granted in a conversation is a **conversational presupposition**.

Peter has not made up his mind yet where to go today, but thinks of going to the park. Both Jane and Peter take a lot of things for granted such as, for example, the existence of the park in the neighbourhood as one of the places to take the children to. This is **world knowledge** and is indicated by grammatical devices such as the use of definite articles. Since such knowledge is obvious from the grammar it is a **conventional presupposition**. Ordinary exchanges such as this contain presupposition elements that speakers can assume to be known or which are clear from the speech situation and which can therefore be taken for granted.

People who do not know each other personally, but who belong to the same national or cultural community, may also share **cultural presuppositions**, which are also part of our conventional presuppositions, for example about places, historical events, national institutions, elections, public figures, and so on. Thus in a television discussion about forthcoming elections the following statement makes perfectly good sense to the viewers:

(13)   Mrs. Garvie: In my street, everybody votes Labour.

This statement is interpreted against a British cultural background in which there are regular democratic elections within a two-party system and in which it is possible to know the voting intentions of one's neighbours, if it is a fairly close-knit community. The same utterance in a completely different context could lead to all kinds of misunderstandings. For example, if Mrs. Garvie, as a British tourist in China, said (13) to a Chinese casual acquaintance, the latter cannot be supposed to know what she is talking about. The Chinese acquaintance may not even be able to conceive that "everybody" cannot be taken as literally everybody, nor that "everybody" includes women and young people but not children — he may not know that not everybody goes to the ballot. The example in (13) thus illustrates that we make a great deal of presuppositions on the basis of the cultural knowledge we have in common with our interaction partners in the same or a similar cultural community.

## 7.3.2 The cooperative principle and maxims of conversation

Considering the fact that in just a few words such as (13) so much information is implied, so much is assumed to be known, and that so much is not to be taken literally, it is amazing that anyone can interpret this utterance at all. But we manage to do so, and on many other occasions like it. This relies on our following a number of "silent" rules or principles, also called "maxims".

According to the language philosopher Grice (1975), human communication is based on the following overriding **cooperative principle:**

(14)   Make your conversational contribution such as is required, at the stage [of the talk exchange] at which it occurs.

The use of the imperative form in (14) does not mean that speakers must do all this, but that these are the internalized rules for cooperative interaction. Within this guiding principle, Grice (1975: 45–6) establishes four specific sub-principles called **maxims of conversation,** which he takes to govern all rational interaction.

a.   Quality:    Try to make your contribution one that is true.
  i.   Do not say what you believe to be false.
  ii.   Do not say that for which you lack evidence.
b.   Quantity:  Make your contribution as informative as is required (for the current purposes of the exchange).
  Do not make your contribution more informative than is required.
c.   Relevance: Be relevant.
d.   Manner:    i.   Be perspicuous (transparent and clear).
  ii.   Avoid obscurity of expression.
  iii.   Avoid ambiguity.
  iv.   Be brief (avoid unnecessary prolixity).
  v.   Be orderly.

Let us first have a closer look at each of these maxims. The first is the **maxim of quality.** It requires that we only give information for which we have evidence. Suppose we ask for the result of a sports contest, e.g. *Do you happen to know who won yesterday?* and our conversational partner does not know the result and gives one of the following answers:

(15)   a.   No, I don't.
      b.   I bet Chelsea did.
      c.   Chelsea did.

In the first answer, our partner is "truthful" since he says he does not have the information. In the second answer, our partner is still "truthful", since by using *bet* he indicates indirectly that he does not know the answer, but that he has good grounds to "assume" that Chelsea won. Only in the third answer is our partner not being truthful, since he presents things as if he has the correct information himself. Note that he is not necessarily lying, but only asserting something to be the case for which he has no evidence.

The second maxim is the **maxim of quantity**. It means that one gives all the necessary information one has for the present needs of the partner — not too much, and not too little. Suppose a driver has run out of petrol on a Sunday and asks you where the nearest petrol station is. You answer with one of (16):

(16)   a.   There is a petrol station round the corner.
      b.   There is a petrol station round the corner, but it is closed on Sunday. The next one is 5 miles ahead.
      c.   The petrol station round the corner is closed on Sunday, but you can fill up there if you have a credit card.

If you know that the petrol station is closed on Sunday and say (16a), you give too little information and thus violate the maxim of quantity. Only the answers in (16b or c) would be cooperative answers.

The third maxim is the **maxim of relevance**, which Grice himself calls the maxim of relation. It can best be illustrated by a deviant case. We often do not answer information questions straightforwardly, probably because we do not know the answer or because we think that the questioner can interpret the answer himself or herself. Therefore, at first sight, the answer in (17b) does not seem to be a relevant one:

(17)   a.   Ann:   Did Tony Blair win the election?
      b.   Bill:   The paper is on the table.

There is indeed no obvious link between Ann's question. and Bill's reply. But on closer inspection, as Grice says, speakers always tend to be cooperative, even if they do not seem to be so. On the assumption that Bill has been cooperative and hence that his utterance is relevant to the question, one can infer, via the maxim of relevance, that the paper contains the answer to the question.

The fourth maxim is the **maxim of manner** and it can also best be illustrated by a negative example. The following dialogue fragment from Lewis Carroll's *Through the Looking Glass* would have to be classified as uncooperative conversation since it seems to flout each sub-maxim of manner: Humpty Dumpty's utterances in (18c,d,f) are not perspicuous or transparent (i), they are ambiguous (ii), not brief (iii); only the maxim 'be orderly' (iv) is not violated.

(18)  a.  "There's glory for you", (said Humpty Dumpty.)
      b.  "I don't know what you mean by glory", Alice said.
      c.  Humpty Dumpty smiled contemptuously. "Of course, you don't, till I tell you.
      d.  I meant, 'There's a nice knock-down argument for you!'"
      e.  "But 'glory' doesn't mean 'a nice knock-down argument'", Alice objected.
      f.  "When I use a word", Humpty Dumpty said in a rather scornful tone, "it means just what I choose it to mean — neither more nor less."

Indeed, this seems like a very uncooperative conversation, in which the partners are fully "obscure" to each other. But this conversational exchange is only obscure if one takes Alice's "literal" point of view, which would exclude all metaphors from our normal cooperative strategies. What Humpty Dumpty suggests to Alice is that she might earn glory from a very good argument. On the basis of the conceptual metaphor ARGUMENT IS WAR, such a good argument has the force of a knock-down blow for the opponent in the discussion and, just like victory in a fight or war, a good argument also brings glory to the winner. So what Alice in (18e) criticizes is the metaphorical use of language. "Glory" indeed does not mean "a nice knock-down argument", as she objects, but the reverse is absolutely true; using "a nice knock-down argument" may indeed mean "glory" for her. We find here a blend of two conceptual metaphors: ARGUMENT IS WAR and WINNING A WAR/ARGUMENT BRINGS GLORY. It is in this sense that we use clusters of metaphors, and instead of obscuring what we say, they just express levels of insight which would be impossible to express with language used in a literal sense.

If we interpreted Grice's maxim of manner in too narrow a sense, the maxim would no longer be tenable. However, if we accept the insight that metaphor and metonymy are part of every-day language and are often necessary to express what we mean, we can see that a number of utterances that seemed to be totally obscure or ambiguous on the surface, are not so in actual fact. We can therefore conclude that the maxim of manner must be extended to include figurative language. In addition, we should realize that the maxim of manner is highly culture-specific and that each culture has different norms and interpretations for the maxim of manner. For example, as we saw in Chapter 6.4, different cultures have very different cultural scripts for saying basically the same thing.

To conclude, even though cooperative principles and conversation "rules" may be realized in very culture-specific ways, it is probable that the cooperative principle can be regarded as a **universal** principle and that the maxims of conversation constitute some fundamental **pragmatic** or **interpersonal universals**.

### 7.3.3 Conversational and conventional implicatures

As the first maxim of conversation, i.e. the maxim of quality says, cooperative speakers are expected to speak the truth. Without this assumption conversation could not work. If speakers were to go about randomly making true and false statements about our world, without any indication to the hearer which are the true statements and which are the statements not to be taken too literally, the communicative process would break down.

But are speakers also expected to speak the whole truth? Are they expected to say as much as they can, as the maxim of quantity (make your contribution as informative as is required, but not more informative) would have us believe? The answer is no. Why would this be so? If speakers are too explicit about their communicative intentions, they enhance the hearer's comprehension of those intentions but the hearer may feel overinformed and thus feel insulted in some way.

Therefore, people in interaction should not be bored with overinformation and hearers must infer to what extent information and communicative intentions in a conversation are only left implicit. Classical examples of implicit communicative intentions are complaints in the context of family scenes as in (19):

(19)  (Wife to husband): You left the door of the fridge open.

Following the maxims of relevance, quantity, and manner, the hearer will "read" more into such an utterance than was explicitly said. Such an utterance will be interpreted as a request to do something about the situation rather than as a description of it. The description stands metonymically for the whole situation that fridges are normally closed and, since this is not the case, action should be taken to bring it about.

Sometimes, people's utterances seem totally irrelevant. However, Grice claims that even such apparent violations of the rules should be interpreted cooperatively. Consider the following example.

(20)  a.  Mathilda:  How do you like my new hairstyle, Francis?
      b.  Francis:  Let's get going, Mathilda.

The radical topic change that Francis makes is an obvious violation of the rule that speakers should say "nothing beyond the truth". A cooperative reply to Mathilda's question would have been "I like it a lot" or "I think it looks awful". Francis' blatant violation of this rule is not simply a case of misunderstanding, but has a meaning of its own. Francis evades a relevant answer to the question and the implication that Mathilda can draw from this is that a relevant answer to her question may very well be too painful.

The kind of implications that follow from the maxims are called **implicatures**. Implicatures come in various sorts, two of which are of special importance: conversational implicatures and conventional implicatures. A **conversational implicature** is the information inferred but not literally expressed in the speech act. The implicatures in (17, 19, and 20) are tied to the conversation, and this makes the implicature context-dependent. The implicature need not be true, or we say that it can be cancelled. The paper in (17) does not necessarily contain the election results about Tony Blair, since it may have been printed too early to give these results.

A **conventional implicature** or an **implicature by convention**, is an implicature that is tied to linguistic expressions. This is why a conventional implicature cannot be cancelled. One of Grice's examples of conventional implicatures is the contrastive meaning of a connective like *but*.

The difference in context-dependency is apparent in examples like (21) and (22):

(21)  The flag is red, but not completely red.

(22)  ?John is a Republican but honest; and I don't mean that there is any contrast between being a Republican and being honest.

In example (21) it is possible to use *but* in order to deny the implicature of the first clause, namely that the flag is completely red. The same holds for the part before the semi-colon in (22), which contains the conventional implicature that there is by definition a contrast between being a Republican and being honest. Therefore, the clause after the semi-colon presents a contradiction, and as a result, the whole sentence is rather questionable (indicated by the question mark).

Let us now look at a conversational implicature which also happens to contain *but*. Suppose two people, Peter and Carl, are playing tennis and after a little while Peter says:

(23)   It's not a sugar spoon you're holding Carl, but a tennis racket.

Peter has used the equivalent of a *not-A-but-B* construction. Such a contrastive construction expresses a correction. Peter's utterance violates the maxim of quality, since he knows perfectly well that nobody is assuming that the thing in Carl's hand is a spoon. Carl therefore infers that the speaker, Peter, is violating a maxim, and, on the assumption that the speaker is cooperative, Carl will try to find out what he ironically intended to convey. The most likely interpretation here is that Carl has been playing the tennis racket as if it were a spoon, i.e. without a real feel for the racket. The absurdity of the suggestion that Carl may have thought that the thing in his hand is a spoon creates the irony of the example.

What happened in these cases is that a conversational implicature was derived, not on the basis of obeying one of the maxims, but on the basis of a violation of the maxims, which is also called **flouting** the maxims. Note that flouting is something different from deception. Flouting involves an open, and hence, obvious violation of the maxims, whereas deception has to do with violations of the maxims which are hidden to the hearer so that the speaker can make him believe that he is saying things which are true. In all cases of figurative, either ironic or metaphorical language, conversational implicatures or flouting, there is always cooperative interaction as long as the speaker's utterance remains relevant. Consequently, of all the maxims of conversation, the maxim of relation "Be relevant" can be considered the most important.

## 7.4  Obligative speech acts and polite interaction

In the previous discussion, we illustrated cooperative principles especially with informative speech acts. There is another basic principle in interaction, i.e. politeness. Although this principle also plays a role in other speech acts, it is most evident in **obligative speech acts** i.e. getting people to do things for you by means of directive speech acts or your offering or promising to do things for other people by means of commissive speech acts. For example, the orders in (24) would be considered very impolite in most situations.

(24)  a.  The door!
      b.  I told you to go and close the door!

The order in (24a) would only be acceptable if someone had forgotten to close the door and the second in (24b) could only be said to a child who has disobeyed a previous order. In the next sections, we will discuss why politeness is so intimately intertwined with obligative acts.

### 7.4.1 Difference between information questions and directives

Even though we use politeness strategies in most of our speech acts, there are differences in motivation and desired consequences between, for example, a directive act such as *May I have the salt, please?* and an information question like *What's the time, please?*

When asking for information, the speaker cannot be sure that the hearer has the necessary knowledge to be able to give the desired information. Therefore, for most information questions we would use the interrogative as in (25a). If the hearer says that he or she does not have the requested knowledge — (as in 25b) — he or she is not likely to be blamed for not being able to provide the information as there is no reason for the first speaker to suspect that the second speaker is not telling the truth:

(25)  a.  Mike:   Can you tell me when the next bus leaves?
      b.  Lady:   I am sorry, I don't know.

Since the lady answers that she cannot give the information, Mike probably assumes she really does not know and is not withholding the information for some other reason. Reasons for withholding information might include keeping a secret, promising not to tell, information about one's sex life or financial matters. In all these situations, the principle of politeness tells us not to intrude. But in any other non-exceptional situation, we feel we can ask all possible information questions. And if the hearer says he or she does not know the answer, we cannot really question this. Therefore asking information questions is less imposing than making requests or giving orders. As long as easy actions such as passing the salt are involved there is no problem, but things become more complex when real work is involved as in (26a).

(26)  a.  Sarah:  Mike, (can you) take the rubbish out, please.
      b.  Mike:   ?No, I don't want to, do it yourself.
      c.  Mike:   Sorry, I can't.

     d.  Sarah:  Why not?

     e.  Mike:  I'm late for my train already.

Based on general knowledge as to what people are able and willing to do, and judging from the perception of the situation, Sarah presumes Mike's willingness and cooperation and expects that he will help her. If he does not do so, she would expect some sort of explanation as in (26c). Therefore, even if Mike does not want to comply with Sarah's order, he is unlikely to say *I don't want to* as in (26b), which therefore is preceded by a question mark, noting an odd utterance. He does not want to appear rude. There are several such strategies available to the speaker to help avoid such unpleasant situations when involved in directive acts.

### 7.4.2 Politeness: Acknowledging the other's identity

Why is it so important to use sentence types with less impact that do not put such a strong obligation, as in (26a), on the hearer? Another example helps to clarify this:

(27)  a.  Sue:         It's my birthday tomorrow. Are you coming to my party?

       b.  Monica:    Well, I'd like to come, but, actually I've got rather a lot of work to finish for the next day.

Here both speakers respect each other's "face". First of all, Sue does not impose too much by avoiding an explicit directive in the imperative form like *Do come to my party tomorrow*, but she uses an implicit directive in the interrogative form to pass on the invitation. Monica also respects Sue's "face". She does not give a direct answer because such an answer could hurt Sue's feelings. Clearly, Monica does not want to come. So she tries to present the situation to Sue as one in which she does not have the choice of saying "yes" but is forced by some important circumstance to reject the invitation.

    This example illustrates that when people talk to each other, they do not only negotiate the meaning of what they are saying to each other, they also continuously negotiate their relationship in that interaction. It is not only important to say to the other person what one thinks, wants or feels. It is just as important to take into account what the other person might think, want or feel about what one says. Will the others be upset if I say what I really want to say? Will they not like me anymore and want to break off the interaction? How can I say what I want to say so that we can continue the interactional relationship? These are questions that very much influence our choice of words in interaction.

In a communicative interaction, participants want to be acknowledged by others. They claim a specific identity as they want to be seen in a specific way, and thus they project a specific image of themselves. This interactional identity is commonly called **face** (where the most visible part of a person stands metonymically for the whole person and his or her identity).

In communicative interaction, we seek to establish and keep our face, not lose it. We hope that our wants and feelings are appreciated by the people we are talking to. We want to be liked and to feel good when interacting with others. In the majority of cases, we also hope to convey that our conversational partners should feel good about themselves, too. To do so, we use positive and negative politeness strategies, i.e. we say a bit more to signal our appreciation of the other's "face" wants.

Let us now have a look at the use of such strategies in conversation for either coming closer ("social accelerating") or distancing ("social braking"). At the beginning of a conversation, we might use ritual phrases like *How are you*, *Nice to see you*, and so on to show our interest in the other person and thus to establish a mutual basis for the present interaction. We signal to each other that the channel is open and we want to communicate. During this "phatic" phase of the interaction, we might engage in a little small talk about things like the weather, sports, or even politics, topics that are relatively neutral as to the wants and feelings of both partners. These "safe topics" are not too important as far as the topic of conversation is concerned, but they are all the more important to establish a mutual basis for interaction.

However, most interactions do not focus on "safe topics" only. One basic reason for taking part in interactions is to convey to others what we think and what we want (the other) to do. Every "less safe" speech act that is directed towards a hearer might threaten his or her face, no matter whether we use informative or obligative acts. When carrying out obligative speech acts, for example, we want to do something or want the other to do something for us. If we do this by means of an explicit form such as the imperative as in (28a), we use a **direct speech act**, i.e. we state our communicative intention openly and directly. This might threaten the other's right to autonomy. If we have the feeling that a direct speech act might be perceived as a face threat by the hearer, there is quite a wide range of implicit directives, which are **indirect speech acts** as in (28b–e) from which we might select something appropriate and less threatening to the other's face.

(28)  a.  Shut the door.
  b.  Can you shut the door, please?
  c.  Will you shut the door, please?
  d.  Would/could you please shut the door?
  e.  Let's shut the door, shall we?
  f.  There's a draught in here.

As already shown in Chapter 6.4, in Anglo culture there are scripts blocking the imperative (28a) and prescribing the interrogative (28b, c, d). Though it may be perfectly acceptable among friends, the use of the imperative in (28a) is not appropriate when the speaker and hearer do not know each other well or when the hearer is of a higher social status or has power over the speaker. The use of the imperative as in *Shut the door* has the strongest impact on the hearer, but it is normally not used. Still, the use of the plain imperative does not count as a face threat per se. There are situations that require such a use of directive speech acts. Imagine for example that someone opens the door of an office, causing a terrible draught, and papers are flying all around the room. This might count as a kind of emergency situation and the secretary might shout: *Shut the door!* Or imagine other direct speech acts like instructions in recipes. We would expect that they read something like *Cook the potatoes and turnips until tender, then drain well.* It would seem rather odd to employ strategies of politeness in this context. The same holds true for instructions in a working environment and task oriented acts: *Give me the nails*, or computer instructions: *Insert diskette and type: Set-up.*

If the speaker is a student, and the hearer a professor, the request to shut the door would be realized rather differently by indirect speech acts, as for example in (28b, c, d). Such, more polite, utterances say more than is necessary and thus seem to flout the maxim of quantity. There are two types of politeness strategies like these. **Positive politeness strategies** signal to the hearer that the speaker appreciates the hearer's needs. For example, a speaker can use an **inclusive *we*** to include both the speaker and the hearer in the action, where, in actual fact, only the hearer "you" is meant to do something as in (28e) *Let's shut the door* or in *We really should close the door.* It can even be employed in prohibitions. So a very polite British policeman might say: *We don't want to park here, do we?* Others include paying compliments like *Oh these biscuits smell wonderful — did you make them? May I have one?* or using in-group address forms such as *Give us a hand, son.*

**Negative politeness strategies**, on the other hand, show the hearer that the speaker respects the hearer's desire not to be imposed upon as in (28b) *Can you shut the door please*. Here, rather than ordering, the speaker asks if the hearer is able to do something. Another possibility would be to ask if the hearer is willing as in (28c). An even more polite form would be the use of the expressions such as *Would you* or *Could you* in (28d). Here the speaker seems to be expressing doubt as to whether the hearer is able or is willing to help so that he need not feel obliged at all. Both, positive as well as negative politeness strategies say something more than really necessary to prevent a possible face threat.

At the politest end of the scale of indirectness, we can express implicit communicative intentions as in the case of (28f) *There's a draught in here*. This highlights the reason why the speaker performs the act. As discussed in the context of (19) and (20), the hearer must infer the conversational implicature, i.e. the door is to be closed and the new hairstyle is not good, respectively. Such implicatures work via the principle of metonymy in that only one element in the interactional situation, i.e. the reason to act, is explicitly mentioned, but this stands for the whole of the speech act, i.e. the carrying out of the implicit request. The **face-threatening act** is still performed, but in an indirect mode.

Moreover, it may also be the case that a request would be thought of as offering such an enormous threat to the face of the hearer (and because of his inappropriate behaviour also a threat to the face of the speaker) that it cannot be uttered at all. If a VIP is making an after-dinner speech, you would probably not utter the request to have the door closed, but avoid the speech act altogether and close it yourself.

If we look at the range of utterances in (28a–f), we can see that positive and negative politeness strategies follow the iconic principle of quantity as introduced in Chapter 1: The more linguistic material is employed, the more polite the strategy tends to be.

## 7.5 Conclusion: Interplay between sentence structure and types of speech act

In Chapter 4 (Section 4.4.1), it was pointed out that there are three basic sentence patterns associated with moods: (a) the subject-verb order for declaratives, with which we make statements, (b) the verb-subject order for interrogatives, with which we ask questions, and (c) the subjectless imperative, with which we give orders:

(29)  a.   Mary has shut the door.
     b.   Has Mary shut the door?
     c.   Shut the door, Mary!!

However, as we have seen now in this chapter, while looking more closely at language as it is actually used in conversation, we have given many examples where the communicative intention does not match with the expected sentence pattern. For example, a declarative statement like *You have left the fridge open* may be meant as an implicit order like "Please, close the fridge". It is especially with obligative speech acts that we often use alternate patterns. To be less direct, we often use a declarative or interrogative sentence pattern.

Table 2 shows some of the possible combinations: Those that are most typical — though not necessarily most frequently used — are connected with full lines, and those which are less prototypical are connected with interrupted lines. We see then that the constitutive (declarative and expressive) speech acts are expressed with only the declarative pattern, but informative speech acts may be expressed with declarative and interrogative patterns, and obligative speech acts may be expressed with all three types: The declarative, interrogative and imperative patterns, each with different stylistic values and effects.

**Table 2.**

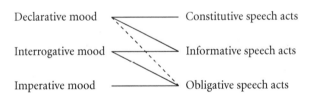

These various possibilities are illustrated in the examples of speech acts in (30).

(30)  a.   Declarative mood
         Const.:      I name this ship the Queen Elizabeth.
         Inform.:     My laptop broke down.
         Oblig.:      You left the door open.
     b.   Interrogative mood
         Inform.:     Do you know when the bus comes?
         Oblig.:      Could you close the door, please?
     c.   Imperative mood
         Oblig.:      Close the door, please.
         Const.:      Have fun!

## 7.6 Summary

Whereas Chapters 1 to 6 focus on the **ideational function** of language, Chapter 7 focuses on the **interpersonal function**. With the exception of its **phatic function, language-in-use** aims at the realization of a specific **communicative intention**, which is realized in the **speech act**. All this is the business of **pragmatics**, the subfield of linguistics analyzing what we do with language. The three main types of 'doing things with language' are constitutive speech acts such as apologizing or sentencing someone, informative speech acts and obligative speech acts.

In **constitutive speech acts** we can distinguish between every-day or informal **expressive speech acts** such as congratulations, apologies, giving comfort and formal **declarative speech acts** such as declaring a meeting open. They have in common that saying the right words at the right time by the right person is the doing of the act and therefore they crucially depend on their **felicity conditions** i.e. the conditions to make a speech act **felicitous**. In many cases the verb indicating the subtype of a constitutive or other type of speech act can be used to both express and describe the speech act and is therefore a **performative verb**.

In **informative speech acts** we either give information by means of **assertive speech acts** or ask for information by means of information questions. We do this on the basis of the **background knowledge** which determines the **conversational presuppositions** the speaker and the hearer make. Otherwise we do this on the basis of **conventional presuppositions**, using the clues of definite articles as in *I'm going to the park* for all the elements the speaker can take for granted because of **world knowledge** or **cultural knowledge**.

With informative speech acts there may be an enormous distance between what is literally said and what is communicatively meant. In order to establish a relation between those two realities, the **cooperative principle** is proposed by Grice. It is assumed that the partners are fully cooperative in some way and that they follow **maxims of conversation**. These are the **maxims of quality, quantity, relevance** and **manner**. The cooperative principle can be seen as a **language universal** and the maxims of conversation constitute **pragmatic universals**, also callled **interpersonals universals**.

As well as implementing these four maxims, we are also called upon to interpret a number of utterances on the basis of the implications they contain. Implications depending on the speech act situation itself are **conversational implicatures**; if they are of a more general nature and depend on grammatical form they are **conventional implicatures**. In a number of cases, we even seem to violate the maxims of conversation, which is called **flouting,** but even then we are cooperative, but express our communicative intention very indirectly.

**Obligative speech acts** carry an obligation placed on the hearer (**directive speech acts**) or on the speaker himself (**commissive speech acts**) and therefore require tact and politeness. A **direct speech act,** especially in the imperative, may be too abrupt and therefore many **indirect speech acts** are used to save the hearer's **face. Negative politeness strategies** inquire after the hearer's ability or willingness to carry out a request, whereas **positive politeness strategies** propose common action, e.g. by means of **inclusive** *we.*

## 7.7 Further reading

Good introductions to the field of pragmatics for beginners are Grundy (1995), and for intermediate students: Levinson (1983) and Blakemore (1992). Cognitive approaches to speech acts in terms of metonymy are Thornburg and Panther (1997), Panther and Thornburg (2003), and Ruiz de Mendoza (2002). The classics of the field are the relatively simple and highly accessible books by Austin (1952) and Searle (1969). The epoch-making paper on the cooperative principle is Grice (1975). The most innovating work on politeness is a long paper by Brown & Levinson (1987). A highly technical, but important study on relevance is Sperber & Wilson (1986). A reader containing many of the basic pragmatic papers is Davis (ed., 1991).

## Assignments

1. Analyze the following utterances. After identifying them as (i) constitutive, (ii) obligative or (iii) informative speech acts, identify the subtype: (i) a declarative or expressive, (ii) offer or directive, or (iii) assertive or information question. Then, finally, for obligative speech acts decide whether they are direct or indirect.

    a. Shall I get you some coffee?
    b. I hereby declare the meeting closed.
    c. (In a book shop): Where is the linguistics department, please?
    d. (In a Bed and Breakfast): Are you ready for coffee now?
    e. (On a shop door): Closed between 12 and 2 p.m.
    f. Oh, Jesus, there he goes again.
    g. What the hell are you doing in my room?
    h. Can't you make a little less noise?

2.   In the following examples "thanks" is said for different reasons and in different situations. Comment on (i) what the reason or occasion is for the thanks, (ii) whether it is a formal or informal situation, and (iii) whether the way it is said is appropriate or not for the situation?

   a.   "Many thanks for your presents."
   b.   Margaret handed him the butter. "Thank you", Samuel said, "thank you very much."
   c.   "Can I give you a lift to town?" — "Oh, thank you."
   d.   "How was your trip to Paris?" — "Very pleasant, thank you."
   e.   The president expressed deep gratitude for Mr. Christopher's service as State Secretary.

3.   In Section 7.2.1 we saw that expressives may differ in degrees of formality. We also saw that we may actually say which act we are performing by naming it with a performative verb. If we look up the two words *sorry* and *apologize* in the DCE, we note different frequencies: *Sorry* is much more frequent in spoken language than *apologize* and *apology*, which are more frequent in written language. In the following examples, examine where and why both forms can be used and where they cannot. Then comment on the relationship between frequency, the different situations these words are used in, and their degree of formality.

   a.   Go say you are sorry to your sister for hitting her.
   b.   I must apologize for the delay in replying to your letter.
   c.   I apologize for being late.
   d.   Your behaviour was atrocious. I demand an apology.

4.   Let's take a closer look again at the fragment in (18) from Lewis Carroll's *Through the Looking-Glass* on "glory" and analyze how its figurative language functions in the giving and receiving of information.

   a.   Why is the information given in (a) "obscure" for Alice? Which conceptual relationship may there be between finding a good argument in a discussion and "glory"?
   b.   Is Alice's speech act in (b) an assertion or an indirect request for information? How else could she have expressed this speech act more directly?
   c.   From (c) it is obvious that Humpty Dumpty interprets Alice's utterance correctly. Which type of implicature (conversational or conventional) is at play here? But in (c) Humpty Dumpty also implies that we do not know what a speaker may mean until he has told us. Which of the two types of implicature does he not seem to be aware of?
   d.   What conceptual metaphor does Humpty Dumpty's explanation in (d) exploit?
   e.   Why does Alice not understand him?

   f.    In (f) Humpty Dumpty makes it sound as if his use of language is quite idiosyn-cratic. What general linguistic principle that he makes extensive use of does he not seem to be aware of?

5.   Which maxim of conversation is flouted in each of the following exchanges?

   a.   A:   What did you have for lunch at school?
        B:   Fish.
   b.   A:   Hello Mary. How are you?
        B:   Well, I went to the doctor's on Monday, and he has now referred me to a specialist. I should have an appointment at the hospital some time in July, if I'm lucky, but you know what the health service is like about arranging appointments. I'll probably be dead by then...
   c.   A:   Can you tell me the time, please?
        C:   Yes.
   d.   A:   Have you got the time, please?
        B:   Yes, If you've got the money!
   e.   A:   Have you put the kettle on?
        B:   Yes, but it doesn't fit!

6.   What is a general characteristic of both positive and negative politeness strategies? Identify the subtype of speech act and the strategy used in the following utterances and give reasons for your answer.

   a.   Please, come quick and see who's coming.
   b.   Could you tell him I am not here?
   c.   Will you please be so kind to keep him off.
   d.   I am sorry, I must go and see my boss now.
   e.   Let's tell him we have a meeting.
   f.   Why don't we tell him we are busy today?

7.   The following series of utterances were made by a mother at 30 second intervals to her eight-year-old child. Which type of politeness strategy does she use? Her degree of politeness reduces with each utterance. Taking the number of words she uses and the difference between direct and indirect speech acts into consideration, explain how this is achieved.

   a.   Could you stop doing that now, please?
   b.   Could you stop that now, please?
   c.   Will you stop that now, please?
   d.   Did you hear me? Stop it!

8. In telemarketing, sales people are often trained to use certain types of speech acts and strategies so that their potential customer, whom they call unexpectedly, will not break off the conversation immediately. The following are two examples of tele-sales training conversations for agents. Analyze each extract in terms of speech acts (obligative, informative, and constitutive) and other possible strategies and suggest why one might be more successful than the other.

    a.    Agent:    It's Pat Searle, Mr. Green, and I am calling from the Stanworth Financial Services Company.

           Mr. Green:    Oh, yes.

           Agent:    I wonder, Mr. Green, would you be interested in getting a better return on your investments?

           Mr. Green:    I'm sorry — no I am not. I am quite happy with my current situation. Good night.

    b.    Agent:    This is Stanworth Financial Services Company. With the current low interest rates, getting a reasonable return on your investments is something of a challenge these days.

           Mr. Green:    Weeell, yeeees.

           Agent:    This is why I felt you might be interested in a new investment product my company has recently launched. It provides a considerably better return than all building society accounts and most other similar types of investment products.

           Mr. Green:    Yes.

           Agent:    Tell me, Mr. Green, how would you feel about receiving details of our new investment product that could provide you with a return of up to nine percent?

# 8    Structuring texts

## Text linguistics

## 8.0 Overview

So far in this book, we have looked at single linguistic expressions such as a word, a morpheme, a sentence, or a speech act. In Chapter 7, we analyzed the ways single utterances may be interpreted as a specific speech act in actual communication. In this chapter, we will go beyond single linguistic utterances and examine how people interpret linguistic expressions as part of a larger whole. The question will therefore be: How are elements of language grouped together in texts?

A text is the spoken or written evocation of an event or series of events. However, the words of a text by themselves never form the whole picture and cannot be the sole object of text linguistics. What matters is not only the words and sentences as they form the text, but our interpretation of that text and the basis for that interpretation. It becomes obvious that a text almost never contains all the clues needed to interpret it, but that we add a lot to the text on the basis of our cultural or world knowledge. This is our text representation, i.e. the interpretation of a coherent whole on the basis of the text elements and of our own mental grasp of the world. Coherence is therefore not, first of all or primordially, based on linguistic expressions in the text, but basically and ultimately, on conceptual links between the various entities referred to in the text and between the various events evoked. The former is known as referential coherence, the second as relational coherence. These will form the main issues in this chapter, which we will end by giving a survey of a fairly large number of coherence relations.

## 8.1 Communication, text, and text linguistics

While writing we mainly or exclusively communicate by words. This is verbal communication. While speaking we not only communicate by words or verbal communication, but also by means of loudness, rhythm and speed. These elements accompanying our words are known as paralinguistic (or paraverbal) communication. Our gestures, facial expressions and body language are non-verbal communication.

In spoken communication the text — the words we speak — is but one of the three means of expression. In written communication the text is almost all there is. In both cases, however, the text is but one aspect or one part of the communication; the other part is what the listener or reader brings with him when he or she interprets this text. This includes the world of the speaker and hearer, their ideas and feelings, as well as their cultural or world knowledge.

**Text** can consequently be defined as the linguistic expressions used in communication between people and the interpretation the hearer or reader makes of them. This definition applies to both oral and written communication, but has the additional condition that text here only denotes the verbal part of the communication, excluding the paralinguistic and non-verbal aspects. This text definition also presupposes the cultural or world knowledge on which the text interpretation is based. Schematically, this definition can be represented as in Table 1.

**Table 1.** Communication, text, and cultural knowledge

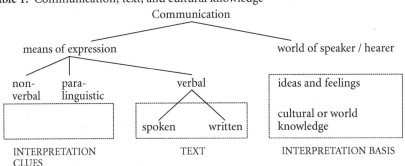

**Text linguistics** is the study of how S (speaker, writer) and H (hearer, reader) manage to communicate via texts, that is how they go beyond the text (words) they produce or have in front of them to see the relations between the sentences, the paragraphs, the sections, etc. In this chapter we will limit ourselves mainly to the relations between sentences. This is an intricate network of relations that warrants its own study, separate from higher relations in the text and text types.

## 8.2   Text representation

In the third part of Swift's *Gulliver's Travels* ('A voyage to Laputa, Balnibarbi, Glubbdubdrib, Luggnagg and Japan'), Gulliver describes a number of scientific projects at the Academy of Lagado. The following describes the second project, which was intended to do away with "words" altogether.

> The other project was a scheme for entirely abolishing all words whatsoever; and this was urged as a great advantage in point of health as well as brevity. For it is plain that every word we speak is in some degree a diminution of our lungs by corrosion, and consequently contributes to the shortening of our lives. An expedient was therefore offered that, since words are only names for things, it would be more convenient for all men to carry about them such things as were necessary to express the particular business they are to discourse on. And this invention would certainly have taken place, to the great ease as well as health of the subject, if the women, in conjunction with the vulgar and illiterate, had not threatened to raise a rebellion, unless they might be allowed the liberty to speak with their tongues, after the manner of their ancestors; such constant irreconcilable enemies to science are the common people. However, many of the most learned and wise adhere to the new scheme of expressing themselves by things, which has only this inconvenience attending it, that if a man's business be very great, and of various kinds, he must be obliged in proportion to carry a greater bundle of things upon his back, unless he can afford one or two strong servants to attend him. I have often beheld two of those sages almost sinking under the weight of their packs, like peddlers among us; who, when they met in the streets, would lay down their loads, open their sacks, and hold conversation for an hour together; then put up their implements, help each other to resume their burdens, and take their leave.

Of course, the idea that we might prefer to converse in "things" rather than "words" may strike us as rather odd, but actually such ideas have outlived the days of Swift considerably. What Swift expresses ironically is also adhered to by philosophers such as Leibniz at a scientific level. Also the logical analyses by the British philosopher Bertrand Russell are based on the Misleading Form Hypothesis.

**Figure 1.** Conversation between sages using things, not words

This hypothesis dictates that natural language is not very well suited to formulate accurate descriptions of the world around us because natural language is ambiguous and misleading. Therefore, it should be emulated by a more exact mode of representing the world: the logical form of sentences.

In this chapter we will show that communication formulated according to the "new scheme of expressing [oneself] by things" differs in a significant number of ways from natural texts, and that "the women, in conjunction with the vulgar and illiterate" were very right to protest against such an unnatural way of communication.

The first thing that is wrong about the Lagadan vision of language is that it assumes that language is merely descriptive, that it only represents certain states of affairs. Such a function has already been referred to as the **ideational function** of language in Chapter 7. It is of course an important one, and in fact until fairly recently it has been the almost exclusive object of semantic studies. But in producing texts, people do other things than merely describe. Texts contain many indications as to the role of the speaker or writer and to the function of the sentences, referred to as the **interpersonal function** in Chapter 7. For one thing, as we saw in Chapter 7, natural texts contain politeness information. For example, the difference between (1a,b,c) is not one of content, as it has the same *ideational* information, but one of appropriateness.

(1)  a.  Would you pass me the butter, please?
     b.  Pass me the butter!
     c.  Pass me the butter, would you?

Texts may also contain information concerning the way they are structured, called the **textual function** of language. For example, a sentence like (2) does not add much to the ideational content of the text, yet it performs an important function in that it guides the reader in processing the text.

(2)  In the following section I will briefly go into the history of car mechanics.

The second reason why the Lagadan version of communication and its interpretation and production is wrong has to do with how it views meaning. It assumes that "words are just names for things", and that therefore each word stands directly for a thing in the world. A Lagadan communication new style consists of a number of objects. In other words, the meaning of a conversation as a whole could then be equated with the collection of the "things" brought to bear by the participants in the conversation while in actual fact texts, whether spoken or written, consist of sentences or rather idea units.

It might be tempting to consider the interpretation of a text as the sum of the interpretation of the individual sentences of a text. However, there is good reason to assume that this view on text interpretation is not correct. For one thing, as (3) illustrates, readers add all sorts of information to the sentences in the text when they process it.

(3)  On our way to the reception, the engine broke down. We were late for the party.

Conversational partners will have no difficulty in understanding that the engine that broke down is part of the car and that the person uttering (3) was in this car. But this car is not mentioned explicitly in the text. Readers or hearers will also assume that there is a causal link between the engine breaking down and being late for the party. These implicit assumptions, called **inferences**, are usually based on the reader's previous experience. (Conversational implicatures, which were discussed in Chapter 7, are a subset of these inferences.) The fact that we always make a great many inferences when we interpret a text is evidence for the fact that a text is more than the sum of the interpretations of the individual sentences.

On the other hand, one can also say that the meaning of a text is also more restricted than the sum of the interpretations of the individual sentences in the text. Texts are usually interpreted with respect to a context. This context can resolve ambiguities or vague allusions in separate sentences. For example, in isolated sentences, the pronouns *him* or *you* may remain unspecified, but in a text such references are fixed.

To conclude, these points can be summarized as follows: A writer or speaker (from now on S) has the intention of conveying a message to a reader or hearer (from now H). In order to realize this intention, S formulates a message consisting of linguistic expressions, called the text. However, one cannot understand the functioning of texts by merely looking at the linguistic information in the text. One also has to study the **representations** that S and H have of the text. Therefore, it is argued here that it is a crucial property of natural language that there is no direct mapping of communicative intentions to linguistic expressions, but that this mapping is mediated through a conceptual level: the level of **text representation**. This is particularly true for the most distinctive characteristic of texts, namely the fact that well-formed natural texts are coherent. **Coherence** is the property that distinguishes texts from arbitrary sets of sentences. Much of the remainder of this chapter will be devoted to an exploration of this notion of text coherence.

## 8.3 Coherence vs. cohesion

A text is called coherent if it is possible to construct a coherent representation of that text. The following is an example of a coherent text.

(4) (a) "The Adventures of Huckleberry Finn" must be pronounced the most amusing book Mark Twain has written for years. (b) *Moreover, it* is a more minute and faithful picture of Southwestern manners and customs fifty years ago than was "Life on the Mississippi", (c) *while* in regard to the dialect *it* surpasses any of *the author's* previous stories in the command of the half-dozen species of patois which passed for the English language in old Missouri.
(San Francisco Chronicle, March 15, 1885)

In this example, a number of elements have been italicized. These are elements that link a clause to its surrounding text. The **cohesion** of a text is the explicit marking of its coherence by means of cohesive links. The following is also an example of a coherent text.

(5)  (a) *Twelve year term of imprisonment.* (b) LONDON, APRIL 10. (c) The London court has convicted a Brighton resident to twelve years imprisonment for accessory to murder. (d) The victim was fatally wounded in a shooting incident in a Winchester restaurant last year.

Even though this mini-text seems quite coherent, there are no words that explain what the situations described in (c) and (d) have to do with each other. Also, none of the concepts mentioned in the fourth sentence repeat any material from the third sentence. In other words, there are no cohesive links (or there seems to be no cohesion) between (c) and (d). Yet, no one would find it difficult to understand. The explanation is that we add the missing links from cultural knowledge, i.e. our knowledge of the world. For this we use the murder script, whereby the term *script* refers to our idea of what a murder case is composed of and is used in a slightly more general sense than it was in the phrase *cultural script* introduced in Chapter 6, which only relates to our norms of behaviour. We know from previous experience that murders come along with murderers, victims, means, motives, murder sites, and the like, and it is this cultural knowledge that allows us to construct a coherent representation of text (5). The example shows, therefore, that it is possible to have coherence without explicit cohesion.

The coherence of a text can be signalled through cohesive links such as word repetition or the use of subordinate or superordinate terms, but the following fragment shows that the presence of such cohesive links is not a guarantee for coherence:

(6)  I bought a Ford. A car in which President Wilson rode down the Champs Elysées was black. Black English has been widely discussed. The discussions between the presidents ended last week. A week has seven days. Every day I feed my cat. Cats have four legs. The cat is on the mat. Mat has three letters.

This text seems to have many cohesive links, mostly word repetitions. Still, it is very difficult to assign it a coherent interpretation. Therefore, we may conclude that coherence is not so much a property of the linguistic expressions in the texts itself, but of the representation that S and H make of this text.

Coherence can be established in one of two ways: By repeated reference to the same referents or 'mental objects' in a text, called **referential coherence**, and by linking text parts with **coherence relations** like "cause-consequence" and "contrast", called **relational coherence**. In the next two sections we will explore these two coherence-creating devices separately.

## 8.4 Referential coherence

Part of the coherence of a text stems from the fact that texts are used to talk coherently about a set of concepts and their referents. Texts contain referential expressions. One of the insights of modern linguistics is that the referents of these text words are not so much things in the outer world as the mental images people have of them. That is why it is possible to refer to things that do not exist but can be thought about, such as unicorns and Santa Claus.

Typical referential expressions are pronouns (*she, my*) and full noun phrases (*the woman next door*). The reference can be to something outside the text, or to other concepts mentioned in the text. The first case is called **exophoric reference** or **deixis**, the second is called **endophoric reference**. Example (7) is a clear case of exophoric reference.

(7)  [Wife to her husband while pointing to the ceiling:]
     Did you speak to *them* upstairs?

The wife's utterance can only be interpreted completely if information about the situational context is available. This is typical of exophoric or deictic elements.

Endophoric elements get their interpretation from the textual context, either the preceding context as in (8), called **anaphoric reference**, or the following context as in (9) called **cataphoric reference**. The terms *anaphoric* and *cataphoric reference* pertain to the use of pronouns to refer to a noun that precedes or follows. In the examples, the referential expressions and their antecedents are marked by the indices *i*.

(8)  Last year we were in [the Alps]$_i$. We think [they]$_i$'re beautiful.

(9)  a.  [That]$_i$'s just my luck: [first my tyre bursts and then the bridge is closed, too]$_i$.

     b.  Did you hear [the news]$_i$? [Clinton will be impeached]$_i$

By depending on the textual context for their interpretation, endophoric elements contribute to the coherence of a text, and that is why it can be said that referential coherence is established through endophoricity.

Not all of the referents in a text are equally prominent. Some are talked about continuously, some are new to the text, and others have a subsidiary role. Careful studies of this **identificational function** of referential expressions have shown that the way in which concepts are referred to depends on the prominence of the concept. For instance, if an object is completely new to the text, it has to be introduced. In a Lagadan conversation this would mean that an object is taken from the bag. In natural language, at least in West European languages, the typical way to do this is by using an **indefinite expression** i.e. an expression with an indefinite article or pronoun. This is found in the typical introductory sentence of fairy tales:

(10)   Once upon a time there was *a little girl.*

Once the referent has been introduced it can be referred to in various ways, depending on the **prominence** of the concept. The more prominent it is, the less linguistic material is needed to identify the referent. If it has constantly been in the 'focus of attention', the natural way of referring to it is by the use of a pronoun:

(10)   a.   She was called Goldilocks.

This is a reduced way of referring to the girl whereas a non-reduced form would be *The girl was called Goldilocks.* An English pronoun contains semantic information only about gender, person and number (pronouns in other languages may give even less information). More information, in the context of (10a), is not needed because the referent can be inferred from the immediate context. Sometimes, if the reference is even further reduced, it becomes **elliptical**:

(10)   b.   Once upon a time there was a little girl Ø called Goldilocks.

If the girl is less prominent, for instance because she was referred to a while ago, meaning that another object has come into focus, more content, e.g. not a pronoun but a full noun phrase is needed to establish **co-reference**, i.e. reference to the same person or object.

(10)   c.   Once upon a time there was a little girl called Goldilocks. She lived in a forest that belonged to a rich and powerful king. The king had a son called Jeremy, who loved hunting. One day, as he was chasing a deer, he saw {$^{??}$her/the little girl}.

It can also be the case that objects or persons have not yet been introduced, but that their 'existence' can be inferred from situational or background knowledge. This we saw in example (3). *The engine* in (3) is presented as if it has been introduced, and in a way it has, because we know from previous experience that one of the ways to get to a reception is by car, and cars have engines.

These examples clearly show the identificational function of referring expressions. There is a strong correlation between the degree of prominence of a referent and the form of referential expressions. Thus these expressions form a signal showing H where to look for the referent of the expression.

Recently text linguistics has realized that an anaphor (i.e. an anaphoric expression) may also have a **non-identificational function**. There are cases in which the form of an anaphor is not in accordance with its referential function, either because it is overly specific, called **referential overspecification,** or because it presents a referent as new although it has already been introduced, referred to as late indefinites. An example of the former can be found in the last sentence of the following fragment from an encyclopaedic text on Goethe.

(11)  He$_i$ was fascinated by humanity and its progeny, and he$_i$ expressed his$_i$ ideas, questions, and struggles by means of poems, songs, plays, prose, maxims, and short essays. Goethe$_i$, besides being an artist, was also a leading physicist.

The use of the full name *Goethe* in the last sentence is a clear case of overspecification. Here the use of *he* would have sufficed for identificational purposes. Every sentence of this fragment is 'about' Goethe, and therefore he is fully in the focus of attention. In this case, though, the name is used rather than a pronoun in order to signal that a new aspect or topic will be discussed. The full name *Goethe* is used now to obtain a specific text-structural effect, namely text **segmentation**, i.e. the structuring of a text into larger conceptual units such as a paragraph. In experimental research it was found that readers experience thematic discontinuity of the text because the name helps to indicate that a new topic is introduced.

**Late indefinites** is the use of indefinite noun phrases or pronouns at a later moment in the text where one would expect a definite expression. Late indefinites also have an informational effect, but of a different nature:

(12)  Girl subdues attacker
     A brave young woman turned the tables on a robber and beat him with an iron pipe which she had wrested from him, then handed him over to

the police in Osaka Wednesday night.

At about 11:25 p.m. Wednesday, *a man* attacked Miss Mayumi Sanda, 23, of Oyodo-cho, Oyodo-ku, Osaka, on a street in the same ward. He struck her several times on the head with an iron pipe and tried to strangle her. [...]

The phrase in question is *a man* in the second sentence. From an identificational point of view this use of an indefinite expression is rather odd. The referent has already been introduced and frequently referred to in the context. Therefore one might expect a pronoun like *he* or a definite phrase like *the man*. The effect of this indefinite phrase renders the text more lively. We experience the event through the eyes of Miss Mayumi, so to speak, and to her the robber is an unidentified person. This use of a late indefinite is called **perspectivization**, which means that a given scene is seen from a given person's perspective. This 'perspectivizing' way of reporting dramatic events has by now become almost standard procedure in English newspapers.

To sum up, we have seen that referential coherence can be established through endophoric reference. Endophoric reference has primarily an identificational function, which means that the referential choice is as a rule in accordance with the informational needs of H. In the case of special, i.e. marked reference, non-identificational effects like text segmentation and perspectivization can be achieved. It is clear that in a Lagadan type of communication only very few of these different means for establishing referential coherence are available.

## 8.5  Relational coherence

Whoever reads or hears a text has not fully understood that text unless he or she has also interpreted the **coherence relations** like "cause-consequence", "contrast", "evidence", and so on between the sentences or clauses of the text. A coherence relation is that aspect of the interpretation of the text that is additional to the interpretation of the sentences or clauses in isolation. This is yet another reason why a Lagadan 'procedure' would not work very well. Such a conversation consists of groups of objects, and there are no objects that can stand for complete situations and events expressed in natural language via event schemata in clauses (see Chapter 4.2). Therefore, since there is no Lagadan equivalent for the notion "clause", there cannot be an equivalent for relations between clauses either.

Below are some examples of such coherence relations. Some are explicitly signalled using words like *because* and *although* as in (13, 15); other coherence relations are left implicit as in (14).

(13)   The unicorn died because it was lonely. (*Consequence-cause*)

(14)   Maggie must be eager for promotion. She's worked late three days in a row. (*Evidence*)

(15)   Although Greta Garbo was called the yardstick of beauty, she never married. (*Concession*)

In (13) the second clause gives the cause for the death of the unicorn. In (14) the second clause does not so much give a cause for a specific state of affairs, but rather evidence upon which a supposition about Maggie is based. In (15) the relation is a so-called concession, i.e. the second clause denies an expectation raised by the first clause. In fact, (15) is quite a famous case. It appeared in an obituary on Greta Garbo in a national Dutch newspaper, *De Volkskrant*. Because the sentence contains the implicature that "beautiful women normally marry", there were many angry letters to the editor about the author's old-fashioned world view.

A coherence relation can be encoded explicitly through the use of **connectives**. The class of connectives consists of subordinating conjunctions (*because, if, although*), coordinating conjunctions (*and, but*), conjunctive adverbs (*so, therefore, yet*) and conjunctive adverbial phrases (*as a consequence, in contrast with this*). An interesting claim of current theories of text linguistics is that the same coherence relations that can occur between clauses can also occur between larger text segments, such as paragraphs and even complete sections. That is why the presence of a coherence relation between two paragraphs (e.g. one containing a hypothesis and one presenting its analysis) is sometimes signalled by complete sentences (*This problem is in urgent need of a solution*). There are also more subtle ways of signalling the coherence relation, for instance by the use of 'relational' content words like the pair *some…others* to signal a contrast relation, or by means of stress and intonation. For example, in (16) there is rising intonation at the end of the first clause and a steep fall in the second clause to signal the concession link between the two clauses.

(16)   John may have written a famous book, but he has absolutely no manners.

Sometimes speakers use connectives that do not seem to "match" the coherence relation. An example is (17).

(17)   (a) Since June 1 Jan Kaal has been editor in chief of the monthly O. (b) Kaal was approached last year by the publisher, Maurice Keizer, (c) after he had written a critical article in *NRC Handelsblad* on the first issue of the magazine.

Obviously the writer of this text intends to say Kaal is now editor in chief because he had written a critical article. However, instead of *because* the connective *after* is used, which specifies only a temporal relation rather than a causal relation between the two events. This is called **relational underspecification**. Underspecification could of course add to the complexity of text interpretation, and apparently speakers use it only if the context provides enough information for H to derive the correct interpretation.

These contextual restrictions are very diverse in nature. One important factor is **genre** or **text type**. In narratives H expects events to be causally related and consequently it is fairly common to leave causal relations underspecified in narratives. By contrast, in testimonies S and H expect each other to be very explicit, and consequently there is little underspecification in texts of this type.

How should one account for the occurrence of underspecified coherence relations? In Chapter 7 the notion of **conversational implicature** was introduced. Participants in a conversation need not express all of the information they intend to convey explicitly, because they can rely on the cooperation of their conversational partners to make the relevant inferences. If, as stated in Chapter 7 (example 16), someone responds to an utterance 'I've run out of petrol' with 'There is a petrol station round the corner', then one can safely assume, on the basis of the maxim of relevance, that the respondent believes that one can get petrol in the petrol station, even though this has not been stated explicitly. If this is not the case, then the respondent may not have said something that is not true, but he or she can certainly be accused of having been uncooperative.

The underspecification of coherence relations can also be explained as a case of conversational implicature based on the maxim of relevance. Mere temporal ordering of events is hardly ever relevant, and as (18) and (19) illustrate, that explains why explicit temporal connectives receive a causal interpretation:

(18)   After John entered the room, Bill jumped out of the window.

(19)   I couldn't work when the television was on.

Similarly, mere simultaneity of states of affairs is hardly ever relevant unless these states are somehow counter to expectation, and that explains why explicit additive connectives have a concessive reading:

(20)   He's only seven years and he can play the Beethoven sonatas.

The principle at work here seems to be that of metonymy. The temporal and the simultaneity relation are metonymies for the causal and the concessive relation, respectively. The proposed analysis of such a metonymic meaning shift in terms of implicatures is supported by the fact that connectives in a great number of languages show traces of similar meaning changes. What seems to have happened is that conversational implicatures have been gradually encoded into the language. This is another instance of grammaticalization. (Also see Chapter 3.3.3.)

(21)   a.   Fr. *cependant* (originally meant 'during this' and now means 'yet'; co-occurrence becomes denied expectation).
       b.   Du. *dientengevolge* (originally meant 'following this' and now means 'as a consequence'; spatial ordering becomes temporal ordering, which becomes causality).
       c.   Ge. *weil* (originally meant 'so long as', and now means 'because'; temporal overlap becomes causality).
       d.   En. *still* (originally meant 'now as before'; simultaneity becomes denied expectation like *but*).

As the list in the next section (8.6) may show, there are a great many different types of coherence relations, and recently there has been an explosive growth of the number of coherence relations mentioned in the literature. Inventories have led to over 300 different ones! A point generally agreed upon, however, is that somehow this proliferation of relations has to be constrained, if only because it is hardly conceivable in a cognitive theory of language how S and H are able to choose from such an unbounded list of fairly abstract relations under normal conditions of language use. One way of constraining this list is by recognizing that these coherence relations can be categorized into general groups along different dimensions and that each grouping of coherence relations has its more central and more peripheral members.

One grouping that frequently occurs in the literature is that such relations are categorized under either **positive relations** as in (13) or (14) or **negative relations** as in (15). In (13), for instance, the underlying regularity is "usually loneliness causes death". This relationship is more or less directly expressed in the clauses of (13). In (15) the relationship is "usually beautiful women marry". This relationship is only indirectly expressed in (15), because one needs a negation to get at the regularity. That is why relations like (13) are called positive, and relations like (15) are called negative. Negative relations can typically be signalled through contrastive connectives like *but*.

Another way to group coherence relations is by looking at the hierarchical relation between the clauses that are linked. A **paratactic relation** is one in which clauses of equal status are linked. A typical example of a paratactic relation is a sequence relation, as in (22), in which one clause describes an event that follows an event mentioned in the previous clause. Paratactic relations are said to be "multi-nuclear", in that all of the clauses (22a,b, and c) are equally central to the text.

(22)   (a) Bring the water and milk to the boil, (b) add the yeast extract (c) and pour in the dry semolina.

A **hypotactic relation**, on the other hand, involves the linking of a dependent clause to an independent one. A typical hypotactic relation is an evidence relation, as in (23).

(23)   (a) John must have stopped smoking, (b) because I haven't seen him with a cigarette all day.

Hypotactic relations are "nucleus-satellite" relations. One clause, containing the main information as in (23a), is the **nucleus**, the other, (23b), is the **satellite**. An argument for this distinction between nuclei and satellites is that a fairly good summary of a text can be obtained by deleting all satellites from the text.

The distinction between nuclei and satellites is a functional one: A nucleus contributes more to the main line of the text than a satellite. Without the nucleus, the satellite usually becomes incomprehensible. By contrast, the satellite usually can be deleted without affecting the main intention of the text. It comes as no surprise that such a central notion as nuclearity has found its way into the language system: Prototypically, the nucleus is expressed in a main clause, and a satellite in a subordinate clause. However, this does not have to be the case. For example, in (24) the main clause is the satellite, giving background information, and the subordinate clause is the nucleus.

(24)   Mac Loyd had just started to study the legacy left by the socialist Heath, when he died.

A third way to group coherence relations is to distinguish between the different conceptual levels described in a clause. We have to do with **ideational** or **content relations** if the two clauses are related at the same "world" level, as in (13) *The unicorn died because it was lonely*, where an event (*it died*) is a natural consequence of a certain situation (*it was lonely*). **Epistemic relations** occur if one of the two clauses relates to the speaker's judgement, e.g. a first clause describes a "worldly" event and in a second clause the speaker states what his reasoning is based upon as in (14) *Maggie must be eager for promotion. She's worked late three days in a row.* In **interpersonal** or **speech act relations** as in (25) the first clause gives a reason why the speaker is uttering the second clause:

(25)   Since we're on the subject, when was George Washington born?

It has been claimed that reflections of such groupings are found in the actual language use of S and H. For instance, in **language acquisition** studies it is found that more concrete relations are mastered before abstract ones; positive coherence relations are mastered before negative relations, and paratactic relations before hypotactic relations. An example of the latter point often occurs in the developing speech of children. *We went to the zoo and saw some lions, then we had a picnic, then we watched the dolphins, and then…* would be replaced more hypotactically later on by *We went to the zoo, and had a picnic before we watched the dolphins.* This provides evidence that such groupings are not merely analytic tools but they are cognitively relevant determinants of actual language use. And that in turn may help to explain the language user's ability to deal with large numbers of coherence relations.

   To summarize, we have seen that interpreting a text implies deriving coherence relations between the text elements. These relations can be marked in a number of ways, but frequently remain underspecified. In that case pragmatic implicatures guide H's interpretation. Groupings of coherence relations were also discussed. Coherence relations can be grouped along varying dimensions, and it may well be that such groupings play an important role in the way language users deal with the large number of coherence relations that can exist between the clauses of a text.

## 8.6 Survey of coherence relations

For the sake of consultation, the following gives an alphabetical listing of coherence relations, which is based on the work by Mann and Thompson (1988). Remember: The nucleus contains the main information, the satellite the additional background information.

Background:    The information in the satellite helps the reader to understand the nucleus.

    a.    The elimination of mass poverty is necessary to supply the motivation for fertility control in underdeveloped countries. [satellite]

    b.    Other countries should assist in this process. [nucleus]

Cause:    The satellite presents a situation that caused the situation presented in the nucleus.

    a.    The United States produce more wheat than needed for internal consumption. [satellite]

    b.    That is why they export the surplus. [nucleus]

Circumstance:    The satellite gives the framework within which the reader is intended to interpret the situation described in the nucleus.

    a.    Probably the most extreme case of Visitors' Fever I have ever witnessed was a few summers ago [nucleus]

    b.    when I visited relatives in the Midwest. [satellite]

Concession:    There is a potential or apparent incompatibility between the situations in the nucleus and the satellite; the situation in the nucleus is more central to the writer's intentions.

    a.    Although this material is toxic to certain animals, [satellite]

    b.    evidence is lacking that it has any serious long-term effects on human beings. [nucleus]

Condition:    The nucleus presents a situation the realization of which depends on the realization of the situation in the satellite.

    a.    You should immediately contact your insurance company [nucleus]

    b.    if there is a change in your personal situation. [satellite]

Contrast:    The situations described in the nuclei are the same in many respects and different in a few respects, and they are compared with respect to the differences (paratactic: Two nuclei).

    a.    Bergoss increased by twelve points, just like Van Hattum, Holec and Smit-Tak. [nucleus]

    b.    By contrast, Philips lost 10 points. [nucleus]

Elaboration:    The satellite presents additional detail about (some element of) the situation described in the nucleus.

a. The next ICLA conference will be held in Stockholm in 1999. [nucleus]
b. It is expected that some 300 linguists from 23 countries will attend the biannual meeting. [satellite]

Enablement:    Comprehending the information in the satellite enables the reader to perform an action described in the nucleus.

a. Could you open the door for me, please? [nucleus]
b. Here's the key. [satellite]

Evaluation:    The satellite gives the writer's evaluation of the situation described in the nucleus.

a. Peace negotiations between Israel and the Palestinians have resulted in a new treaty. [nucleus]
b. This is the best of possible results of the latest U.S. peace initiative. [satellite]

Evidence:      Comprehending the information in the satellite will increase the reader's belief of the information in the nucleus.

a. 20-year old Bill Hamers is the murderer of his father. [nucleus]
b. Witnesses have seen him at the murder scene. [satellite]

Justification: Comprehending the information in the satellite will increase the reader's readiness to accept the writer's right to present the information in the nucleus.

a. I am the chairman of this meeting. [satellite]
b. You're out of order. [nucleus]

Motivation:    Comprehending the information in the satellite motivates the reader to perform the action described in the nucleus.

a. Come and join us on our trip to Disney World. [nucleus]
b. It'll be fun. [satellite]

Purpose:       The satellite presents a situation that is to be realized through the activity in the nucleus.

a. To get the latest version of Qedit, [satellite]
b. send in the registration card. [nucleus]

Result:        The nucleus presents a situation that caused the situation presented in the satellite.

a. The explosion destroyed the factory and a large part of the environment. [nucleus]
b. There were 23 casualties and more than 2,000 people are still in hospital. [satellite]

Restatement:   The satellite gives a reformulation of the information in the nucleus.

a. A well-groomed car reflects its owner. [nucleus]
b. The car you drive says a lot about you. [satellite]

Sequence:  (paratactic) The nuclei present a succession of situations.

    a.  Soak the beans for at least 12 hours. [nucleus]

    b.  Cook them until soft. [nucleus]

Solutionhood:  The situation described in the nucleus is a solution to the problem described in the satellite.

    a.  You cannot make optimal use of ethernet possibilities? [satellite]

    b.  Choose a computer with a PCI bus. [nucleus]

## 8.7 Summary

**Text** is defined as the **verbal** part of communication, excluding the **paralinguistic** and **non-verbal** part of the communication. The text as such or the linguistic elements only make sense if they are interpreted by readers/listeners using their cultural or world knowledge. This interpreted text is the reader's **text representation**, which goes far beyond what is said in the text but also contains the **inferences** the hearer makes. The object of **text linguistics** is precisely text representation, not texts.

Alongside ideational and interpersonal functions there is also a **textual function**, structuring the relations in a text. The main property of a text is **coherence** and it is this (partially hearer-imported) property that makes a text interpretation possible. **Coherence relations** are often realized by **cohesive links** such as pronouns and word repetitions. But **cohesion** by itself does not guarantee coherence so that we conclude that coherence is a purely conceptual matter.

The two main manifestations of coherence are **referential coherence**, i.e. the continuing reference to the same entities figuring in a text, and **relational coherence**, i.e. the coherence between various events. Referential coherence is constituted by either **exophoric reference** or **deixis**, i.e. pointing to entities in the speech situation, or by **endophoric reference**, i.e. reference to entities evoked in the text. Within endophoric reference, one can refer backwards to entities already named, which is **anaphoric reference**, or forward to entities to be named later, which is **cataphoric reference**.

The primary function of referential coherence is that of **identification**. Entities are referred to on the basis of their **prominence**. In general, the more prominent an item is at a given point in discourse, the more reduced or elliptic the form can be to refer to that entity. If an item is completely new and not yet prominent, it is introduced by an **indefinite expression**. Recently **non-identificational functions** of anaphoric expressions have received much attention, too.

We often witness a **referential overspecification**, i.e. using a definite noun phrase or full name when a pronoun would do, or on the contrary there are **late indefinites** for entities already introduced before. Overspecification serves the fuction of text **representation**, late indefinites that of **perspectivization**.

Alongside referential coherence, linking entities in a text, we see relational coherence taking care of the **coherence relations** between events. Coherence relations may be left implicit, or they may be made explicit by means of **connectives** such as conjunctions or adverbial phrases. But some connectives do not express the real coherence relation that is intended. In this case we have to do with **relational underspecification**. These phenomena are strongly linked to the **text type** and **genre**.

Over time, these implicit relations, originally based on conversational implicatures can become part of the conventional meaning of an item, which is known as the process of grammaticalization. The number of possible coherence relations is so big that it hardly makes sense to suppose that humans can command them all. Therefore there must be groupings of coherence relations such as **positive** vs. **negative relations, paratactic** vs. **hypotactic** relations, **ideational** vs. **interpersonal relations**, etc. Hypotactical relations reflect a conceptual distinction between a **nucleus** and a **satellite:** The former contributes more to the main line of a text than the latter.

## 8.8  Further reading

Collective volumes with cognitive approaches to text linguistics are Van Hoek, Kibrik, Noordman (1999), Couper-Kuhlen ans Kortmann (2000), ans Sanders, Schilperoord, and Spooren (2001). Coherence as a property of text representation rather than of the linguistic information in the text is discussed extensively by Brown and Yule (1983). Example (6) is quoted from Enkvist (1978). Referential coherence has been treated in many approaches. Among the dominant ones is Grosz and Sidner (1986). Prominence and accessibility of referents are a major topic in Du Bois (1980). Experimental work on the segmenting function of overspecified noun phrases is reported by Vonk, Hustinx and Simons (1992). 'Late indefinites' are analyzed by Ushie (1986), who is also the source of example (12).

Among the most influential works on relational coherence is that by Mann and Thompson (1988). Traugott and König (1991) give a clear analysis of underspecified coherence relations. The question of how coherence relations are to be grouped is treated by Sanders, Spooren and Noordman (1992).

Much work exists on the hierarchical aspects of text structure. Van Dijk and Kintsch (1983) give a classic treatment of the subject, at the cross-roads of text linguistics and psycholinguistics. Martin (1992) discusses text types and many other aspects of text structure within the framework of systemic-functional linguistics.

## Assignments

1. As we saw in this chapter, pronouns are usually used for highly prominent referents, and full NPs for less prominent referents. In the following sequences, either an NP or a pronoun could be used, but with different effects. Which one do you feel is the more likely to be used in the sentences below? Why? What would the effect be if the less likely one is used?

   a. A ninety-year-old man and an eighty-year-old woman were sitting on the park bench. They/The couple were making love furiously.

   b. Dr. Smith told me that exercise helps. Since I heard it from the doctor/her, I'm inclined to believe it.

2. Relational coherence can be established by different kinds of connectives: Subordinating conjunctions (*because, if, although*), coordinating conjunctions (*and, but*), conjunctive adverbs (*so, therefore, yet*) and conjunctive adverbial phrases (*as a consequence, in contrast with this*). Find the connectives in the following fragment and identify the subtype.

   If you want to make the best use of this book, you should note the following. This book can be used either as a straightforward handbook for its recipes, or as a full course in modern vegetarian cookery because the recipes are all described in enough detail for anyone with only a little cooking experience to be able to follow them. In addition, we have tried to anticipate, and provide remedies for, any snags which might occur.

3. First read the following monologue (based on an example of Prince, 1981) and try to establish what and whom the speaker is talking about. Then give an analysis of the referential coherence in the text by answering the questions below.

   a. Well, a friend called me;

   b. a friend of hers who I know,

   c. last week she called

   d. and said: "Well, you have company.

    e.   Jan fell down four flight of steps."

    f.   They have a house like this,

    g.   and she was going to a luncheon

    h.   and the women were honking the horn outside.

    i.   She heard them, right?

    j.   And usually she lets the door open

    k.   but she didn't this time.

    l.   So she comes running down the steps

    m.   and she fell down four

    n.   and landed on her side.

    o.   Her right side's fractured.

    i.   First underline all the referential expressions (pronouns and full noun phrases) in the text.

    ii.   Identify each referential expression as presenting *new information* (N) or as presenting information that has already been introduced (*given information*: G).

    iii.   Identify each referential expressions as presenting exophoric (EX) reference or as presenting endophoric reference (EN).

    iv.   Classify the given endophoric elements as cataphoric (C) or anaphoric (A).

    v.   As you saw in this chapter, endophoric elements may be conceptually prominent (and realized by a pronoun or ellipted) or non-prominent (usually realized by full noun-phrases). In this text, however, this correlation between prominence and linguistic form is clearly broken by the use of *they* in (f). Explain how the hearer is able to make sense of this form.

4.   After reading the following text make an analysis of the relational coherence in the text by answering the questions below.

    (1)  a.   Four hundred U. S. Marines have just completed a 100-mile march from Lake Hemet, California, to Camp Horno at Camp Pendleton,

         b.   the first march of that length by the camp's Marines since 1985.

    (2)  a.   Marching merrily at the head of the column was Colonel Peter Miller,

         b.   who said he had to take 19-year-olds with McDonald's and Taco Bells under their belts

         c.   and give them a touch of reality.

    (3)  a.   Tough as the hike was

         b.   – with full packs, Marines averaged 4 miles per hour –

         c.   there were few concessions,

         d.   including 10-minute breaks every 3 miles.

    (4)  a1.   The colonel,

         b.   a former British Marine,

a2. found one of the biggest challenges was not a physical one:

c. A 250-page environmental impact report had to be filed in advance with the communities the hike was to pass through.

i. Identify the nuclei (lines that contain the main story line) in each sentence in the text.

ii. Are all of the nuclei main (or independent) clauses?

iii. In each sub-part there can be nuclei and satellites. Of the following sets, which one is the nucleus and which one the satellite?

<table>
<tr><td>1a–1b</td><td>3a–3b</td></tr>
<tr><td>1ab–2ac</td><td>3c–3d</td></tr>
<tr><td>2a–2bc</td><td>1ab–4abc</td></tr>
<tr><td>2b–2c</td><td>4a–4b</td></tr>
<tr><td>1ab–3abcd</td><td>3ab–3cd</td></tr>
<tr><td>4ab–4c</td><td></td></tr>
</table>

5. The coherence relation (see Section 8.6) between most of these sets is one of Elaboration, but there is also one each of Cause, Concession, and Evidence. Identify the coherence relation in each set.

# 9 Language across time
## Historical linguistics

## 9.0 Overview

So far in this book, we have looked at different language forms and language uses separately as they are used at one particular point in time, usually the present time. In this chapter, we will examine how language changes over time.

In order to understand language change one must start from the reality that there is not "one" English language, but many different kinds of English, like any other language, with variations arising from generational, social, regional or ethnic factors. Any of these may introduce new forms or new meanings or cause older ones to disappear. When such processes are more widely accepted, it can be said that language change has occurred.

If we look back at earlier phases of a language, e.g. Middle English, we are surprised at how much we still understand of it. With the help of translations and explanations of individual words or phrases (called *glosses*) along and under the text, we may even understand most of it. Going even further back, i.e. to Old English, we find that we understand very little or nothing, so that we need a full translation of the text. If we go so far back in history that no texts are available, historical linguistics tries to reconstruct the first and earliest ancestors of a group of languages, such as the ancestor of all Germanic languages, i.e. Proto-Germanic or even the ancestor of almost all the languages spoken from India to Western Europe, called Proto-Indo-European. This is possible because of the regularity principle, the assumption that changes take place in all cases where the same conditions are met. Since all linguistic expressions can be thought of as categories and since a category, be it a phoneme, a word, a morpheme or a syntactic construction, is in most cases structured in the form of a radial network, we can locate language change more exactly. Changes can occur within or across radial networks, or in our more abstract representations of a whole category, i.e. in a schema. Many changes, such as -s plural markers in English, are due to analogy. Finally, the question arises as to the cause of language change. Although the prestige of a particular variety plays an important part, language changes can never be predicted.

## 9.1 Language change and language variation

Language change is very strongly interwoven with **language variation**. Language variation means that a given language like English is not one uniform and homogeneous system, but that it contains many, slightly or strongly diverging subsystems or varieties.

Here **language variety** means the total number of grammatical, lexical and phonological characteristics of the common core language as used by a certain subgroup of speakers. Thus we have regional groups, which each have their own **dialect**. But in linguistics the term *dialect* is no longer reserved for regional dialects only; it has become a synonym of variety. A regional dialect is therefore also referred to as a **regiolect**. Other groups in society are socially determined and have their own **sociolect**, e.g. those of the lower, working, middle and upper classes. The **standard variety** of a given language, e.g. British English, tends to be the upper class sociolect of a given central area or regiolect. Thus Standard British English used to be the English of the upper classes (also called the Queen's English or Public School English) of the Southern, more particularly, London area. The notion of Standard English is related to the written language and mainly covers syntax, morphology, and lexicology. Differences in pronunciation are subsumed under the notion of **accent**. The British standard accent is known as R. P., i.e. **Received Pronunciation**. Nowadays English as spoken on the BBC can be regarded as the standard accent. This is a southern, upper middle class variety which differs considerably from that of the older Royals, or public school inmates. The clipped vowels of the Royals' English are known as 'advanced RP, which is used by very few people (under 5 per cent) in the UK today. There are now also many regional standard accents that are accepted as BBC English.

In American English, the standard variety is less geographically identifiable, and known as **General American**. It is the standard of educated people all over the United States, and is found notably in the speech of radio and television news broadcasters.

In addition to regiolects and sociolects there are also **ethnolects**. This is the variety of a given ethnic group such as Black English and Hispanic English in the United States, or Jamaican English, Punjabi English, and many other Englishes in Great Britain. Most important, especially in view of language change, are age differences in languages, sometimes referred to as **aetalect** (from Latin *aetas* 'age'). The language peculiarities of a single speaker are known as **idiolect**.

When it comes to language variety due to age, lexical items in particular play an important role. Often parents claim not to understand what their children are saying, and children don't want to sound "old" like their parents. Young people in the United States and elsewhere, especially college students, are currently using the expression *to be like* in place of *to say* when they are reporting a conversation:

(1) So he's like 'I didn't know that!' And I'm like 'but I told you all about it last night!'

In Britain younger speakers use items like *stuff, there you go* or *sorry* in innovative ways, which are not always understandable to older speakers:

(2) a. A: What are you doing in your new job?
       B: Oh, I'm in banking. That sort of *stuff*, you know.
    b. A: (Junior bank clerk to elderly lady), *There you go* madam. This is the form to be filled in.
       B: Where am I supposed to go, young man?
    c. A: May I introduce myself — Dr. Efurosibina Adegbija.
       B: *Sorry*, what was your name?

The item *stuff* already has a wide range of meanings such as 'things' (*Get all the stuff in your car*), 'activities' (*a lot of stuff to do in the weekend*), 'equipment' (*camping stuff*), 'character' (*he's the right stuff*), etc. Now in (2a) the speaker extends this range of vague meanings to typical banking activities. *Stuff* now seems to have acquired the meaning of 'typical things, characteristic activities associated with a given domain'. In (2b) the young speaker has replaced (playfully, but it is a very general tendency now) the traditional ritual *here you are* when handing something over by *there you go*, meaning the object transferred. But this meaning seems to go unnoticed by some few elderly people. The expression is fairly entrenched, especially in Scotland. The use of *sorry* has been and is being extended from the sense of "apology" to that of a request for repetition. This had already happened to the formula "I beg your pardon", which now only has one meaning, i.e. that of a request for repeating the thing just said. Such facts can help us see wider tendencies for items to undergo language change. It is all very much a question of how productive a form (or meaning) is within a certain age group, or to what extent it is only passively understood, or not used at all. Table 1 summarizes the relevant factors.

Table 1. Possibilities of language change

| Forms | Teenage use | | | Senior use | | |
|---|---|---|---|---|---|---|
| | productive | passive | unknown | productive | passive | unknown |
| *I'm like* (AmE) | ✓ | | | | | ✓ |
| *There you go* (BrE) | ✓ | | | | ✓ | ✓ |
| *stuff* | ✓ | | | | ✓ | |
| *sorry* | ✓ | | | ✓ | ✓ | |
| *jolly* | | | ✓ | ✓ | ✓ | |

Some expressions, such as *I'm like*, are unlikely to become quickly entrenched in language use, as most people, especially the elderly, are unlikely to encounter it on a regular basis. Others like *there you go, stuff* and *sorry* are gradually accepted since they are understandable to senior language users and may remain as the younger speakers who use them actively become older. An opposite case is illustrated by items like *jolly* (*good*), a form currently disappearing from the language, since, although it is either still productively used or at least passively understood by older speakers of English, the new teenage generation simply does not use it at all and understands it less and less.

However, people of different generations, regional areas, social classes, and ethnic groups can usually understand each other, even though it may at times take a bit of effort. This fact suggests that native speakers do not only have a command of their own variety of the language and of the standard variety, often learned at school, but that they have a passive command of other varieties too. This capability is called a **pandialectical competence**, which, as we will see later in this chapter, may also include a passive command of a historical variety that is not too remote in time.

The enormous influence of language variety on language change is especially clear in the evolution of the Romance languages, like French, Spanish, Italian, and Portuguese. Late Latin or early Romance (before its separation into the various Romance languages) is the further development of a social variety (soldiers' language) of Latin and includes many different geographical or regional varieties (see survey in Chapter 10, Table 6). The different regional varieties of vernacular Latin are partly due to the contact and intermingling of Roman soldiers and public service people with the speakers of different languages and cultures in areas of Europe which were (or had been) part of the Roman Empire.

This influence of first language uses, habits, and grammatical patterns upon an imposed or adopted new language is called a **substratal influence**, with the influencing language called a **substratum**. For instance, speakers in Gaul (present France, Belgium, Switzerland, etc.) learned to speak the new Latin language with many of the speech habits and grammatical patterns of their native Gallic languages and carried them over into the new variety of Latin, i.e. the one that they spoke. Later generations no longer learned to use Gallic as a native language but only the Latin/Romance variety as it had been influenced by Gallic.

In addition to these social and regional differences, there is also the time factor. In Italy and Romania, areas of the Eastern Romance language group, the progress of new varieties of Latin had begun much earlier than in the Western group, especially the Ibero-Romance group (Spanish, Portuguese) and the Gallo-Romance group (French). Up to a certain point, we can say that these languages are all ethnolectic variations of Late Spoken Vulgar Latin. Later Germanic tribes conquered the Western Romance provinces (now France, parts of Spain, Belgium, and Northern Italy). The later influence of Germanic languages, due to settlements in these areas by the invading Germanic tribes, is thought of as a **superstratal influence** or the presence of a **superstrate** language. These varieties of Germanic brought new vocabulary, phonemes and even grammatical structures to the existent Latin in these regions before they disappeared themselves.

There is however an insurmountable problem. The first texts in the new Romance varieties or languages did not appear until the 9th century. So when did the various Latin spoken varieties become Romance spoken varieties? Any written text reflecting Late Spoken Latin as Early Spoken Romance would at that time be frowned upon as "bad Latin", since the petrified form of Classical Latin or even the non-classical Vulgar Latin of the Bible was there to set a permanent standard. In fact, hardly a single early Romance text was produced for a couple of centuries, leaving us with just a few written texts as brief examples of early Romance or Proto-Romance.

Still, there is good evidence that in a number of cases, soldiers' slang for a given referent was more successful at surviving than the Classical Latin variant. In Modern French, for example, *tête* 'head' comes from Late Latin *testa* 'jug', which was used in an informal way in soldiers' slang to refer to the "head". This is a typical instance of metonymy combined with metaphor: the 'jug' is a prototypical container, which comes to stand for the mental faculty containing all of man's experiential wisdom. This *testa*-metaphor superseded the classical word *caput* in French, whereas *caput* survived in other regions and was the basis for Spanish *capeza*.

## 9.2 Methods of studying historical linguistics

To search for information about previous stages of a language and study the changes that have taken place in a language, linguists have two main methods at their disposal, depending on the available data. If there are written documents, linguists may use the **philological method**, but if no written texts are available and if the older language forms can only be discovered by means of comparison, linguists must use **reconstruction**. The written records used in **philology** may be legal documents, literary, technical or religious works, personal letters, or a variety of other materials. They may also be rather minimal texts, in the form of inscriptions, graffiti, or gravestones. Whatever the genre and content, philologists attempt to uncover and clarify the linguistic and cultural information provided by these texts.

Although language is in continuous change, as the examples in Table 1 have shown, there is also very great historical continuity. Not only do we understand quite a lot of texts from 400 years ago, such as the works of Shakespeare, but we may also be able to understand — to a varying degree — texts dating back 600 years, such as Chaucer's *Canterbury Tales*. This fact is in accordance with one of Whorf's most central theses, i.e. the fact that languages offer to their speakers "habitual patterns" and are only very slow to develop and change (see Chapter 6.1.1). Whereas most forms of culture are strongly subject to change, language especially grammar, is so deeply entrenched in the mind that it will not change very substantially over years, not even over centuries. Thus, with a little effort speakers of English can read a text written by Geoffrey Chaucer at the end of the 14th century — in 1387 to be exact. The text uses a number of vocabulary items which may have to be explained to us, but the general gist of the text and all the concrete details still seem to be accessible.

The following fragment from the *Canterbury Tales* is taken from the Prologue, in which each of the characters taking part in the horseback pilgrimage to Canterbury is briefly characterized by the general story-teller, Chaucer himself. With refined irony he describes the physical and moral appearance of the prioress, who in spite of her religious function as the leading nun of a priory, behaves very much like an aristocratic lady.

(3)  **A Middle English Text**

|  | Ther was also a Nonne, a PRIORESSE, | |
|---|---|---|
| | That of hir smylyng was ful symple and coy; | *unaffected; modest* |
| 120 | Hire gretteste ooth was but by Seinte Loy; | *Eligius* |
| | And she was cleped madame Eglentyne, | *called* |
| | Ful weel she soong the service dyvyne, | |
| | Entuned in hir nose ful semely, | *suitable to the occasion* |
| | And Frenssh she spak ful faire and fetisly; | *elegantly* |
| 125 | After the scole of Stratford atte Bowe, | |
| | For Frenssh of Parys was to hire unknowe. | |
| | At mete wel ytaught was she with alle: | *dinner* |
| | She leet no morsel from hir lippes falle, | |
| | Ne wette hir fyngres in hir sauce depe; | |
| 130 | Wel koude she carie a morsel and wel kepe | |
| | That no drope ne fille upon hire brest. | |
| | In curteisie was set ful muchel hir lest. | |
| | Hir over-lippe wyped she so clene | |
| | That in hir coppe ther was no ferthyng sene | *cup; spot* |
| 135 | Of grece, whan she dronken hadde hir draughte. | |
| | Ful semely after hir mete she raughte. | *food; reached* |
| 146 | Of smale houndes hadde she that she fedde | |
| | With rosted flessh, or milk and wastel-breed, | |
| | But soore wepte she if oon of hem were deed, | |
| | Or if men smoot it with a yerde smerte; | *struck* |
| | And al was conscience and tendre herte, | *tender feelings* |
| 157 | Ful fetys was hir cloke, as I was war. | *well-made* |
| | Of smal coral aboute hire arm she bar | *carried* |
| | A peire of bedes, gauded al with grene, | *balls* |
| 160 | And theron heng a brooch of gold ful sheene, | |
| | On which ther was first write a crowned A, | |
| | And after *Amor vincit omnia.* | |

Notes

123 Intoned in her nose in a very seemly manner.
125 The Prioress spoke French with the accent she had learned in her convent (the Benedictine nunnery of St. Leonhard's, near Stratford-Bow in Middlesex).
132 She took pains to imitate courtly behaviour, and to be dignified in her bearing.
147 *wastel-breed*, fine wheat bread.
157 I noticed that her cloak was very elegant.
159 A rosary with 'gauds' (i.e. large beads for the Paternosters) of green
161 *crowned A*; capital A with a crown above it.

(from Geoffrey Chaucer, *Canterbury Tales*. Edited by A. C. Cawley, London: J. M. Dent & Sons, New York: E. P. Dutton & Co. 1975)

To be able to read such older texts, the writing system must be interpreted first, in the sense that often the use of the letters of the alphabet must themselves be identified, as must their value in the language in question. Orthographic problems that pose themselves in this fragment from the Canterbury Tales are, amongst others:

– the use of different symbols (i, y) for the same sound: (119) hire smylyng was ful symple
– the use of two spellings for the same word, i.e. *well:* (122) *ful weel,* (127) *wel* taught.
– the mixed use of *k* and *c* for the sound /k/: (130) *koude,* (145) *kaught in a trappe,* (119) *coy,* (121) *cleped,* (130) *carie,* (134) *coppe.*
– the use of doubling for long vowels: (120) *ooth,* (122) *soonge.*

It is only a century later that the fixation of English spelling could come about especially thanks to the first printed books published by William Caxton (1476). But even more puzzling than the orthography is the pronunciation, which in the case of Middle English has been entirely reconstructed and is available on records (see Strauss, n.d.). The most important thing is that this text was written before the general change of all vowels in English, known as the **Great Vowel Shift**. In this process the long English vowels, which up till then had been pronounced much the same as in French or German, became diphthongs or were raised, i.e. pronounced higher in the mouth. For instance, in Middle English the vowels of *late, see, time, boat, foot,* and *house* were still pronounced as the sounds /a/, /e/, /i/, /ɔ/, /o/ and /u/, respectively, but due to the Great Vowel Shift they were changed into the direction of their present pronunciations.

Historical linguistics thus examines the written texts for the light they may shed on whatever level or aspect of the language in a given period and deduces the grammar of that particular historical phase. A typical instance of this approach is Fernand Mossé's *A Handbook of Middle English* (1952, 1968), which not only provides a number of texts of all possible varieties of Middle English, but also suggests the "grammar of Middle English" as derivable from these written sources. One part of this grammar is the various classes of strong and weak verbs, a part of English grammar which has undergone quite a few changes. Strong verbs (also misleadingly called *irregular verbs*) are verbs like *speak*, which have a vowel change to form the past tense form (*spoke*) and the past participle form (*spoken*) (Table 2). Moreover, the past participle ends in -*n*. There are about seven distinct patterns with different vowel change, called strong verb classes. The Chaucer fragment in (3) contains forms from most of these, indicated by italics and the line in which each form occurs.

Table 2. The classes of strong verbs in Middle English

|  | Infinitive | Past singular | Past plural | Past participle |
|---|---|---|---|---|
| Class I | write | wrot (wrat) | writen | (y)*write(n)* (161) |
| Class II | fresen | fres | fruren | (y)froren |
| Class III | drink | drank (dronk) | drunken | (y)drunke(n), *dronken* (135) |
| Class IV | speke | *spak* (124) | spaken | (y)spoken |
| Class V | see | *saugh* | sene | (y)sene (134) |
| Class VI | take | tok | token | (y)taken |
| Class VII | falle | fel (fil) (131) | fallen | (y)fallen |

A brief look at the Chaucer fragment has shown that historical linguists can learn a great deal about the spelling practices, pronunciation, and grammar by examining older texts carefully. But if no written text is available, they must use the method of reconstruction, which allows them, by examining the earliest documented stages of related languages, to extrapolate backwards in time and reconstruct a parent language. **Reconstruction** is based on a small set of principles, which are related to the structure of language. The first of these principles is that groups of languages are genetically related to each other (to be discussed further in Chapter 10); that is, they evolve over time from a single ancestor. Such groupings are referred to as language families, consisting of language groups. A very large language family is, for instance, **Indo-European,** which encompasses Indian and Iranian languages as well as European languages such as Latin, Greek, the Germanic languages, etc. The genetic relatedness of these languages can be seen in a large number of words with similar sound structure as shown in Table 3.

Table 3.

| | Sanskrit | Latin | Greek | English |
|---|---|---|---|---|
| a. | | *labium* | | lip |
| | | *decem* | *deka* | ten |
| | | *genu* | *gonu* | knee |
| b. | *bharmi* | *fero* | *phero* | bear |
| | *dhava* | *vidua* | *étheos* | widow |
| | | *vehere* | *okheo* | vehicle |
| c. | *pitár* | *pater* | *patér* | father |
| | *dantas* | *dentis* | *odontos* | tooth |
| | | *cor* | *kardia* | heart |

The second of these principles is that, given the same set of circumstances, or linguistic environment, a general **sound shift** will occur, i.e., a sound will change in the same way in each word. This is often called the **regularity principle** (or more precisely, the principle of regular sound equivalence). Based on this assumption (which is what this principle really is, although it is true over vast numbers of cases), we can understand an important change in the Germanic languages, known as **Grimm's Law** (Table 4).

Words with the same initial (or medial) consonants in Sanskrit, Latin, Greek show regular correspondences with Germanic (here English) consonants:

Table 4. Grimm's Law or the First Germanic Sound Shift

| **Indo-European**<br>a. voiced stops | | | b. voiced stops | c. voiceless stops | |
|---|---|---|---|---|---|
| | non-aspirated | aspirated | | non aspirated | aspirated |
| Labials | /b/ | /b$^h$/ | | /p/ | /p$^h$/ |
| Dentals | /d/ | /d$^h$/ | | /t/ | /t$^h$/ |
| Velars | /g/ | /g$^h$/ | | /k/ | /k$^h$/ |
| | ↓ | ↓ | | ↓ | |
| **Germanic**<br>voiceless stops | | | voiced stops | voiceless fricatives | |
| Labials | /p/ | /b/ | | /f/ | |
| Dentals | /t/ | /d/ | | /θ/ | |
| Velars | /k/ | /g/ | | /χ/ | |

(a) voiced stops, if non-aspirated, become voiceless, (b) aspirated voiced stops change into unaspirated voiced stops in Germanic, e.g. English, and (c) voiceless stops all become fricative. It is this type of comparison which has also allowed the reconstruction of the sound system of the ancestor of these four language groups, i.e. **Proto-Indo-European.**

In order to reconstruct Proto-Indo-European, we can compare different languages to each other. It is also possible to apply the reconstruction method to data within the same language, which is is called **internal reconstruction.** Although the transition from Latin to the Romance languages, occurring from the 5th to the 8th century, is a millenium younger than the Germanic sound shift, which must be located two and a half millenia back, we have almost no written documents of the early phases of the Romance languages and can only rely on the methods of internal reconstruction. The method is most often applied within verbal or nominal paradigms, e.g. forms of the verb in one tense, such as the six persons for *amare* 'to love': *amo* 'I love', *amas* 'you love', *amat* (s)he loves', *amamus* 'we love', *amatis* 'you two love', *amant* 'they love'. The underlying premise is that where there is later variation in the forms, an earlier version of the paradigm shows unity.

Let us examine, for example, the French verb *devoir* 'to have to, to be obligated', which exemplifies a series of changes in verb paradigms of a rather large set of Modern French verbs with alternations in present indicative stem forms. Here, and in all other verbs of this class, from the earliest documenta-tion, the vowel of the stem alternated between a diphthong in the singular forms and the third person plural, and a simple vowel (in fact, one which is much reduced) in the first and second person plural. The forms of *devoir* are cited, for simplicity, in Modern French:

(4)  a.  *je dois*        *nous devons*
         *tu dois*        *vous devez*
         *il doit*        *ils doivent*

Given the force of the regularity principle, we expect that at some time in the history of this verb, there was one verb stem for the entire paradigm rather than this alternation. Although there are no documents for pre-French, or Proto-Romance, classical Latin provides the clue. The Latin verb *debere*, with the same meaning, does indeed have a single stem vowel:

(4)  b.  *'debeo*        *de'bemus*
         *'debes*        *de'betis*
         *'debet*        *'debent*

Further investigation of Latin, and particularly its system of accentuation, allows us to complete the story. At some undocumented point in the history of very early Romance (French is only one example), vowels in stressed position were diphthongized. This was the case in all of the singular and third person plural forms where stress was on the first syllable, that is, on the stem. In the first and second person plural, where stress was on the vowel before the ending, acting as a link between stem and tense and person markers, the stem vowel did not diphthongize, giving rise to this irregular pattern in all attested forms of French from the 9th century onwards. In addition to *devoir* as set out above, we see the same pattern (cited here in the first person singular) with stress on the stem vowel and hence diphthongization, and the first person plural with stress on the later syllable and hence no diphthong in the stem: *je reçois/nous recevons* from *recevoir* 'to receive; *je bois/nous buvons* from *boire* 'to drink'; *je peux/nous pouvons* from *pouvoir* 'to be able'.

## 9.3 Typology of language change

Language change may occur in all of the units of language discussed so far in this book: the use of particular sounds may change, words and morphemes may change their meanings, and syntactic patterns such as word order patterns may change. These changes occur in four different types. First of all changes can take place within radial networks, i.e. a more prototypical or central element in a category may become peripheral and a peripheral element may become more central. Next, changes may occur across radial networks so that elements switch from one category or network to the other. Third, we may witness changes in schemas. And finally a number of changes are due to analogy.

### 9.3.1 Changes within a radial network

Changes within a radial network may occur at the two ends, either in the sound system of a language, or else in the semantic system. Sound change may be purely phonetic and bring about no changes in the phonemic system of the language. Among these changes are such processes as **assimilation,** where sounds are pronounced to sound more like each other. In the history of Italian, for example, the Latin consonant cluster /kt/ becomes /tt/, as in the past participle *factum* 'having been done', which becomes the Italian *fatto*. Again, we cannot claim any change in the overall system; one isolated sound combination has been modified.

Other kinds of phonetic change may involve **dissimilation**, whereby two sounds become less like each other so that the first /r/ in Latin *peregrinatum* becomes /l/ in the French *pèlerin*. English *pilgrim* shows the same dissimilation, but differs from French *pèlerin*, because it was not borrowed from French, but directly from Latin.

Another frequent phenomenon is **metathesis,** where sounds seem to change places, e.g. the order of the segments /r/ and /l/ in Latin *miraculum* as compared to the Spanish word *milagro*. A typical English example of metathesis is the verb to *ask*, which in Old English was *aksian*; the order of [k] and [s] has changed over time.

On the semantic side, changes in categorization may occur, first, within the category or radial network or in the interaction of categories. These categories or networks develop in the native speaker to represent not only lexical items, but also sounds, morphemes, compounds, phrases, or whole grammatical constructions. Within the network, the items may be **rearranged** so that what used to be more prototypical is less so, or vice versa. A case in point is the evolution of the words *dog* and *hound*. In the 14th century the basic level term in English is still *hound* (compare German *Hund* and Dutch *hond*). Thus in the Chaucer fragment the prioress is described with her "hounds":

(5)   *Of smale houndes hadde she that she fedde*
      *With rosted flessh, or milk and wastel-breed.*

It is not clear which kind (or subtype) of dog is meant here, but they might even be small poodles. In Middle English a *dog* is just another subtype, just like *poodle*, but perhaps a very frequent one, as represented by the sub-species *mastiff*, 'a large, strong dog often used to guard houses' (DCE). This 'dog' type of 'hound' was so frequently met that it became the prototype of the category "hound". It was so much wanted that it was also exported quite a lot and gradually this very prototypical type of "hound", replaced the category name itself, which from the 16th century onwards is *dog*. The change in the radial network can be represented as in Table 5.

The same kind of development over time can be seen in grammatical forms as well. The English comparative form *older* is a recent form in contrast to the earlier regular form *elder*. It has, however, become the prototypical comparative, with the accompanying relegation of *elder* to the rather specialized ecclesiastical meaning "a non-ordained person who serves as an advisor in a church" or to the fixed kinship expressions *elder brother/sister/sibling*. We will return to this particular form below in the discussion of analogical change and umlaut.

Table 5. Change within a radial network

a.   14th century                                b.   16th century

9.3.2 Changes across radial networks

The number of examples of phonetic realizations or allophones of a given phoneme, e.g. /t/ may be so extensive that we speak of phonemes as categories which may also change internally or across two or more networks. In Ch. 5.5 on 'Phonemes and Allophones', Figure 3 illustrates two allophones for /p/. Let us apply the same line of reasoning to /t/. The prototypical realization of /t/ as in non-initial position is the unaspirated [t], which in word-initial position becomes [tʰ]. But immediately preceding a /k/, e.g. in *cat-call*, /t/ is in some dialects realized as a glottal stop [ʔ] + [t], i.e. [kæʔtkɔl], which may be reduced even more so that the cluster /t/ and glottal stop can even change to a glottal stop in this environment. In medial position between two vowels (e.g. city) /t/ may be realized as a flap, [ɾ], e.g. [sɪɾɪ], which may be reduced as in *pretty good* [prɪɾɪ gud] to [prɪɪ gud], whereby /t/ is now ɵ. This symbol stands for a **zero form**, which means a linguistic form which does not show up, but is structurally

Table 6. The radial network of the phoneme /t/

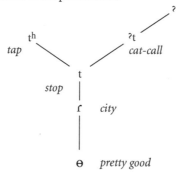

given. The radial network for these realizations can be represented as in Table 6.

A very typical example of change in a lexical network is the item *bead*, which now means 'one of a set of small usually round pieces of glass, wood, plastic etc. that you can put on a string and wear as jewellery' (DCE). In Middle English, however, *bead* had a much more specific meaning: 'one of small perforated balls forming the *rosary* or *paternoster*, used for keeping count of the number of prayers said' (SOED). This is what the prioress is said to be wearing on her arm (158–161):

(6)   *Of smal coral aboute hire arme she bar*
      *A peire of bedes, gauded al with grene,*
      *And theron heng a brooch of gold ful sheene,*
      *On which ther was first write a crowned A,*
      *And after* Amor vincit omnia.

As the gloss on (159) on page 210 says, the rosary contains beads of different colours and sizes: *gauds*, that is large beads in green, for the *Our Fathers*, and small beads for the *Hail Marys*. Apart from the technical fact about this aid to prayer, the rosary as a whole is already linked to the notion of jewellery, since there is a brooch of gold attached to it with an inscription probably referring to worldly love. Chaucer's art in portraying the prioress by means of her rosary here anticipates the category change to follow later. *Bead* as a stem is related to German *beten* 'pray' or Dutch *bidden* 'pray' and in its etymological sense is synonymous with Dutch *bede, gebed* 'prayer' or German *Bitte, Gebet* 'request/ prayer'. From this meaning it has undergone a metonymical change to the ball that stands for one single prayer in a set of fifty balls. From this still religious domain it has then shifted to the purely ornamental domain, e.g. a necklace. We can represent this change across radial networks as in Table 7.

Table 7.  Lexical change across networks

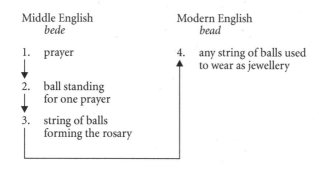

In grammar an existing network may **split** into two parts or the opposite may happen: two networks may be merged into one. The first of these changes can be illustrated by the history of the English indefinite article *a/an* and the numeral *one*. Where once the article *an* was simply the phonetically reduced form of the numeral *one* occurring in unstressed position, speakers of modern English now perceive them as two entirely different words, members of different grammatical classes, and therefore of quite different categories.

In opposite fashion, categories may **merge**, as happened over time to many pronominal cases in European languages. At one point in the history of English personal pronouns, the masculine third person singular dative (indirect object) form *him* was distinct from the accusative (direct object) *hine*. Through a series of sound changes, *hine* and *him* merged in form and eventually lost distinctions of meaning as well, so that English has a non-subject/non-possessive pronoun *him*, which contrasts with the subject form *he* and the possessive form *his* in this much reduced paradigm.

### 9.3.3 Changes in schemas

The notion of "schema" or "**schematic meaning**" has only been used so far in the context of morphology for the analysis of the suffix -*er* in Chapter 3 (13) and in the syntactic notion of "event schema" in Chapter 4.2. We will now apply this notion to any linguistic category. Just as a category has more central or prototypical members, less central and even marginal members, it also has a highly abstract, schematic representation, which applies to all the members of the category. Given the many different types of chairs, for example, we must have an abstract idea of a chair. This might be something like "construction to sit on for functional use", keeping all the meanings together. **Changes in schemas** may take two routes based on the nature of the change over time: a schema may develop a new form or else a new schema may arise. We will illustrate the former type of change (new arrangement of the schema) with grammar and the lexicon, and the latter type with phonology.

Let us consider the basic word order within a clause, an aspect of grammar which plays an important role in the syntax of a given language. In Old English, like modern German or Dutch, the order of the basic sentence is SVO (Subject – Verb – Object) in an unmarked (main) clause, but SOV (or SCV; Subject – Complement – Verb) in a subordinate clause as (7a), or VSO in a main clause following a subordinate clause or an adverbial adjunct (7b):

(7)  a.  *Þa se biscop to Þam cyninge com,* (SCV)
         'When the bishop to that king came'
         When the bishop came to that king.

     b.  *Þa sealde he him stowe and biscopseðl* (VSO)
         'then gave he him house and bishop's seat'
         he gave him a house and the diocesian town.
         (Dürrmüller and Utz, 1977:5)

In present-day English these three word order patterns have been reduced to SVO only. Whereas in Old English and Modern German or Dutch the schema of SENTENCE is a highly variable one, the present-day English schema of SENTENCE is comparatively strict and inflexible.

   A similar evolution can be seen in the networks of some lexical items. Let us have a look at the meaning of *meat* in Middle English and in present-day English. In the Chaucer fragment the item *mete* occurs twice (127, 136).

(8)  a.  *At mete wel ytaught was she with alle*
         *She leet no morsel from hir lippes falle,*

     b.  *Ful semely after hir mete she raughte*
         'In an elegant way for her food she reached'
         She reached for her food in an elegant way.

From the context it is quite obvious that the word *mete* in both (8a) and (8b) does not refer to "meat" in the present-day sense, but to food in general. The evolution in the lexical networks of *meat* can be represented as in Table 5.

   In Middle English, there are three extensions from the prototypical "food" sense of *mete* (1). The second sense (2), shows a specialization in the direction of the "food part" or "edible part" of things. As part of the third sense (3), there is a further specialization in the direction of "food in the form of animal flesh". In the fourth sense, the food metonymically stands for the whole meal, just like in *at table*, the place where the meal is taken, stands for the whole meal. Most of these meanings are still used in the 16th and 17th century English of Shakespeare, but in contemporary English only the third sense "animal flesh used for food" exists, so that *meat* is now no longer polysemous to the same degree. What once was a complex radial category, has become a much simpler category. However, the archaic sense is still evident in some fixed expressions like *meat and drink,* and *mincemeat.* At the same time, the meaning of *flesh* has changed and no longer applies to 'meat' in the present-day English sense, but only to the surface part of the body of men or animals.

**Table 8.** From a radial network of polysemy to monosemy

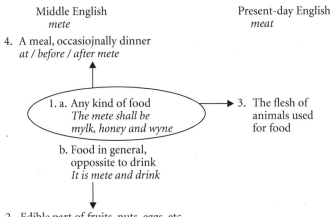

There is also the possibility of the development of a new schema, often arising from the split of a category into two new ones or the merger of two into one. Within phonology, this kind of change is often called **phonologization**, i.e. the creation of new phonemes. As was argued in Chapter 5, a phoneme is thought of as a category of sounds, with the prototypical allophone as the centre around which others are arranged. The phoneme itself is therefore schematic.

When a new phoneme is created, a new schema emerges which may, at first, have only one allophone, which is prototypical by default. Let us look at two examples drawn from the history of the Germanic languages. First, there is a series of changes, called the Second Germanic Sound Shift. When you compare English, Dutch, and German words beginning with [p], [t], and [k] with each other in Table 9, you can see that some German words are different.

**Table 9.** Dutch and English versus German consonants

| | | | | Loanwords | |
|---|---|---|---|---|---|
| English | German | English | German | Dutch | German |
| | Initial | | Medial | | |
| Pound | Pfund | pepper | Pfeffer | piste | Piste |
| token | Zeichen | eaten | Essen | tante | Tante |
| — | — | make | Machen | Kinepolis | Kino |

What has happened in German is that the voiceless stops /p/, /t/, /k/ first underwent aspiration to become similar to English /pʰ, tʰ, kʰ/; these then became affricates /pf, ts, k$_\chi$/ and in medial position simplified to the fricatives /f, s, χ/.

In Dutch, initial voiceless stops have remained unaspirated, but in English, as is well known, they are aspirated. In German loan words too they are aspirated stops, as in *Piste, Tante, Kino*. But in all words existing at the time of the Second Sound Shift, the voiceless stops became affricates in initial position and fricatives in medial position.

**Table 10.** Second Germanic Sound Shift

| | Voiceless stops | | | |
|---|---|---|---|---|
| | Unaspirated ⟶ | Aspirated ⟶ | Affricates ⟶ | Fricatives |
| Labials | p ⟶ | pʰ ⟶ | pf ⟶ | f |
| Dentals | t ⟶ | tʰ ⟶ | ts ⟶ | s |
| Velars | k ⟶ | kʰ ⟶ | kχ ⟶ | χ |

The second process, is a transformation of a back vowel to a fronted vowel because of assimilation, known as **umlaut** or **mutation**, and led to the creation of new phonemes. In Old English this was the case in the plural of a set of words like *foot, foti* or *goose, gosi*, where the plural affix /i/ caused the stem vowel to change. The /ɔ/ assimilated to a new rounded front vowel /ø/ (føti, etc.), which since that time changed again to an unrounded and raised vowel, yielding the present plural forms *feet* and *geese*. Umlaut occurred much more frequently in German because there were three affixes with /i/: to form a plural as in *Kuss/ Küsse* 'kiss/kisses', to form a diminutive as in *Kuss/Küsschen* 'kiss/little kiss', or to form a comparative as in *dumm/dümmer* 'stupid/more stupid'. Here too /i/ triggered assimilation in a preceding back vowel. A back vowel is usually rounded anyway, and in this context, the back vowel became front without losing its rounding. Later, the /i/ suffix, which had triggered the umlaut originally, became a schwa as in *Küsse* or disappeared as in *Küsschen*. The two steps are summarized in (9).

(9)  a.  u > y / -i

   b.  i >/ ø # (Note ø = zero)

   (This reads as follows: /u/ becomes /y/ in the context of /i/, and /i/ then disappears [becomes zero])

As a result, the front rounded vowel was no longer triggered automatically by context and thus became a new phoneme. At this point, to return to the notions of radial networks and schemas, /y/ no longer belonged to its original category as a rather unprototypical, fronted allophone of the back vowel /u/, but became the central element of a new network in its pronounced form and a new schematic phoneme.

### 9.3.4  Analogical change

Speakers also seem to have a desire for forms and constructions to be transparent, that is, for the parts to be recognizable in a larger unit, which may cause analogical change. **Analogical change** is the process through which individual speakers note resemblances between sounds, forms, or constructions and decide (though not on a fully conscious level) to make them even more alike. For analogical change to occur, there must be a more or less conscious reanalysis of the items in question. (Such an analogical reanalysis is in fact the correct name for what has traditionally been called 'folk etymology' (see p. 13)).

For example, in Middle English, the plural -s was already quite frequently used, but it was not yet the only plural marker. Chaucer still used the -en plural in *eyen* 'eyes'. Later most -en plural markers became -s. This change is a clear case of analogy since the change to -s was motivated by the already well established presence of that marker. Another example is the change from *elder* to *older*, now the regular comparative of *old*. However, *elder* used to be the regular form. What happenend is that the base form *old*, when followed by -er, changed to an umlauted vowel ([ɔ] > [ø] > [e]). Later, *older* came into existence again, probably because speakers considered it a better instance of a comparative since it is made up of the totally transparent base *old* instead of one which was partially transformed by sound changes.

Other analogical changes are motivated by a desire not only for transparency, but also for a one-to-one correspondence between form and meaning. Consider, for example, the kinds of analogical morphological change which are involved in the substitution of a regular plural for an irregular (*cows* for the older plural *kine*) or of a weak past tense for a strong one (*lighted* for *lit*). In these cases, it is not only the desire for transparent parts but also the desire for a distinct — and unique — plural marker in one case and a distinct past tense marker in the other that motivated the change.

Strangely enough, though, an irregular form that is used very frequently, often does not change. For example, the present tense forms *am, is, are* of the verb *to be* in English or their equivalents in most European languages, which are also very irregular, show no sign of changing to anything more regular. Also, very infrequent forms will stay stable since they are often used only in fixed expressions, so that if, for example, an English speaker knows the verb *smite* at all (an archaic verb meaning 'to strike'), the chances are great that he or she will also use the past tense form *smote* as in the Chaucer fragment (149) and not transform it to a much more regular *\*smited*. We may conclude that analogical change is most likely to occur with forms that are in the middle range in terms of frequency and level of recognition.

## 9.4 Causation and predictability

As can be concluded from the sections above, all languages change all the time. We will now turn to a more fundamental question: why should language ever change at all or what are the **final causes** for language change? Thinking, for instance, of strong verb changes, we can add to this question the matter of predictability: Can we know in advance when change will take place and in what direction?

Perhaps the easiest way to answer the first question is to turn it around and point out that all human institutions change; why should language be different? But if language is viewed as a series of mental structures and cognitive phenomena, we might counter by pointing out that other features of the human mind remain constant; there is no evidence, for example, that there has been any change in the memory capacity of human beings during the last centuries. But as an examination of texts shows, the English/French/Russian of the present is quite different from what it was four or six hundred years ago. Language may change slowly, but often over some thousand years the change is so fundamental that it is no longer understandable, as the Old English sentence in (7) demonstrates.

One answer to the question of final causes is found in the work of William Labov (1973), who was among the first to link language change with variation (see Section 9.1). The basis for his claim was that languages always have some low level of variation at work since people do not pronounce things *exactly* the same each time they say them or even state the same things in exactly the same way. Some of these variations are identified with four social groups: different ages, education, economic background, and gender. As such they take on a certain identification which may finally be marked as having some kind of

**prestige**. It is important to note that prestige does not necessarily (or often) refer to a higher social class or older age group, but may in fact be hidden from any obvious norms. The pronunciations and in-group lexical use for certain subculture phenomena like *grass* (for marijuana) may come from, for example, the speech of punks, or drug dealers, or gangsters. Whatever the source of the prestige, others imitate the pronunciation or word use. The form then spreads across the speech community, usually as one of several variants, although with added social value. But occasionally the form may remain until the others are no longer remembered by speakers; here we have real change.

This is what has happened to the retroflex /r/ variant since the Second World War in the United States. Now this retroflex /r/ has also become very popular in the language of city youngsters in the provinces of South and North Holland in the Netherlands, where uvular /r/ is the general norm. But will the innovation of retroflex /r/ stay and spread?

One of Labov's best-known studies involves details of the pronunciation of the natives of Martha's Vineyard, an island off the coast of Massachusetts in New England. He studied, in particular, the degree of **centralization** of the first element of the diphthongs [aɪ] and [au], i.e. a pronunciation in the direction of /æ/ or /ɛ/ among natives of the island, i.e. people who stayed there throughout the year. The diphthongs of these speakers were more centralized than those of the many summer visitors who owned or rented houses and lived the rest of the year on the mainland, although sometimes quite close to Martha's Vineyard. Looking in more detail at the data taken from the island natives, Labov found that the degree of centralization was greater with a younger group of speakers and that in fact there was a correlation between age (or lack of it) and degree of centralization. He concluded that the centralized variety of the diphthongs had taken on prestige; the younger the speakers, the more important it was to them to sound less like summer visitors and to identify more with the island. Here we can see how what was originally a more or less random variant in pronunciation took on prestige when it was identified with a specific group. It then spread and became more entrenched.

Labov also pointed out in some of his work the importance of differentiating within analyses of language change between the **actuation** of the change, that is, the way in which it starts, and its **spread** across a speech group. Most of his studies, like the one just described, deal more specifically with spread than with the initial stages of a change. Work by Rudi Keller (1990 [1994]) expands this account of final causation to include a theory of actuation. Language, for Keller, is not like a natural phenomenon which changes through unconscious, unintentional forces e.g. the course of rivers when they change through erosion or as a result of earthquakes. We can see something of a parallel here to what was said above about mental structures like memory. Neither is language a social institution which can be changed intentionally by its users the way a law might be. Rather, it is what he calls a 'phenomenon of the third kind', changed by its users, but not intentionally. He compares language change to kinds of events like traffic jams. No one wants to cause one intentionally, but each driver's actions, motivated by other forces such as a desire not to hit the car in front of themselves, contribute to what is eventually an undesirable situation.

What actuates language change in this model is an intention on the part of speakers to be successful in communicating something to their hearers. To attain success, they must balance the need for full comprehension — and therefore a need to use a form of language which will not be too different from that of their listeners — and enough novelty to call attention to what is being said. It is precisely in this seeking out of novelty that change is actuated. When a speaker of English talked about *seizing upon* an idea for the first time (as opposed to a physical object), there was enough similarity between ideas and objects for other speakers to understand the innovation, but at the same time enough innovation for the speaker to be viewed as clever or particularly eloquent. From there we can return to Labov's model: the novel expression is imitated by individuals, and then spreads across other speakers who for some reason identify that group as having sufficient prestige to be a model of language use.

Because of the multiple cognitive and social variables involved in any kind of change, and particularly because the likelihood of linguistic variation leading to change is rather low, it is very difficult to talk about historical linguistics as predictive. Theories (cognitive or other) make no claims about being able to state what changes will take place until some variation is so clearly entrenched that prediction is merged with description. Nobody at present can make any prediction as to what will happen to the retroflex /r/ in North and South Holland or in Dutch as a whole. The question of *when* change will occur is just as delicate. Even if a set of circumstances seems to guarantee that a change will take place, nothing may happen for literally centuries.

The expression of future action in Latin, for example, can be described in retrospect as a highly unstable morphological system, with two entirely different ways of marking this tense (one with an infix and the other with a change of vowel in the ending) depending on the verb class. It took many years, however, for change to occur, as based on when the change appeared in written records. Presumably Latin speakers learned and used this somewhat uncomfortably diverse system over centuries without being bothered by it. A similar situation arose in English. Although the use of *do* in interrogative, negative and emphatic sentences arose at the end of the 16th century (e.g. in Shakespeare's English we find both *what read you* and *what do you read*) it was only at the end of the 18th century that the new system as we know it now emerged in stable form.

The Polish linguist Kuryłowicz (1945–49 [1995]), in discussing analogical change, uses the image of a drainage system: we may find that downspouts, gutters, sewers are all in place, but if it doesn't rain, nothing happens. In this chapter the downspouts are the various mechanisms of change, and the rain is the set of social and cognitive variables which may bring about a given change. Everything has to be lined up just right!

## 9.5 Summary

**Historical linguistics** is the branch of linguistics which studies language change. **Language change** can only be understood against the background of **language variation**, the fact that "the" language does not in fact exist, but is composed of a number of **language varieties**, or dialects. One of those is the **standard variety** as used in syntax and lexis, and the standard accent, i.e. **Received Pronunciation** in Britain and **General American English** in the United States. But in addition to the standard variety, most speakers command one or several of the other varieties such as **regiolects, sociolects, ethnolects** or **aetalects**. The peculiarities of a single speaker form his or her **idiolect**. Age varieties or aetalects may particularly influence language change: not only do younger speakers make many innovations, but they also give up a number of forms, productively used or only passively understood by older speakers. In spite of continuous change, there is also a great deal of continuity so that we can still partially understand texts of 400 or even 600 years ago. This is due to our **pandialectical competence**, which means that we understand passively more dialects, both geographical and temporal, than we productively use ourselves. The influence of first language uses, habits, and grammatical patterns upon the new language adopted by people who are conquered is called a **substratal influence**, with the influencing language called a **substratum**. The influence of the language of the conquerors on the language of the conquered is called **superstratal influence** with the influencing language called a **superstrate** language. The methods used in historical linguistics are the **philological method** for written texts, and **reconstruction** for all those periods and languages without written records. The historical linguist compares language forms in the various languages and tries to reconstruct (part of) the ancestor language, which is indicated by the form *proto* 'first, earliest stage in a language'. This stage may have to be situated 1,000 to 3,000 years back in time, e.g. **Proto-Indo-European, Proto-Germanic, Proto-Western-Germanic, Proto-Romance**. Reconstruction is based not only on **genetic relatedness**, but also on the **regularity principle**. The so-called sound laws, or statements of regularity, such as **Grimm's Law**, summarize what are really closer to majority rules than laws in the physical sense. If reconstruction is applied not across languages, but to various phases of the same language we speak of **internal reconstruction**. Language change can be studied at any level, i.e. in the lexicon, morphology, etc. Since linguistic categories appear as **radial networks,** it is especially those networks that can be studied in their historical evolution. Within categories we as language users also build up a **schema**, i.e. the most abstract representation of that category applying to all its members. Language change can occur in networks, across networks and in schemas. First we have **changes within radial networks**. Here minor phonetic changes may occur such as **assimilation, dissimilation,** and **metathesis**. Within a category's network the items may be **rearranged**: the most prototypical member *dog* has superseded the whole original category *hound*, which has now become a relatively peripheral member of the category *dog*. **Changes across networks** are found in the set of allophones for a given phoneme, e.g. the phoneme /t/ may comprise allophones like glottal stops [ʔ] as in *cat-call*, or flaps [ɾ] in *pretty* [prɪɾɪ], or even a **zero form** as in [prɪɪ]. The radial network for *bead* has undergone a most radical change-over from the domain of "prayer" to that of "jewellery". In grammar, an existing category, e.g. the form *one*, may **split** into two or three categories (numeral, impersonal pronoun and in a reduced form as the article *an*). Conversely, two different categories, e.g. the masculine pronoun forms *him* and *hine*, may **merge** into one category.

Changes in schemas may reduce existing variations of word order as in Old or Middle English with their SOV, OSV, VOS orders, into SVO as the sole sentence type. Similarly the radial network of a lexical item like *meat* may be reduced to only one meaning instead of several. Also new schemas may be created, called **phonologization** for phonemes. The **umlaut** or **mutation** as for example the German rounded vowel /y/ in *Kühe* 'cows' is a case in point. The Old English equivalent to *Kühe* was *kine*, but due to **analogical changes** plural endings in *-ne* have been done away with so that ME *eyen* is now *eyes* and OE *kine* is now *cows*.

Coming back to the initial question of **final causes**, why languages change at all, one possible answer is that of the **prestige** that a given variant may acquire, which then is **spread**. This is exemplified, for instance, by the **centralization** of the first elements in diphthongs used by native speakers of a holiday island to emphasize their nativeness. But even if all the elements necessary for a change are present, the change may not reach **actuation**. Language change is actuated by the speaker's desire to be both comprehensible and attention-getting. However, a change can never be predicted.

## 9.6 Further reading

Introductions to Old English are Quirk and Wrenn (1973) and Dürrmüller and Utz (1977). Middle English texts and grammars have been published by Mossé (1968) and Cawley (1975). For the sound track of *The Canterbury Tales (Prologue)*, see Strauss (n.d.). Generally accessible introduction to causation in language history is Keller (1990). More general, theoretical approaches are Hock (1986), Hock and Joseph (1996) and Trask (1996). The link between historical sound changes and present-day variation in language was established by several scholars but most notably by Labov (1973) and Trudgill (2002). A collection of cognitive-linguistic approaches to historical linguistics is offered in Kellermann and Morissey (1992). The links among prototypes, schemas, and change in syntax are explored in Winters (1992). An approach related to that of cognitive linguistics is Kuryłowicz (1945; translated into English by Winters 1995).

## Assignments

1. Check in some older dictionaries whether the words in italics in the following sentences are present already and whether they have their present-day meanings. What can you conclude from this?

   a. He is a real *anorak* ('boring person')
   b. This machinery has highly *sophisticated* equipment ('clearly designed, advanced')
   c. This teacher knows how to keep the children *on their toes* ('alert')

2. Consider the following Chaucerian passage, dated ca. 1380. What characteristics show you that it is not a modern text? Be specific about the differences, what they are and how you recognize them:

   If no love is, O God, what fele I so?
   And if love is, what thing and which is he?

If love be good, from whennes cometh my woo?

3. If there are double forms for the past tense and the past participle, British English more often uses the strong form and American English the weak form e.g. *burnt* vs. *burned*; *dreamt* vs. *dreamed, knelt* vs. *kneeled, leant* vs. *leaned, leapt* vs. *leaped, spat* vs. *spitted*. Do you see a possible explanation for this phenomenon?

4. In each case, say which aspect in Grimm's Law has operated, e.g. the Indo-European voiceless stop has become a voiceless fricative in Germanic.

   | | **Sanskrit** | **Latin** | **English** |
   |---|---|---|---|
   | a. | *ajras* | *ager* | acre |
   | b. | *pad* | *pedis* | foot |
   | c. | *dva* | *duo* | two |
   | d. | *trayas* | *tres* | three |

5. What kind of change is illustrated in each of the following examples?
   a. Latin *in* + *legitimus* ⇒ modern English *illegitimate*
   b. Latin adjectival suffix *-alem* yielding English *glottal, palatal*, but also *velar*
   c. Old English *brid* ⇒ modern English *bird*
   d. English *mouse/mice*, but *Mickey Mouses*
   e. English *horse* vs. German *Roß*, Dutch *ros* 'horse'
   f. English *three* vs. *thirteen, thirty*, German *dreizehn*
   g. English name *Bernstein* vs. German *Brennstein*, or English *burn* vs. German *brennen*.
   h. English *thunder* vs. Dutch *donder* vs. German *Donner*
   i. English *cellar* vs. German *Keller* vs. Dutch *kelder*
   j. English *adventure* vs. French *aventure*, Dutch *avontuur*.

6. Compare the plural forms of the Proto-West-Germanic words *mus* and *kuh* in English, German and Dutch and say what similar or different processes took place in each language.

   | | | | |
   |---|---|---|---|
   | a. | West Germanic: | *mus – musi* | *kuh – kuhi* |
   | b. | English: | *mouse – mice* | cow OE *kine*/NE *cows* |
   | c. | German: | *Maus – Mäuse* | *Kuh – Kühe* |
   | d. | Dutch: | *muis – muizen* | *koe – koeien* |

7. Compare the use of the morpheme *full* in Modern English (see Ch. 3.3.1) with its entirely different use in the Chaucer fragment in (3). First collect all the instances from the Prioress fragment. Is it a bound or a free morpheme, a function word or a content word? What is its meaning in the Chaucer fragment? Can you call this an instance of grammaticalization? Which English word has later taken over the function of Chaucer's *ful*?

(3) **A Middle English Text**

| | |
|---|---|
| Ther was also a Nonne, a PRIORESSE, | |
| That of hir smylyng was ful symple and coy; | *unaffected; modest* |
| 120 Hire gretteste ooth was but by Seinte Loy; | *Eligius* |
| And she was cleped madame Eglentyne, | *called* |
| Ful weel she soong the service dyvyne, | |
| Entuned in hir nose ful semely, | *suitable to the occasion* |
| And Frenssh she spak ful faire and fetisly; | *elegantly* |
| 125 After the scole of Stratford atte Bowe, | |
| For Frenssh of Parys was to hire unknowe. | |
| At mete wel ytaught was she with alle: | *dinner* |
| She leet no morsel from hir lippes falle, | |
| Ne wette hir fyngres in hir sauce depe; | |
| 130 Wel koude she carie a morsel and wel kepe | |
| That no drope ne fille upon hire brest. | |
| In curteisie was set ful muchel hir lest. | |
| Hir over-lippe wyped she so clene | |
| That in hir coppe ther was no ferthyng sene | *cup; spot* |
| 135 Of grece, whan she dronken hadde hir draughte. | |
| Ful semely after hir mete she raughte. | *food; reached* |
| | |
| 157 Ful fetys was hir cloke, as I was war. | *well-made* |
| Of smal coral aboute hire arm she bar | *carried* |
| A peire of bedes, gauded al with grene, | *balls* |
| 160 And theron heng a brooch of gold ful sheene, | |
| On which ther was first write a crowned A, | |
| And after *Amor vincit omnia.* | |

**Notes**

123 Intoned in her nose in a very seemly manner.

125 The Prioress spoke French with the accent she had learned in her convent (the Benedictine nunnery of St. Leonhard's, near Stratford-Bow in Middlesex).

132 She took pains to imitate courtly behaviour, and to be dignified in her bearing.

147 *wastel-breed,* fine wheat bread.

157 I noticed that her cloak was very elegant.

159 A rosary with 'gauds' (i.e. large beads for the Paternosters) of green

161 *crowned* A; capital A with a crown above it.

(from Geoffrey Chaucer, *Canterbury Tales.* Edited by A. C. Cawley, London: J. M. Dent & Sons, New York: E. P. Dutton & Co. 1975)

# 10 Comparing languages
## Language classification, typology, and contrastive linguistics

### 10.0 Overview

Chapter 6 on Cross-cultural semantics has already looked into some similarities and differences in the lexicon, grammar and cultural scripts of various languages and cultural communities. This chapter will now systematically explore the whole area of the comparison between languages from various points of view.

A first viewpoint is an external one and concerns the identification and status of languages. How do we count the number of languages and how can we be sure whether a given variety is a mere dialect or a real language? Which are the internationally most important languages in the world and what criteria can we use for this comparison?

Alongside this external comparison we can compare languages and classify them according to origin and relatedness. Where did languages originate and how did they spread? Which are genetically related languages and which are not, i.e., how do a number of languages belong to the same language group, to the same language family and to the same language stock?

A third viewpoint is that of language typology, which is also applicable when if languages are not genetically related, because they can be allocated to certain structural types based on linguistic criteria such as, for instance, word order phenomena. All languages have common properties, i.e., are subject to a number of constraints called language universals.

Finally, languages can also be compared for more practical purposes such as supporting foreign language learning, translating, and writing bilingual dictionaries. This is done in contrastive linguistics where two or more languages tend to be compared and contrasted in greater detail than is possible in language typology.

## 10.1 External comparison: Identification and status of languages

### 10.1.1 Establishing and counting languages

It is still impossible to state exactly how many languages are spoken in the world today. Estimates range from 5,000 to 6,000 so that one might ask whether linguists cannot be more accurate in this regard. There are, however, various reasons for this uncertainty.

The first reason is that some parts of the world such as Africa and Australia are still linguistically underexplored. We still lack data on many of the languages spoken there, because linguistic observation needs time, funds and knowledge to be carried out. Some recently explored areas have turned out to contain a vast number of languages. Comrie (1987a) reports that now New Guinea unexpectedly shows linguistic relevance in that it hosts about one fifth of the world's languages, and some have still not been definitively identified. The same holds for a number of African or Australian languages.

Secondly, one often cannot state if two contiguous linguistic varieties are different languages or simply regional dialects of the same language. Even in Europe, where there is virtually no more uncertainty, language or dialect status has traditionally been and still is the result of political rather than linguistic decisions.

### 10.1.2 Linguistic identification of languages and dialects

One of the most frequently applied criteria for the identification of a language has been **mutual intelligibility**: if speakers can understand each other, they are assumed to speak the same language or dialects of the same language; if they don't, they probably speak different languages. We can easily detect evident contradictions even in the European regions we know. Within the German language territory, for instance, northern dialects are almost unintelligible to southern speakers and vice versa. Italians of the Alpine region need subtitles to understand dialect dialogues in Mafia films. On the other hand, the border between Germany and Holland, which is the dividing line between two official languages, i.e. German and Dutch, crosses a territory where neighbours can easily understand each other. A significant amount of mutual intelligibility also exists between Scandinavian languages. Danes and Norwegians understand each other perfectly, each speaking their own language. It seems therefore that mutual intelligibility sometimes characterizes relatively close dialects or languages.

Another problem with intelligibility is that understanding another language or another dialect is more often than not a matter of degree or percentage, often depending on familiarity, exposure and willingness to understand. There can be situations in which only one of the two partners understands the other. The solution to the problem of language boundaries, dialect boundaries and mutual intelligibility is the concept of a **dialect continuum**. Even if they are included in different official languages, neighbouring dialects in a dialect continuum may be fully understandable. But two very distant dialects falling under the same official language need not be mutually intelligible. However, all these dialects form a continuum. As we see in Table 1, there could be evidence for a dialect continuum from the North Sea, or the Baltic Sea, as far down as Tyrol.

**Table 1.** Some realizations of the utterance "how are you now"

|  | Written (sub)standard | Phonetic realisation |
|---|---|---|
| Bavarian | *wia geht's da jetzat?* | via gɛts da ietsat |
| Standard German | *wie geht's dir jetzt?* | viː geːts diʋ iɛtst |
| Low German | *wo geit di dat nu?* | voː gait di dat nuː |
| Dutch | *hoe gaat het met u?* | huː xaːt hɔt met y |
| Danish | *hvordan har du det nu?* | voʋdan haː du deː nuː |
| Norwegian | *hvordan har du det no?* | vurdan har dy deː noː |

Alongside a geographical continuum we also have a **historical continuum**. Some languages disappear and new ones emerge as a consequence of the evolution from a former stage into a new one. This is the case with classical Latin, which eventually died out as a spoken language, whereas spoken vulgar Latin in a few centuries split into many different Romance languages. Conventionally, we accept that a language is extinct when nobody speaks it anymore, but **language death** need not happen abruptly as a consequence of the death of the last speaker. More frequently, there will be a slow transition in the community of speakers, who gradually give up an old language while using a new one. So there might well be a stage in which the old language is still latent in the competence of a certain number of speakers in the community. Conversely, how can we determine the birth date of a new language, if it has been gradually developing as a variety of an existing one? We speak of Romance languages as an offspring of Latin, but at the same time admit just one Hellenic language, i.e. (modern) Greek. An important difference is that Greek has not been influenced by different substrata (see Chapter 9.2).

Identifying and counting languages is therefore a very difficult task, even if left exclusively in the hands of linguists. Data collections still need to be completed, and criteria are not sufficiently precise, let alone clear as to how they are applied. As we will see, however, language definition and consequently language classification depends in its turn on the progress and results of sociolinguistic and diachronic research.

10.1.3 The political and international status of languages

The sixteenth century, i.e. the beginning of Modern Times in history, saw the rise of a new concept of the state. It was shaped by great and powerful kings like Henry VIII in Britain, François I in France, and Emperor Charles V or his son Philip II in Spain. Both language and religion were also powerful levers in this new idea of a state, which was summarized in the slogan "One kingdom, one language, one religion."

Since a number of languages have so much public and political relevance, decisions on what should be labelled as a language are made by political authorities in collaboration with — or instead of — linguistic experts. A country may recognize just one official language. An **official language** is any variety or a language which has been officially recognized (even if only implicitly) by a state. The linguistic definition of a language does not always coincide with what is described as a language from a political or sociological point of view. A clear instance of a language policy and the choice of an official language is Serbo-Croatian. Both in (Small) Yugoslavia and in Croatia it is used, but in Serbia it is written in the Cyrillic (Russian) alphabet, in Croatia in the Latin alphabet. Linguistically speaking it is one language, politically it is two.

In France it has always been the traditional French language policy to have only one official language, also in colonial times. Other countries may, however, adopt more than one language as their official languages, e.g. Great Britain (English, Welsh), Spain (Spanish, Catalan), Belgium (Dutch, French, German) or Switzerland (German, French, Rhaeto-Romance). A country may even attribute language status to what other states would regard as a dialect. In Europe this could be the case of Letzeburgesch, which many linguists consider as a German dialect. But Letzeburgesch has, in contrast with other German dialects, a rich literary tradition and it is extensively used in the media, especially in television, and is therefore not comparable in status to German dialects. However, it remains a purely political decision to promote it as the third official language of Luxemburg, and consequently also as one of the official languages of the European Union.

In various countries in Asia, varieties of Malay are treated as dialects or as official languages. In Malaysia general communication relies on one or the other dialect form of Bazaar Malay, but the superordinate official language is Standard Malay. In Indonesia politicians decided long before independence that they would not take one of the bigger national languages, e.g. Javanese with its 70 million speakers, as the national language, but an Indonesian form of Malay. This was successfully developed into a standard language and is now called Bahasa Indonesia.

Official language status does not imply typological or statistical relevance, but contributes in the long term to establishing rules and enriching the lexicon of the **institutionalized language**. In many countries where minorities are granted linguistic autonomy there are particular **language laws** determining the obligatory or optional use of the languages and the different degrees in the official status of those languages.

From a global perspective, if we try to determine which languages are the most important ones in the world, our findings will vary according to the criteria we apply. If we only take the number of speakers, the languages of Asia are dominant as Table 2 shows. But if in addition to the number of speakers we also use other criteria such as the number of countries in which a given language has official language status, in how many different continents it is spoken, or the strength of the economy in its original country (expressed in billion US Dollars), the picture is quite different (Table 3).

It is clear from all these figures that English ranks highest. Given its large number of native speakers, its official status in so many countries and its spread on all continents it is only natural that English has now become the "world language".

**Table 2.** The most widely spoken languages (in million speakers) (according to Grimes 1996)

| | | | |
|---|---|---|---|
| Mandarin Chinese | 885 | Portuguese | 175 |
| English | 450 | Russian | 160 |
| Spanish | 266 | Arab | 139 |
| Hindi/Urdu | 233 | Japanese | 126 |
| Bahasa Indonesia | 193 | French | 122 |
| Bengali/Assam | 181 | German | 118 |

**Table 3.** The most "international" languages of the world

| Language | Native speakers[1] | Official language in countries | Spoken on number of continents | GNP in billion US Dollars in core countries[2] | |
|---|---|---|---|---|---|
| English | 300 | 47 | 5 | 1,069 | UK |
| French | 68 | 30 | 3 | 1,355 | France |
| Arabic | 139 | 21 | 2 | 38 | UAR |
| Spanish | 266 | 20 | 3 | 525 | Spain |
| Portuguese | 175 | 7 | 3 | 92 | Portugal |
| German | 118 | 5 | 1 | 2,075 | Germany |
| Indonesian Malay | 193 | 4 | 1 | 167 | Indonesia |

[1]Grimes (1996); [2]Fischer Weltalmanach (1997).

## 10.2 Spread and classification of languages

Whereas the socio-political criteria discussed in the previous section help to identify and classify languages according to their importance, language-internal criteria are used to classify languages by the degree of relatedness amongst them. Genetic relatedness of languages tells us indirectly more about human migration patterns.

### 10.2.1 The genesis and spread of languages

The comparison between languages is one of the many important tools used to help find the answers to some fundamental questions about the origin, the nature and the evolution of language. This is also a field which concerns many sciences at the same time.

Did language originate together with mankind? According to Jean Aitchison (1996) this evolution happened east of the Great Lakes in East Africa, now Kenya, some 200,000 years ago. Over a period of many millennia language just stayed dormant. Then 50,000 years ago languages began to develop and spread like wild fire. From East Africa people did not only migrate to Western and Southern Africa, but also to Northern Africa and the Near East. After a bifurcation, groups of people migrated to Europe and to Central Asia, to South East Asia, Australia and New Zealand; other groups migrated to Northern Asia, through the Behring Strait to Alaska, North, Central and South America; from Central Asia ever increasing numbers of new people migrated to the West, and to Europe. One of the largest language families in the world is the Indo-European family. Figure 1 offers a general view of these migrations.

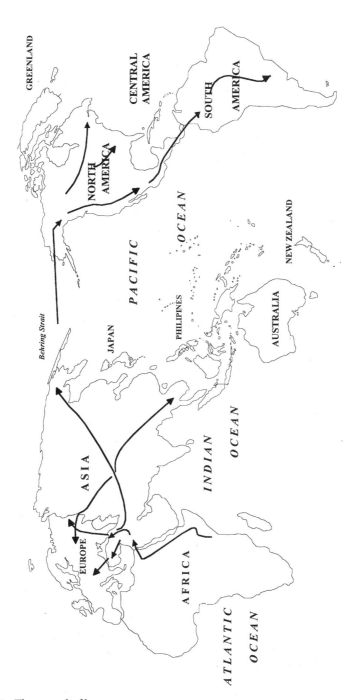

**Figure 1.** The spread of languages

Not only linguistics, but many other sciences such as physiology, ethology (study of the behaviour of animals), evolution theory, anatomy, anthropology, human geography, neurobiology study these issues. In fact only an **interdisciplinary** approach, in which various disciplines co-operate, can deal with the genesis and spread of languages and can provide data of this kind.

### 10.2.2 Genetic relatedness of languages

Language classification has a rich tradition of trying to identify **language families**. This metaphor suggests the existence of a genetic relatedness between a number of languages, reflecting the relations between the members of a human family. Languages that show a large number of common features in phonology, lexicology, morphology and syntax stem from a common ancestor. Thus, a number of languages from India, such as Hindi, Iranian languages, Slavonic languages, Greek, Latin, Celtic languages, Romance and Germanic languages are all members of one big language family, i.e. the Indo-European language family. Establishing language families therefore means historical research and **reconstruction** of older language forms, called **proto-language** and of the great lines of historical **sound shifts** or **structural changes** that have caused language differentiation. The latter were discussed in Chapter 9 on historical linguistics.

Here in this section we will concentrate on the results of historical differentiation. In addition to the notion of language family, language classification now uses a more complex taxonomy. At the top we have the category of a **phylum**, i.e. a language group which is unrelated to any other group. The next lower level of classification is that of a (language) **stock**, i.e. a group of languages belonging to different language families which are distantly related to each other. **Language family** remains a central notion, emphasizing the internal links between the members of such a family. In a number of cases, e.g. in the case of Indo-European, the levels of phylum, stock and family coincide, but as Tables 4 and 5 show, in the many complex language situations in Africa, Asia and the Americas, these distinctions are necessary. Language families are further subcategorized into **branches**, e.g. the Western European branch of the Indo-European family, branches are subcategorized into **groups**, e.g. the Romance and Germanic groups in the Western European branch, and groups may branch into **subgroups**. These terms are displayed and illustrated for a number of African languages in Table 4. Table 5 gives a classification of the world's major linguistic areas. Table 6 offers a survey of the Indo-European family.

We see in Table 4 that the notions of "family" and "branch" coincide for Bantu languages. Although Bantu is distantly related to other Niger-Congo languages, Bantu itself is only one family. This family is, however, composed of many more groups than are shown here, and each group also contains many more subgroups. Thus, for instance, the group of Nguni languages in South Africa encompasses most speakers of African languages in that country, i.e. those of the major languages Zulu and Xhosa and also those of the somewhat minor languages Ndebele and Swazi.

**Table 4.** Taxonomic levels in language classification; examples from Africa (after Moseley/Asher 1994:292)

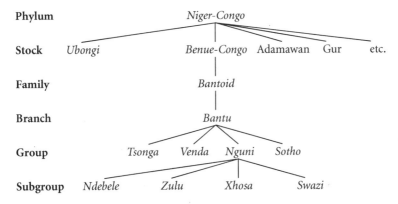

Table 5 displays some systems of relatedness for various languages all over the world. Here, the notion of a "phylum" becomes of paramount importance. But since we also want to refer to geographical regions, we will be using the notion of a set of language phyla. The classification of the first set, i.e. the African sub-Saharan languages in three different phyla implies that no genetic relatedness holds between these three phyla, i.e. Niger-Congo, Khoisan and Nilo-Saharan. This in its turn implies that these people migrated to these parts of Africa long before the birth of "language", which, according to Aitchinson (1996) may be placed between 150,000 and 50,000 B.C.

Things are quite different in the second set of languages in the Middle East and North Africa, which all belong to one stock, i.e. the Afro-Asiatic stock. This implies that families and languages in this second set may be distantly related (Somali) or relatively closely related (Hebrew and Arabic) to each other.

In fact, the Afro-Asiatic stock is the only set of the six sets of languages that can be shown to have distantly related members (Comrie 1987b:155). Consequently,

**Table 5.** The world's major linguistic areas

1.  Sub-Saharan languages
    1.1. Niger-Congo phylum, e.g. Bantu family
    1.2. Khoisan phylum, e.g. Khoekhoe branch, e.g. Nama
    1.3. Nilo-Saharan phylum, e.g. Nilotic family
2.  Africa and Middle East: Afro-Asiatic stock
    2.1. Cushitic family, e.g. Somali; some Ethiopian languages
    2.2. Ancient Egyptian and Coptic: now extinct
    2.3. Semitic family, e.g. Arabic group, Hebrew, Aramaic
    2.4. Berber family
    2.5. Chadic family, e.g. Hausa
3.  Nostratic languages
    3.1. Indo-European phylum (see Table 6)
    3.2. Kartvelian phylum: e.g. South Caucasian, Georgian
    3.3. Uralic phylum, e.g. Finnish, Estonian, Lapp, Hungarian
    3.4. Altaic phylum, e.g. Turkic group (e.g. Turkish), Mongolian group
4.  Austric languages
    4.1. Austro-Asiatic phylum, e.g. Mon-Khmer subgroup
    4.2. Dravidian phylum, e.g. Tamil, Telugu
    4.3. Sino-Tibetan, e.g. Chinese family, Tibetan-Burman family
    4.4. Korean, Japanese
5.  Australasian and Pacific languages
    5.1. Austronesian phylum (800 languages), e.g. Malay stock, Indonesian, Javanese
    5.2. Papuan languages (750 languages in Papua New Guinea)
    5.3. Australian phylum (250 languages), e.g. Pama Nyungan stock, e.g. Mbabaram
    5.4. Polynesian group
6.  Amerindian languages
    6.1. North American languages (selected families or stocks)
        6.1.1. Eskimo-Eleut family
        6.1.2. Athapaskan family, e.g. Navaho
        6.1.3. Wakashan family, e.g. Kwakiutl, Nootka
        6.1.4. Uto-Aztecan stock, e.g. Hopi
    6.2. Mezo-American languages, e.g. Mayan family
    6.3. South American languages

with the exception of the 2nd set, the six sets listed in Table 5 are rather geographical divisions. Thus the 3rd set, the **Nostratic languages,** a term proposed by the Danish linguist Pedersen (1924), reflects an older approach to language classification, whereby many scholars tended to assume that all languages of the world are genetically related. But today most scholars require very sound empirical evidence before admitting any statement of relatedness. The presentation in Table 5 is a compromise between the two views in the sense that it may be useful to have some geographical sets without committing oneself to any genetic relatedness between the members in a geographical set.

Table 6 displays the Indo-European phylum, which has only one stock and one family, but two main branches, i.e. the *Satem* branch and the *Kentum* branch. These two words stand for "hundred" in Old Iranian, a member of the Eastern branch, and in Latin, a member of the Western branch, respectively. On the basis of the many documents available, the Proto-Indo-European form *k'mto* has been reconstructed, where /k'/ represents a palatal stop (whereas /k/ is a velar stop). This palatal stop /k'/ has become a palatal fricative /ʃ/ and later /s/ in the **Satem languages**. But palatal /k'/ has become a velar /k/ in the **Kentum languages** as in Greek *hekaton*, Latin *centum*, whereby /k/ has later become /h/ in most Germanic languages (see Grimm's Law in Chapter 9).

As already stated in Table 5, the Indo-European family is placed together with several other phyla into the set of Nostratic languages without implying any relatedness between them. As one can see in Table 6, the categories *phylum*, *stock*, and *family* coincide here. This means that the Indo-European languages form "one phylum", not related to any other set or family, "one stock" not even distantly related to other languages, and "one family". In the older view the four members of the set of Nostratic languages in Table 5 would at least be seen as "stocks", i.e. as distantly related sets of families.

Genetic relatedness is generally assumed on empirical grounds for nearly all groups of Indo-European languages. Written documents are largely available and allow scholars to reconstruct the evolution of the various branches, groups and subgroups, as was shown in Chapter 9 for the two sound shifts.

While some similarities between languages can clearly be explained on grounds of genetic relatedness, others may be the result of chance. Chance similarities are generally assumed when isolated items of geographically and/or historically distant languages are involved. Comrie (1987a: 8) discusses the case of the word *dog* in Mbabaram, an Australian Aboriginal language (see Table 5; 5.3), which happens to mean "dog". Since borrowing from English can be excluded and a satisfactory etymological explanation via a Proto-Australian form is possible, it would be wrong to assess genetic relatedness between Mbabaram and English just on the basis of this one item. This conclusion is undisputed in this special case, because we know a lot about English and its development. In cases in which languages are less well documented, it may be hard to decide whether similar items are relevant for classification or just coincidentally similar.

Table 6. Indo-European Languages

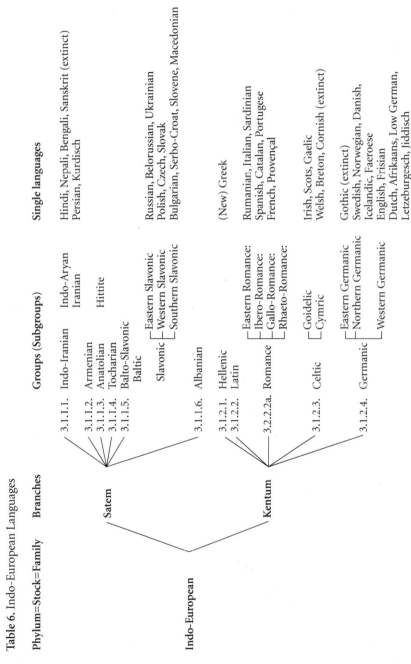

| Phylum=Stock=Family | Branches | Groups (Subgroups) | | Single languages |
|---|---|---|---|---|
| | Satem | 3.1.1.1. Indo-Iranian | Indo-Aryan | Hindi, Nepali, Bengali, Sanskrit (extinct) |
| | | | Iranian | Persian, Kurdisch |
| | | 3.1.1.2. Armenian | | |
| | | 3.1.1.3. Anatolian | Hittite | |
| | | 3.1.1.4. Tocharian | | |
| | | 3.1.1.5. Balto-Slavonic | | |
| | | Baltic | | |
| | | Slavonic | Eastern Slavonic | Russian, Belorussian, Ukrainian |
| | | | Western Slavonic | Polish, Czech, Slovak |
| | | | Southern Slavonic | Bulgarian, Serbo-Croat, Slovene, Macedonian |
| Indo-European | | 3.1.1.6. Albanian | | |
| | Kentum | 3.1.2.1. Hellenic | | (New) Greek |
| | | 3.1.2.2. Latin | | |
| | | 3.2.2.2a. Romance | Eastern Romance: | Rumanian, Italian, Sardinian |
| | | | Ibero-Romance: | Spanish, Catalan, Portugese |
| | | | Gallo-Romance: | French, Provençal |
| | | | Rhaeto-Romance: | |
| | | 3.1.2.3. Celtic | Goidelic | Irish, Scots, Gaelic |
| | | | Cymric | Welsh, Breton, Cornish (extinct) |
| | | 3.1.2.4. Germanic | Eastern Germanic | Gothic (extinct) |
| | | | Northern Germanic | Swedish, Norwegian, Danish, Icelandic, Faeroese |
| | | | Western Germanic | English, Frisian |
| | | | | Dutch, Afrikaans, Low German, Letzeburgesch, Jiddisch |

## 10.3 Language typology and language universals

**Language typology** is the branch of linguistics that aims to find the common properties between various languages, whether genetically related to each other or not. Amongst the different approaches within typology, we will focus on the issue of **language universals**, i.e., properties common to all languages.

Universals were dealt with in Chapters 6 and 7. In Chapter 6, universal concepts, listed in Table 2 were discussed as 'the alphabet of human thought'. This claim entails that the human conceptual apparatus has developed in such a way that a small set of some 60 concepts are the essential ones to be shaped in language generally, in any one language and in all languages of the world. The linguistic form or word class assumed by a unit in any given language is immaterial. The expression for the concepts "I" and "you" need not be a pronoun, but it may also be a bound morpheme such as the suffix -*i* in Latin *veni* 'I have come' or -*is* in *venis* '*you* have come'. The Amerindian language Nootka is said to have no nouns and, just like Latin, expresses the reference to the speaker (*I*) and to the hearer (*you*) by means of affixes on the verb.

We can generalize these facts and state that the universal concepts are linguistically expressed either as lexical items (free morphemes) or as affixes (bound morphemes). Here we are dealing with **ideational universals**. Language is primordially used as a means of communication, which would suggest that there must also be **interpersonal universals** regulating the way we communicate with one another. The maxims of conversation, at least those of quality, quantity, and relevance (see Chapter 7.3.1), can be claimed to be some of the interpersonal or **pragmatic universals**.

However interesting and convincing these types of language universals may be, they do not contain any internal complexity, in that they are just a list of statements that can, if enough research can be organized, either be confirmed or refuted in the 5,000 or 6,000 languages of the world. But the type of universals that language typology has traditionally been interested in is of a more complex nature. It rather tries to inspect a number of elements from the general systems of sounds, words, morphemes, syntactic structures etc. that may be found in all the languages of the world and to decide in what combination or succession they have to be chosen if they are chosen at all. A very clear example is that of basic colour terms.

It was originally thought that colour terms were the most language-specific, arbitrary elements in language. But the two researchers Berlin and Kay (1969) examined a large number of languages and found a remarkable regularity in the distribution of basic colour terms all over the world (also see Heider 1972). All languages have at least two basic colour terms, i.e. those displaying the greatest attention such as "black" and "white" (or "dark" and "light"). If a language has three terms, the third is "red". If four or five, they are either "yellow" or "green" or both. The sixth term is "blue". The next term is "brown" and subsequently we get four possibilities from either "purple", "pink", "orange" or "grey". This can be summarized as in Table 7.

**Table 7.** Lexical universal: Distribution of colour terms

| Stage 1 | Stage 2 | Stage 3 | Stage 4 | Stage 5 | Stage 6 |
|---|---|---|---|---|---|
| white black | < red | yellow *or* green | < blue | < brown | grey pink orange purple |

The order in the growth of colour terms implies that the opposition between two extremes is the most salient basis on which to build concepts. In languages that have only equivalents for "white/black" or "light/dark", this opposition is more salient than the distinction between the single colours, which can anyway all be seen as "light (green, blue, etc.)" or "dark (green, blue, etc.)". More recent research (Kay et al. 1991) has shown that the situation is not so straightforward, e.g. that the four colours of the sixth stage may appear much earlier than those of the other stages. Still, it is rather the principle that matters i.e. that there is a great deal of systematicity in the development of colour terms, even if the details are not yet completely understood.

A similar principle could by way of hypothesis be applied to the use of the vowel system in a language. One universal says that a language must have at least two vowels. We could go one step further and hypothesize that if there are only three vowels in a language, they must be the three cardinal vowels in greatest opposition to each other, i.e. /a/ and /u/ or /i/, which according to Kelz (1976) is the case in Guarani. If there are four, either /e/ or /ɔ/ will be added; if five, they will be /i, a, u, e, ɔ/, which is the case in Spanish. So, in analogy with the colour terms discussion, the hypothesis could be set up that the vocal system of languages shows a similar, systematic elaboration.

A similar order has been set up in morphology for the affixes, where the most common preference is the use of suffixes, followed by the use of prefixes, next infixes and we could tentatively add circumfixes, as in the the morpheme

Table 8. Phonological universal: Distribution of basic vowels

| /i, u/ | /e/ |
|---|---|
| < | |
| /a/ | /ɔ/ |

Table 9. Morphological universal: Preference for affixes

| suffix | < | prefix | < | infix | < | circumfix |
|---|---|---|---|---|---|---|

for the perfect, e.g., ***have worked***. See Table 9.

In past research, especially syntactic (or grammatical) universals were highlighted in language typology. Here Greenberg (1966) summarizes the insights that already prevailed at that time. First Greenberg presents the results of the inquiry into word order such as SVO, etc. The thinking behind Greenberg's universals now appears to be very much comparable to the approach in terms of prototypes. Like all categories, universals can also be claimed to have central (or prototypical) members, less central members and marginal or peripheral members. Thus for the various possible word orders we could also set up a preference hierarchy as in Table 10. This table summarizes Greenberg's (1966:107) results for 30 languages.

Table 10. Syntactic universal: Preference for word order types

| SVO | < | SOV | < | VSO | < | VOS | < | OVS |
|---|---|---|---|---|---|---|---|---|
| (13) | | (11) | | (6) | | | | |

The numbers give the frequencies of the word order types in 30 languages, selected from all possible stocks.

As these facts reveal, SVO and SOV are the prototypical or central word orders, and VSO is less central, but still very frequent. These three word orders share the principle that the subject precedes the direct object. As was shown in Chapter 4, we can see a conceptual priority in the energy flow from an Agent to a Patient or from some other control relation i.e. a Possessor or Experiencer to a Patient. This conceptual priority is also reflected in the great majority of preferred word orders in the world's languages. The opposite pattern, in which the object precedes the subject, is extremely marginal: VOS is found in the Amerindian language Cœur d'Alène and both VOS and OVS in the Amerindian languages Siuslaw and Coos (Greenberg 1966:110).

The implicit thinking in terms of prototypes is also clearly manifest in the way the list of 45 universals are stated by Greenberg (1966: 110). It contains all sorts of restrictions such as *almost always*, *with overwhelming greater than chance frequency*, etc. We quote four of the first five universals from this list (Greenberg 1966: 110) in Table 11.

**Table 11.** Syntactic universals

| | |
|---|---|
| 1. | In declarative sentences with nominal subject and object, the dominant order is almost always one in which the subject precedes the object |
| 3. | Languages with dominant VSO order are always prepositional. |
| 4. | With overwhelming greater than chance frequency, languages with normal SOV order are postpositional. |
| 5. | If a language has dominant SVO order and the genitive follows the governing noun, then the adjective likewise follows the noun. |

The type of universals in Table 11, no. 3 to no. 5 are **implicational universals**. This means that a given type of word order for S, V, and O will also imply a given order between other elements in other phrases, e.g. between the place of the preposition, which in theory can be put either before a noun (prepositional) or after a noun (postpositional). If a language has the verb before the object (VO) as in *climb the tree*, then it will probably have the preposition before the noun as in *up the tree*. But if a language like Hungarian has SOV order as in *on the tree climb,* then it will probably have the adposition after the noun as in *the tree up*. This is then a postposition. As nos. 3 and 4 state, VSO order implies prepositional order, but SOV order implies postpositional order: if V comes last, the adposition also comes last. This is illustrated by the Hungarian sentence *Zoltàn a fa alatt fut* 'Zoltàn the tree under runs (he)' in which the prepositional phrase *a fa alatt* 'the tree under' has a postposition, just like the sentence has the verb *fut* in end-position.

Now, if languages share such implicational universals, our conclusion to this effect need not imply any genetic relatedness. Postpositions are indeed common not only to languages in the Uralic phylum like Hungarian (Table 5; 3.3) but also to those in the Altaic phylum like the Turkic group and the Mongolian languages, and even Japanese and Korean. On this basis, it was proposed in the twenties to consider all these languages as members of the Altaic phylum. But this provides too little evidence to assume genetic relatedness.

We will now summarize the various types of universals in a comprehensible table (Table 12).

Table 12. Types of universals

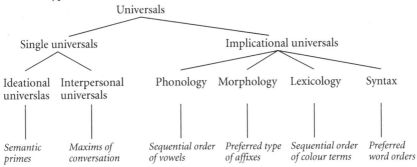

## 10.4 Contrastive linguistics

As we saw in the preceding section, the search for language universals involves the comparison between and among many, often hundreds of languages. Even though this search has led to important assumptions for theoretical linguistics and interdisciplinary research, the focus on similarities in a great number of languages is a different concern from that of **contrastive linguistics**, which focuses on contrasts between two or more languages.

Contrastive linguistics can therefore check more precisely how far a specific element applies to two or more languages. This kind of in depth comparison often reveals multidimensional correspondences, creating new cognitive perspectives. Moreover, contrastive linguistics has some very practical applications: Its findings aim at contrastive grammars, lexicons, phonologies of two or more languages and are useful for foreign language learning, translation, and bilingual dictionaries.

### 10.4.1 "Comparative" or "contrastive?"

Let us start with a rather common pattern of English, i.e. the progressive form of the verb. If we look for a corresponding form in other European languages, e.g. Italian, we may decide to stay with verb morphology, and conclude that only a few languages can express the same function in (nearly) the same way:

(1)  Progressive and equivalents

    a.  English:     What are you doing? I am writing a card.

    b.  Italian:      *Cosa stai facendo? Sto scrivendo una cartolina.*

                        'What you-stay doing? I-stay writing a card'

                        or: *Cosa fai? Scrivo una cartolina.*

                        'What you-do? I-write a card'

    c.  Dutch:      *Wat ben je aan het doen? Ik schrijf een kaart.*

                        'What are you on the doing? I write a card'

    d.  German:    *Was machst du gerade? Ich schreibe eine Karte.*

                        'What make you right-now? I write a card'

All these examples express that the speaker focuses on the internal phasing of an event. When you look at the translation of "What are you doing", you can see that English, Italian and Dutch with their progressive or gerundial verb constructions have more in common with each other than English has with German, which can only use a simple present tense and the adverb *gerade*.

The English progressive may also express that the focus is on the duration of an event. Let us check how this sense can be translated into Italian, Dutch and German:

(2)  a.  English:    He has been crying for an hour.

     b.  Italian:      *Sta piangendo da un'ora* or: *piange da un'ora.*

                        'He-stays crying since an hour' or:

                        'He cries since an hour'

     c.  Dutch:      *Hij schreit al een uur.*

                        'He cries already an hour'

                        *Hij is al een uur aan 't schreien.*

                        'He is already an hour on the crying'

                        *Hij heeft al een uur geschreid.*

                        'He has already an hour cried'

                        *Hij is al een uur aan 't schreien geweest.*

                        'He has already an hour on the crying been'

     d.  German:    *Er weint (schon) seit einer Stunde.*

                        'He cries (already) since an hour'

                        *Er weint jetzt (schon) eine Stunde.*

                        'He cries now (already) an hour.

                        *Er hat eine Stunde lang (stundenlang) geweint.*

                        'He has an hour long (hours long) cried'

However, the English progressive construction has other senses besides focusing on the internal phasing or on the duration of an event. In English, the progressive pattern can also express intentionality, but the Italian gerundial and the Dutch progressive cannot:

(3) a. English:    I am not taking the train today.
     b. Italian:    *Non intendo prendere il treno oggi.*
                 'Not I-intend to take the train today'
     c. Dutch:    *Ik ga vandaag niet de trein nemen.*
                 'I go today not the train take'
     d. German:    *Heute nehme ich den Zug nicht.*
                 'Today take I the train not'

The various uses of the English progressive can be seen as members of a radial category as suggested in Table 13.

**Table 13.** Radial network of some senses of the English progressive

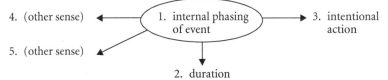

To conclude, our comparison started from one morphological pattern, i.e. the English progressive, but needed to consider at least two different semantic functions (internal phasing of an event and duration) to be fully explained. At the same time it showed how partial and deceptive correspondences across languages can be. Italian present tense, just like Dutch and German present tense, may cover both internal phasing and duration, whereas English present tense does not. Starting from German, we probably would not have thought of putting semantic categories like internal phasing and duration together.

It has been expedient to consider both similar and dissimilar patterns across languages, although the actual increase in linguistic knowledge is instigated by the latter, i.e. contrastive approach. Since such contrasts seem to highlight relevant features in numerous fields, contrastive linguistics constitutes an important branch of linguistics.

### 10.4.2 Methodological aspects of contrastive linguistics

In the fifties **contrastive linguistics** was originally conceived as a sub-field of behaviorism, as a correlate for behavioristic language learning. It was assumed that within the **target language**, i.e. the foreign language being learnt, those features which significantly diverge from the mother tongue or **source language** would represent a serious obstacle in the learning process, and that they should be submitted to a specific learning effort. It seemed that language learning errors were being predicted. This claim obviously had to be adjusted as the relationship between language structure and learning difficulty became clearer. Not only is there no correlation between degrees of linguistic dissimilarity and mental effort required, but also proficiency can often be affected by mistakes concerning minor differences rather than major ones. Describing a language is not exactly the same as describing states and processes in the mind of a foreign language learner.

However, empirical data show that foreign language learning must take into account any previously acquired linguistic structures and previously established linguistic categories. A learner dealing with new linguistic data inevitably must revise old categories, schemas and prototypes at all levels of his language competence. This revision means adapting an old mental situation to specific data from a foreign language. This is where the need for contrastive studies arises. Tools are required which help clarify what kind of dissimilarities are to be found where, and make these explicit for language learners and translators.

One can compare languages in many different ways, starting from categories of traditional grammar, from lists of words or phrases, from a whole vocabulary or from a collection of texts. The way in which correspondences and discrepancies are highlighted and explained is determined by the theoretical framework one chooses.

In the examples given above we started from a morphological pattern in English and tried to determine the conceptual categories it conveys. We could also have started from conceptual categories, asking for example how internal phasing and duration are realized grammatically in English, Italian, Dutch and German. The answer is summarized in Table 14.

For the purpose of language learning or translation it also seems appropriate to develop tools based on familiar linguistic elements such as words, phrases, especially selected semantic fields, and text types. Vocabulary information should be the outcome of an extensive check of all instances of usage concerning an item or an idiomatic expression (both as a heading and as a proposed

Table 14. The expression of "internal phasing" and "duration"

|  | Internal phasing | Duration |
|---|---|---|
| a. English | Progressive | Perfect Progressive (+ duration adjunct) |
| b. Italian | Gerund/Present (+ time point adjunct) | (Gerund) Perf. + duration adjunct |
| c. Dutch | Progressive/Present (+ time point adjunct) | Pres/Progr/Perf/Perf Prog. + duration adjunct |
| d. German | Present + time point adjunct | Pres/Perfect + duration adjunct |

translation). To meet this need we can rely neither on the linguistic competence of one or a few dictionary authors nor just on previous lexical work. We must combine these sources with a carefully designed and constantly updated **corpus** (or a set of corpora), i.e. a wide collection of written or spoken texts covering as many varieties as possible.

The first step is the search for all possible variants of a single word or phrase within the same language. This step may show that some words, syntactic forms and idiomatic expressions have disappeared, some others have emerged and others have never been taken into account. It may show also that some are statistically so reduced that we may practically ignore them, and others are so limited and specialized that we may use them only in very particular circumstances. We may register that some words, syntactic forms or expressions tend to evoke **connotations**, i.e. typical emotional associations, including negativity, enthusiasm, distance, taboo, etc. A typical instance of a negative connotation associated with a syntactic form is the use of the progressive in combination with *why ... always* as in (4a), which is in strong contrast with the neutral sense of the *why ... always* question in (4b).

(4)  a.  Why are you always coming late?
     b.  Why do you always come late?

It is in other words impossible to use (4a) with a positive connotation. It is also impossible to ask a neutral information question in the progressive. Compare *Are you always coming late?* and *Do you always come late?*

The next step is the contrastive one. If we already know where to begin the search for equivalent items in the other language, we try to gather the same amount of data on variants and **collocations**, i.e. typical contexts in which a word or idiomatic expression occurs. Otherwise we browse texts parallel or comparable to the ones we have analyzed in the first language, until we find at least a partially matching item to start from. After acquiring the amount of new information we need, the two resulting sets of data are interfaced. This is where the real comparison begins.

### 10.4.3 Contrasting verb phrases

As stated in Chapter 4, verb phrases are crucial for the semantic and the syntactic classification of event schemas and sentence patterns. All basic sentence patterns can be seen as possible variants of phrases with a verb as head. To classify combinations between a verb and specifically compatible nouns (including the subject) means classifying all sentence patterns in which that verb can occur. If we perform a parallel classification for the verbs of two languages, we create an invaluable tool. This classification is certainly feasible, given the limited number of verbs in European languages.

We will now try to — partially — interface the English verb *to count* with the German verbs *rechnen* 'calculate' and *zählen* 'count', using a simplified set of examples. Counting is a central activity of human beings. In advanced cultures, formalized and empirical sciences have produced precise and generalized definitions for all mental operations related to counting. Consequently in the vocabulary of major languages, one would expect to find clear-cut groups of nominal and verbal expressions and easy matching across their meaning.

(5) a. The porter counted our bags.
    b. *Der Gepäckträger zählte unsere Taschen.*

(6) a. I count to three before screaming.
    b. *Ich zähle bis drei, dann schreie ich.*

(7) a. Fifty dogs, counting the puppies.
    b. *Fünfzig Hunde, wenn man die Welpen mitrechnet/mitzählt.*

(8) a. He still counts as a child.
    b. *Er zählt noch als Kind.*
    b'. *Er wird doch noch als Kind gerechnet.*

(9) a. I do not count him as a friend.
    b. *Ich würde ihn nicht gerade zu meinen Freunden rechnen/zählen.*

(10) a. Your feelings count little with him.
    b. *Deine Gefühle zählen doch kaum für ihn.*

(11)  a.  Do not count on me.

     b.  *Zähle nicht auf mich/Rechne nicht mit mir.*

We see that English *count* is matched in German by two different verbs, i.e. *zählen* and *rechnen*, both of which are extended by particles or prepositions such as *mit, zu, auf,* etc. This means that German expresses the various senses of English *count* by making use of its greater morphological flexibility.

But in order to see the similarities and contrasts between English and German more sharply, let us draw up a radial network for *count* and the sentence patterns and meanings it is used in (see Table 15).

**Table 15.** Radial network for *to count*

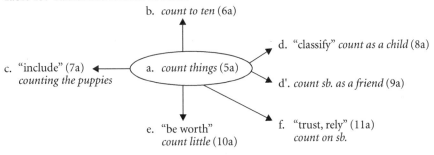

We start from the principle that there is straight semantic correspondence between verbs in two contrasted languages if we find the same semantic roles for the subject and object or complement in the two languages. This condition is very much satisfied in the correspondences for each of the six meanings, but the differences between the six meanings are also spelled out by particles and prepositions in German, and only to a certain degree in English. We can analyze the examples in reduced form again.

(5)  count objects '*Dinge zählen*'      Agent + Patient

(6)  count to three '*bis drei zählen*'    Agent + Goal

The "goal" function of *three* is clear if one considers the expression *count from 1 to 10.* In the next three cases *to count* is used in an extended sense, which can be paraphrased as "include" in (7) and as "classify" in (8), (9).

(7)  counting the puppies      '*die Welpen mitrechnen/mitzählen*'
     Agent + Patient.

(8)  sb. counts as a child          '*jemand zählt als Kind/wird als Kind*
     Patient + Essive               *gerechnet*'

(9)  count sb. as a friend          '*jemanden zu seinen Freunden*
     Agent + Patient + Essive       *rechnen/zählen*'

In the extended meanings, German can use both *rechnen* and *zählen*, but if no Agent is involved at all, as in (8), *zählen* is used; if the agent is explicit or implicit, *rechnen als* is possible. This is not the case in (10), since here an Experiencer, not an Agent is involved.

(10)  count little                  '*kaum zählen*'
      Patient + (Experiencer)

The Experiencer need not be expressed, but is implicitly always understood in this figurative sense. Also the last sense (11) is fully figurative.

(11)  count on sb/sth.              '*auf jemanden/etwas zählen*';
      Agent + Goal                  '*mit jemandem rechnen*'

However useful a tool these analyses in terms of role configurations may be, we must realize that they do not work for **idiomatic expressions**. A case in point is the German expression *rechnen mit* 'count on', which can be a real equivalent of English *to count on*, as in *mit einer Erbschaft rechnen* 'count on an inheritance', but which can also be used in an idiomatic way and have negative connotations as in *mit dem Schlimmsten rechnen* 'expect the worst', or *es ist mit starken Regenfällen zu rechnen* 'heavy rain is expected'. Although this negative connotation of *rechnen mit* 'take into account the eventuality of a negative event' is analyzable as an "experiencing" schema and has the role configuration Experiencer + Patient, it is not a regular syntactic pattern, but rather a highly idiomatic expression, in many respects unique.

These observations are just a small part of what might be detected with a thorough contrastive analysis of just a couple of verbs in English and German. Even in such a fundamental semantic field like "count", we notice that the English verb *to count* semantically corresponds to two different German verbs. These correspondences are fully analyzable in terms of role configurations. But what also emerges here, is the essential role of idiomaticity. In each language there are a large number of idiomatic expressions and idiomatic uses of verbs and other words which are completely unique and cannot be analyzed in a general systematic way by means of role configurations. In such expressions there is no productive use of any of the role configurations, but a purely ad hoc configuration. This is precisely the meaning of the term *idiomatic expression*. So the heuristic value of the use of role configurations is that it can show which senses of a verb are productive and regular, and which use is highly **idiosyncratic**. Still, all these idiomatic uses form a very substantial part of language. Radial networks can aptly represent these relations between the various senses of words — both productive and idiosyncratic ones.

## 10.5 Summary

Languages are compared with one another because of different theoretical interests. One major concern is language-external and relates to the identification and status of languages: how many languages are there in the world and what criterion can we use to count them? **Mutual intelligibility** is not a fully reliable criterion, since in a **dialect continuum**, two neighbouring **dialects**, even if they belong to two different languages may meet the criterion, whereas distanced dialects of the same language may not. The status of a variety as a regional dialect or as an **official language** is often a matter of political decision. But once a variety has become the **institutionalized language**, it may be widely extended both lexically and grammatically and may be enforced by **language laws**.

A second major type of language comparison is on the basis of **language classification**, which encompasses the study of the origin and spread of language(s) and groups languages on the basis of genetic relatedness. **Genetic relatedness** of languages leads to the setting up of **language families** and the reconstruction of their **proto-language**, such as e.g. **Proto-Indo-European**. In addition to the notion of language family, new notions constituting a taxonomy have been developed. At the highest level of such a taxonomy is the **language phylum**, i.e. a group of languages not related to any other group, but which is geographically or historically defined. Language phyla consist of **language stocks**, the members of which are very remotely related to each other. Language stocks may consist of one or more **language families**, e.g. the Indo-European family. A language family consists of **branches**, e.g. the **Satem languages** and the **Kentum languages** as the two main branches of the Indo-European language family. A branch may consist of **groups**, e.g. the Kentum branch consists of a Germanic and a Romance group; each of them consists of **subgroups**.

A third concern is that of **language typology**, which searches for common properties of a number of languages or of all languages. In the latter case, language typologists aim for **universals of language**. These may be found at every level of language. At the level of lexicology and morphology we find **ideational universals** such as semantic primes. At the level of interaction we find **interpersonal** or **pragmatic universals**. At all levels of language structure we may find **implicational universals**.

Finally in addition to the external, classificatory, and typological comparison of languages, there is also a contrastive approach. **Contrastive linguistics** specializes in the description of the differences or contrasts between two or more languages with a practical purpose in mind: it aims at providing support for foreign language learning, translation projects and bilingual dictionaries. A contrastive approach can start from a language form in the **source language** such as the progressive form in English, and then explores what uses or meanings it can express and how these meanings are expressed in the **target language(s)**, e.g. by a comparable morphological form or by a different contextual constraint. Methodologically, contrastive linguistics needs huge **corpora** of texts, both written and spoken. By listing all the **collocations** of a given word or word group, i.e. the contexts in which it can occur and repeating this for the two or three languages concerned, the comparison of items, e.g. in terms of **role configurations** can pinpoint precisely to what extent items converge and diverge. If the analysis in terms of role configurations no longer applies systematically, we are in the **idiomatic** area of language use, a very large and important area, but unique in its use and not amenable to real generalizations.

## 10.6  Further reading

Language-external comparisons are made in Comrie (1987) and Coulmas (1995). The international "story" of English is told in Mc Crum, Cran and Mac Neil (1986). Excellent introductions to the interdisciplinary research on the origin, spread and evolution of language are Aitchison (1996) and Beakin (1996). Information on the history of language classification is given by Robins (1973) and Hoenigswald (1973). The latest atlas of all the languages of the world is Moseley and Asher (1994). A good introduction to language typology is Ramat et al. (1987); a general survey is Shopen (1985); a cognitive view is presented in Croft (1999). The first classical work on universals of language was edited by Greenberg (1963) and analyzed in Greenberg (1966, 1973). Later work concentrated more on semantic universals as Comrie (1981) and Goddard and Wierzbicka (eds. 1994). A good introduction to contrastive linguistics is James (1980). Cognitive analyses are legion: a more theoretical foundation is

Krzeszowski (1990); specific analyses of single areas are covered in Barcelona (2001), Boas (2001), Turewicz (1997), Uehara (2003), and Van Langendonck and Van Belle (1998).

## Assignments

1. Is there any reason to say that the many varieties of English all over the world will not constitute one language since not all these varieties are mutually understandable? Compare with the Germanic dialects in Table 1.

2. Using the facts of Table 3, explain why English and French are the two most international world languages. What makes them different from Arabic and Spanish, but also from each other? Or would you claim that Spanish is "more international?" Can you relativize the figures for French and Spanish in Table 3? And why can the biggest language, Chinese, never become the first world language?

3. The expressions *language death*, *language attrition* and *birth of a new language* can be seen as realizations of the underlying conceptual metaphor LANGUAGE IS A LIVING ORGANISM. Consult any book on language evolution, e.g. Aitchison (1991, 1996, 1997), Beakin (1996), or even Darwin (1859), and try to find a few more instances of this metaphor. Here is a possible fragment to work on.

   > Yet there is one extra worry to add in, language loss. Ninety per cent of the world's languages may be in danger. Around 6,000 languages are currently spoken in the world. Of these, half are moribund in that they are no longer learned by the new generation of speakers. A further 2,500 are in a danger zone, in that they have fewer than a hundred thousand speakers. This leaves around 600, a mere ten per cent of the current total, as likely survivors a century from now. Of course, languages inevitably split, just as Latin eventually split into the various Romance languages. So some new languages may emerge. But the diversity will be much reduced. The splendiferous bouquet of current languages will be withered down to a small posy with only a few different flowers (Aitchinson 1997: 95).

4. For each of the three European languages (a) Greek, (b) Finnish, and (c) Welsh find out what language family branch and group they belong to. Making use of Tables 5 and 6, what is the name of the family (or branch), and what are some of the "sister" languages in the same family? Do you have enough information to draw a family tree? For example, English comes from (western) Germanic, as do Dutch, German. The tree is as follows:

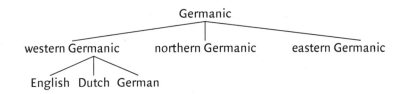

5. Which European languages listed in Table 6 have official status and which do not? Underline all the non-official languages and give reasons why these languages have no offical status.

6. Translate the English sentences of (5) to (11) into a language of your choice (except German).

    (5)     The porter counted our bags.

    (6)     I count to ten before screaming.

    (7)     Fifty dogs, counting the puppies.

    (8)     He still counts as a child.

    (9)     I do not count him as a friend.

    (10)    Your feelings count little with him.

    (11)    Do not count on me.

If you use more than one different verb, can you see a possible system, e.g. one verb for the literal meanings of *count* ((5)–(6)), another verb for the extended meanings ((7)–(8)–(9)) and still other possibilities for the figurative meanings ((10)–(11))?

# References

Aitchison, Jean. 1991. *Language Change: Progress or Decay?* Cambridge: Cambridge University Press.

Aitchison, Jean. 1996. *The Seeds of Speech. Language Origin and Evolution.* Cambridge: Cambridge University Press.

Ammon, Ulrich (ed.) 1994. *English only? In Europa/in Europe/en Europe.* Tübingen: Niemeier.

Andersen, Henning. 1973. Abductive and deductive change. *Language* 49: 765–793.

Austin, J. L. 1962. *How to Do Things with Words.* Oxford: Oxford University Press.

Bally, Charles. 1920. Impressionisme et grammaire. In: *Mélanges d'histoire littéraire et de philologie offerts à M. Bernard Bouvier.* Geneva: Sonor. Microfilm, British Museum, pp. 261–279.

Barcelona, Antonio (ed.) 2000. *Metaphor and Metonymy at the Crossroads: A Cognitive Perspective.* Berlin and New York: Mouton de Gruyter.

Barcelona, Antonio. 2001. On the systematic contrastive analysis of conceptual metaphors: Case studies and proposed methodology. In Pütz, Martin, Niemeier, Susanne; Dirven, René (eds), *Applied Cognitive Linguistics II: Language Pedagogy.* Berlin and New York: Mouton de Gruyter, pp. 117–146.

Barzini, Luigi G. 1964. *The Italians.* London: H. Hamilton.

Bauer, Laurie. 1988. *Introducing Linguistic Morphology.* Edinburgh: Edinburgh University Press.

Beakin, Mike. 1996. *The Making of Language.* Edinburgh: Edinburgh University Press.

Béal, Christine. 1994. Keeping the peace: A cross-cultural comparison of questions and requests in Australian English and French. *Multilingua* 13(1/2): 35–58.

Berlin, Brent and Paul Kay. 1969. *Basic Color Terms. Their Universality and Evolution.* Berkeley and Los Angeles: University of California Press.

Berlin, Brent, Dennis E. Breedlove and Peter H. Raven. 1974. *Principles of Tzeltal Plant Classification.* New York: Academic Press.

Berlin, Brent. 1978. Ethnobiological classification. In: Rosch, Eleanor and Barbara B. Lloys (eds.) *Cognition and Categorization.* Hillsdale, New Jersey: Lawrence Erlbaum Associates, pp. 9–26.

Blakemore, Diane. 1992. *Understanding Utterances. An Introduction to Pragmatics.* Oxford: Blackwell.

Boas, Hans C. 2001. Frame Semantics as a framework for describing polysemy and syntactic structures of English and German motion verbs in contrastive computational lexicography. In Rayson, Paul; Andrew Wilson, Tony McEnery, Andrew Hardie, and Shereen

Khoja (eds), *Proceedings of the Corpus Linguistics 2001 Conference*. Lancaster, UK: University Centre for computer corpus research on language.

Bonafante, Guliano. 1997. *The Origin of the Romance Languages*. Heidelberg: C. Winter.

Bowerman, Melissa. 1996. The origins of children's spatial semantic categories: Cognitive versus linguistic determinants. In: Gumperz, John and Steven C. Levinson (eds.), pp. 145–176.

Brisard, Frank (ed.) 2002. *Grounding: The Epistemic Footing of Deixis and Reference*. Berlin and New York: Mouton de Gruyter.

Brown, Gillian and George Yule. 1983. *Discourse Analysis*. Cambridge: Cambridge University Press.

Brown, Penelope and Steven C. Levinson. 1987. *Politeness. Some Universals in Language Usage*. Cambridge: Cambridge University Press.

Bybee, Joan L. 1985. *Morphology: A Study of the Relation between Meaning and Form*. Amsterdam and Philadelphia: John Benjamins.

Catford, John C. 1990. *A Practical Introduction to Phonetics*. Oxford: Clarendon Press.

Cawley, A.C. 1975 [1958]. *Geoffrey Chaucer: Canterbury Tales*. London: Dent, New York: Dutton.

Choi, Soonja and Melissa Bowerman. 1991. Learning to express motion events in English and Korean: The influence of language-specific lexicalization patterns. *Cognition* 41: 83–121.

Chomsky, Noam. 1965. *Aspects of the Theory of Syntax*. Cambridge, MA: The M.I.T. Press.

Clark, Eve V. and Herbert H. Clark. 1979. When nouns surface as verbs. *Language* 55: 767–811.

Comrie, Bernard. 1976. *Aspect*. Cambridge: Cambridge University Press.

Comrie, Bernard. 1981. *Language Universals and Linguistic Typology*. Cambridge: Cambridge University Press.

Comrie, Bernard. 1984. *Tense*. Cambridge: Cambridge University Press.

Comrie, Bernard (ed.) 1987a. *The World's Major Languages*. London: Routledge.

Comrie, Bernard (ed.) 1987b. *The Major Languages of South Asia, the Middle East and Africa*. London: Routledge.

Cooper, William E. and John R. Ross, 1975. Word order. In: Grossman, Robin E., L. James San and Timothy J. Vance (eds.) *Papers from the Parasession on Functionalism*. Chicago: Chicago Linguistic Society, pp. 63–111.

Coulmas, Florian (ed.) 1995. *Language Politics and Accomodation*. (Special issue of the *International Journal of the Sociology of Language* 116: 1–193).

Coulson, Seana. 2000. *Semantic Leaps: Frame-shifting and Conceptual Blending in Meaning Construction*. Cambridge: Cambridge University Press.

Couper-Kuhlen, Elizabeth and Bernd Kortmann (eds.). 2000. *Cause, Condition, Concession, Contrast: Cognitive and Discourse Perspectives* (Topics in English Linguistics 33). Berlin and New York: Mouton de Gruyter.

Croft, William. 1999. Some contributions of typology to cognitive linguistics and vice versa. In Janssen, Theo and Gisela Redeker (eds.) *Cognitive Linguistics: Foundations, Scope, and Methodology*. Berlin and New York: Mouton de Gruyter, pp. 61–93.

Croft, William and Alan Cruse. 2004. *Cognitive Linguistics*. Cambridge: Cambridge University Press.

Goldberg, Adèle E. 2002. Surface generalizations: An alternative to alternations. *Cognitive Linguistics* 13: 327–356.

Cruse, Allan. 1986, 1991. *Lexical Semantics*. Cambridge: Cambridge University Press.

Cuyckens, Hubert, René Dirven, and John Taylor (eds.) 2003. *Cognitive Linguistic Approaches to Lexical Semantics* Berlin and New York: Mouton de gruyter

Cuyckens, Hubert, Thomas Berg, René Dirven, and Klaus-Uwe Panther, (eds.) 2003. *Motivation in Language: Studies in Honor of Günter Radden.* Amsterdam and Philadelphia: John Benjamins.

Darwin, Charles. 1859. *The Origin of Species.* London: Hurrey.

Davis, Steven (ed.) 1991. *Pragmatics. A Reader.* New York and Oxford: Oxford University Press.

Dirven, René and Ralf Poerings (eds.) 2002. *Metaphor and Metonymy in Comparison and Contrast.* Berlin and New York: Mouton de Gruyter.

Du Bois, Jack W. 1980. Beyond definiteness: The trace of identity in discourse. In: Chafe, Wallace (ed.) *The Pear Stories: Cognitive, Cultural and Linguistic Aspects of Narrative Production.* Norwood, N. J.: Ablex, pp. 203–274.

Dürmüller, Urs and H. Utz. 1977. *Altenglisch. Eine Einführung.* Tübingen: Niemeier.

Edwards, J. and M. Lampert (eds.) 1993. *Talking Data: Transcription and Coding in Discourse Research.* Hilldale, N. J.: Lawrence Erlbaum.

Enkvist, Nick E. 1978. Coherence, pseudo-coherence, and non-coherence. In: Östman, J. O. (ed.) *Cohesion and Semantics.* Åbo, Finland: Åbo Academi Foundation.

Fauconnier, Gilles. 1994. *Mental Spaces: Aspects of Meaning Construction in Natural Language.* Cambridge, MA: Bradford.

Fauconnier, Gilles. 1997. *Mappings in Thought and Language.* Cambridge: Cambridge University Press.

Fauconnier, Gilles and Eve Sweetser (eds.) 1996. *Spaces, Worlds and Grammars.* Chicago: University of Chicago Press.

Fox, Barbara. 1987. *Discourse Structure and Anaphora. Written and Conversational English.* Cambridge: Cambridge University Press.

Geeraerts, Dirk. 1987. On necessary and sufficient conditions. *Journal of Semantics* 5: 275–291.

Geeraerts, Dirk. 1988. Where does prototypicality come from? In: Rudzka-Ostyn, Brygida (ed.) *Topics in Cognitive Linguistics.* Amsterdam: John Benjamins, pp. 207–229.

Geeraerts, Dirk. 1993. Vagueness's puzzles, polysemy's vagaries. *Cognitive Linguistics* 4: 223–272.

Geeraerts, Dirk. 1997. *Diachronic Prototype Semantics: A Contribution to Historical Lexicology.* Oxford: Clarendon Press.

Geeraerts, Dirk and Hubert Cuyckens (eds.) Fortcoming. *Handbook of Cognitive Linguistics.* Oxford: Oxford University Press.

Geeraerts, Dirk, Stefan Grondelaers and Peter Bakema. 1994. *The Structure of Lexical Variation. Meaning, Wording, and Context.* Berlin: Mouton de Gruyter.

Giegerich, Heinz J. 1992. *English Phonology: An Introduction.* Cambridge: Cambridge University Press.

Gimson, A. C. 1989. *An Introduction to the Pronunciation of English.* London and New York: Routledge.

Givón, Talmy. 1982. Tense-aspect-modality: The creole prototype and beyond. In: Hopper, Paul (ed.) *Tense and Aspect.* Amsterdam and Philadelphia: John Benjamins.

Givón, Talmy. 1990. *Syntax: A Functional-Typological Introduction.* Vol. 2. Amsterdam and Philadelphia: John Benjamins.

Givón, Talmy. 1993. *English Grammar.* Vols. 1 & 2. Amsterdam and Philadelphia: John Benjamins.

Goddard, Cliff and Anna Wierzbicka (eds.) 1994. *Semantic and Lexical Universals: Theory and Empirical Findings.* Amsterdam and Philadelphia: John Benjamins.

Goddard, Cliff and Anna Wierzbicka. 1996. Discourse and culture. In: van Dijk, Teun A. (ed.) *Discourse: A Multidisciplinary Introduction.* Thousand Oaks, CA, London and New Delhi: Sage.

Goddard, Cliff. 1998. *Semantic Analysis: A Practical Introduction.* Oxford: Oxford University Press.

Goffman, Erving. 1981. *Forms of Talk.* Philadelphia: University of Pennsylvania Press.

Goldberg, Adele E. 1995. *Constructions: A Construction Grammar Approach to Argument Structure.* Chicago: University of Chicago Press.

Goldberg, Adèle E. 2002. Surface generalizations: An alternative to alternations. *Cognitive Linguistics* 13(4): 327–356.

Greenberg, Joseph H. (ed.) 1963. *Universals of Language.* Cambridge, Mass.: MIT Press.

Greenberg, Joseph H. 1966. *Language Universals. With Special Reference to Feature Hierarchies.* The Hague and Paris: Mouton.

Greenberg, Joseph H. 1973. The typological method. In: Sebeok, Thomas A. (ed.) *Current Trends in Linguistics.* Vol. II: *Diachronic, Areal and Typological Linguistics.* The Hague and Paris: Mouton, pp. 149–194.

Grice, H. Paul. 1975. Logic and conversation. In: P. Cole and J. Morgan (eds.) *Syntax and Semantics.* Vol. 3: *Speech Acts.* New York: Academic Press.

Grimes, Barbara F. (ed.) 1996. Languages of the world: Top 100 languages by population. *Ethnologue.* 13th Edition, Tucson, AZ: Summer Institute of Linguistics (SIL).

Grosz, Barbara J. and Candice L. Sidner. 1986. Attention, intention and the structure of discourse. *Computational Linguistics* 12: 175–204.

Grundy, Peter. 1997. *Doing Pragmatics.* London: Arnold.

Gumperz, John J. and Stephen C. Levinson (eds.) 1996. *Rethinking Linguistic Relativity.* Cambridge: Cambridge University Press.

Haiman, John (ed.) 1985. *Iconicity in Syntax.* Amsterdam and Philadelphia: John Benjamins.

Hampe, Beate (ed.) (with the assistance of Joseph E. Grady) Forthcoming. *From Perception to Meaning: Image Schemas in Cognitive Linguistics.* (Cognitive Linguistics Research). Berlin and New York: Mouton de Gruyter.

Heider, Eleanor. 1972. Universals in color naming and memory. *Journal of Experimental Psychology* 93: 10–20.

Heyvaert, Liesbet. 2003. *A Cognitive-Functional Approach to Nominalization in English.* Berlin and New York: Mouton de Gruyter.

Hock, Hans Heinrich. 1986. *Principles of Historical Linguistics.* Berlin and New York: Mouton de Gruyter.

Hoenigswald, Henry M. 1973. The comparative method. In: Sebeok, Thomas A. (ed.) *Current Trends in Linguistics.* Vol. II: *Diachronic, Areal and Typological Linguistics.* The Hague and Paris: Mouton, pp. 51–62.

Hopper, R. 1992. *Telephone Conversations.* Bloomington, Indiana: Bloomington University Press.

Humboldt, Wilhelm von. 1988[1838]. *On Language: The Diversity of Human Language-structure and its Influence on the Mental Development of Mankind.* Translated from German by Peter Heath). Cambridge: Cambridge University Press.

Ikegami, Yoshihiko. 1987. Source vs. Goal: A case of linguistic dissymmetry. In: Dirven, René and Günter Radden (eds.) *Concepts of Case.* Tübingen: Gunter Narr, pp. 122–145.

Indurkhya, Bipin. 1992. *Metaphor and Cognition. An Interactionist Approach.* Dordrecht: Kluwer Academic Publishers.

Ishiguro, Hide. 1972. *Leibniz's Philosophy of Logic and Language.* London: Duckworth.

James, Carl. 1980. *Contrastive Analysis.* Harlow, Essex: Longman.

Janda, Laura A. 1993. *A Geography of Case Semantics. The Czech Dative and the Russian Instrumental.* Berlin and New York: Mouton de Gruyter.

Janssen, Theo and Gisela Redeker (eds.) 1999. *Cognitive Linguistics: Foundations, Scope, and Methodology.* (Cognitive Linguistics Research 15). Berlin: Mouton de Gruyter.

Katamba, Frances. 1982. *An Introduction to Phonology.* London: Longman.

Kay, Paul, Brent Berlin and William Merrifield. 1991. Biocultural implications of systems of color naming. *Journal of Linguistic Anthropology* 1(1): 12–25.

Keller, Rudi. 1990. *Sprachwandel.* Tübingen: Gunter Narr. Translated into English as *On Language Change* by Brigitte Nerlich. 1994. London and New York: Routledge.

Kellermann, Günther and Michael D. Morrissey (eds.) 1992. *Diachrony within Synchrony: Language History and Cognition* Frankfurt: Peter Lang.

Kelz, H. 1976. *Phonetische Probleme im FU.* Hamburg: Buske.

Krzeszowski, Tomasz P. 1990. *Contrasting Languages: The Scope of Contrastive Linguistics.* Berlin and New York: Mouton de Gruyter.

Kuryłowicz, Jerzy. 1945–49. La nature des procès dits analogiques. *Acta Linguistica* 5: 17–34. Translated with an introduction into English by Margaret E. Winters. 1995. *Diachronica* 12: 113–145.

Labov, William. 1973. The social setting of linguistic change. In: Sebeok, Thomas A. *Current Trends in Linguistics.* Vol. II: *Diachronic, Areal and Typological Linguistics.* Berlin: Mouton de Gruyter, pp. 195–252.

Ladefoged, Peter. 1993. *A Course in Phonetics.* London: Harcourt Brace Jovanovich.

Lakoff, George and Mark Johnson. 1980. *Metaphors We Live by.* Chicago and London: The University of Chicago Press.

Lakoff, George. 1987. *Women, Fire and Dangerous Things: What Categories Reveal about the Mind.* Chicago: University of Chicago Press.

Lakoff, George and Mark Johnson. 1999. *Philosophy in the Flesh: The Embodied Mind and its Challenges to Western Thought.* Chicago: University of Chicago Press.

Langacker, Ronald W. 1987. *Foundations of Cognitive Grammar.* Vol. I. *Theoretical Prerequisites.* Stanford, CA: Stanford University Press.

Langacker, Ronald W. 1991a. *Foundations of Cognitive Grammar.* Vol. II. *Descriptive Application.* Stanford, CA: Stanford University Press.

Langacker, Ronald W. 1991b. *Concept, Image, and Symbol: The Cognitive Basis of Grammar.* Berlin: Mouton de Gruyter.

Langacker, Ronald W. 1999. *Grammar and Conceptualization.* Berlin: Mouton de Gruyter.

Lass, Roger. 1991. *Phonology: An Introduction to Basic Concepts.* Cambridge: Cambridge University Press.

Lee, Penny. 1996. *The Whorf Theory Complex.* Amsterdam: John Benjamins.

Lehrer, Adrienne and Keith Lehrer. 1995. Fields, networks and vectors. In: Palmer, Frank R. (ed.) *Grammar and Meaning. Essays in Honour of John Lyons.* Cambridge: Cambridge University Press.

Lehrer, Adrienne. 1974. *Semantic Fields and Lexical Structure.* Amsterdam: Holland Publishing Company.

Lehrer, Adrienne. 1990. Prototype theory and its implications for lexical analysis. In: Tsohatzidis, Savas L. (ed.) *Meanings and Prototypes.* London and New York: Routledge.

Leibniz, Gottfried Wilhelm. 1981[1765]. *New Essays Concerning Human Understanding.* Translated by Remnant, Peter and Jonathon Bennet. Cambridge: Cambridge University Press.

Levinson, Stephen C. 1983. *Pragmatics.* Cambridge: Cambridge University Press.

Locke, John. 1976[1690]. *An Essay Concerning Human Understanding.* Abridged and edited with an introduction by John W. Yolton. London: Everyman's Library.

Lucy, John. 1992a. *Language Diversity and Thought. A Reformulation of the Linguistic Relativity Hypothesis.* Cambridge: Cambridge University Press.

Lucy, John. 1992b. *Grammatical Categories and Cognition. A Case Study of the Linguistic Relativity Hypothesis.* Cambridge: Cambridge University Press.

Luria, A.R. and L.S. Vygotsky. 1992. *Ape, Primitive Man and Child. Essays in the History of Behaviour.* (Translated from Russian into English by E. Rossiter). Hemel Hempstead: Harvester Wheatsheaf.

Mann, William C. and Sandra A. Thompson. 1988. Rhetorical structure theory: Toward a functional theory of text organization. *Text* 8: 243–281.

Marchand, Hans. 1969. *The Categories and Types of Present-day English Word Formation. A Synchronic-Diachronic Approach* (2nd edition). München: Beck.

Martin, Jim R. 1992. *English Text.* Amsterdam and Philadelphia: John Benjamins.

Matthews, Peter H. 1991. *Morphology.* Cambridge: Cambridge University Press.

Mc Crum, Robert, William Cran and Robert Mac Neil. 1986. *The Story of English.* New York: Viking Penguin.

Mey, Jacob L. 1993. *Pragmatics.* Oxford: Blackwell.

Moseley, Christopher and R.E. Asher (eds.) 1994. *Atlas of the World's Languages.* London: Routledge.

Mossé, Fernand. 1968. *A Handbook of Middle English.* (Translated by James A. Walker). Baltimore: The John Hopkins Press.

Nathan, Geoffrey S. 1994. How the phoneme inventory gets its shape: Cognitive grammar's view of phonological systems. *Rivista di Linguistica* 6: 275–287.

Nathan, Geoffrey S. 1996. Steps towards a cognitive phonology. In: Hurch, B., Rhodes, Richard A. (eds.) *Natural Phonology: The State of the Art.* Papers from the Bern Workshop on Natural Phonology. Berlin: Mouton de Gruyter, pp. 107–122

Nathan, Geoffrey S. 1999. *An Introduction to Cognitive Phonology.* Course book.

Nerlich, Brigitte. 1990. *Change in Language: Whitney, Bréal and Wegener.* London: Routledge.

Newman, John. 1996. *Give. A Cognitive Linguistic Study.* Berlin and New York: Mouton de Gruyter.

Niemeier, Susanne, and René Dirven (eds.). 2000. *Evidence for Linguistic Relativity* (Current Issues in Linguistic Theory 198). Amsterdam and Philadelphia: John Benjamins.

Nöth, Winfred. 1990. *Handbook of Semiotics.* Bloomington: Indiana University Press.

Ogden, C.K. and I.A. Richards. 1923. *The Meaning of Meaning*. London: Routledge and Kegan Paul.

Panther, Klaus-Uwe and Günter Radden (eds.) 1999. *Metonymy in Language and Thought*. Amsterdam and Philadelphia: John Benjamins.

Panther, Klaus-Uwe and Linda L. Thornburg 2002. The roles of metaphor and metonymy in English *-er* nominals. In: Dirven, René and Ralf Poerings (eds.), pp. 279–319.

Panther, Klaus-Uwe and Linda Thornburg (eds.). 2003. *Metonymy and Pragmatic Inferencing* (Pragmatics and Beyond NS 113). Amsterdam and Philadelphia: John Benjamins.

Paulussen, Hans. 1995. Compiling a trilingual parallel corpus. *Contragram*. Ghent: University of Ghent, pp. 10–13.

Pedersen, Holger 1931 [1923]. *Linguistic Science in the Nineteenth Century. Methods and Results*. Oxford: Oxford University Press.

Peeters, Bert. 1994. Semantic and lexical universals in French. In: Goddard, Cliff and Anna Wierzbicka (eds.), pp. 423–444.

Peirce, Charles S. 1931–58. *Collected Papers*. Vols. 1–8. C. Hartshorne and P. Weiss (eds.) Cambridge, Mass.: Harvard University Press.

Phillips, John A.S. 1989. *Coping with Germany*. Oxford: Blackwell.

Posner, Roland. 1986. Iconicity in syntax: The natural order of attributes. In: Bouissac, Paul, Michael Herzfeld and Roland Posner (eds.) *Iconicity: Essays on the Nature of Culture: Festschrift for Thomas A. Sebeok on His 65th Birthday*. Tübingen: Stauffenberg, pp. 305–337.

Pütz, Martin and Marjolijn Verspoor (eds.). 2000. *Explorations in Linguistic Relativity* (Current Issues in Linguistic Theory 199). Amsterdam and Philadelphia: John Benjamins.

Radden, Günter and René Dirven. 2005. *Cognitive English Grammar*. Amsterdam and Philadelphia: John Benjamins.

Radden, Günter and Klaus-Uwe Panther (eds.) Forthcoming. *Motivation in Grammatical and Lexical Structure*. Berlin and New York: Mouton de Gruyter.

Ramat, Anna G., O. Carruba, and G. Bernini (eds.) 1987. *Papers from the 7th International Conference on Historical Linguistics*. Amsterdam and Philadelphia: John Benjamins.

Ransom, Evelyn. 1986. *Complementation: Its Meanings and Forms*. Amsterdam and Philadelphia: John Benjamins.

Robins, R.H. 1973. The history of language classification. In: Sebeok, Thomas A. (ed.) *Current Trends in Linguistics*. Vol. II: *Diachronic, Areal and Typological Linguistics*. The Hague and Paris: Mouton, pp. 3–43.

Rosch, Eleanor. 1977. Human categorization. In: Neil Warren (ed.) *Studies in Cross-Cultural Psychology*. Vol. 1. New York: Academic Press, pp. 3–49.

Rosch, Eleanor. 1999. Reclaiming concepts. *Journal of Consciousness Studies* 6: 61–77.

Ryder, Mary Ellen. 1991. Mixers, mufflers, and mousers: The extending of the '-er' suffix as a case of prototype reanalysis. *Berkeley Linguistics Society* 17(1): 299–311.

Prince, Ellen F. 1981. Towards a taxonomy of given-new information. In: Peter Cole (ed.) *Radical Pragmatics*. New York: Academic Press, pp. 223–255.

Quirk, Randolph and C.L. Wrenn. 1973. *An Old English Grammar*. London: The John Hopkins Press.

Rudzka-Ostyn, Brygida (ed.) 1988. *Topics in Cognitive Linguistics*. Amsterdam and Philadelphia: John Benjamins.

Ruiz de Mendoza, Francisco J. and José Luis Otal Campo. 2002. *Metonymy, Grammar, and Communication*. Albolote (Granada): Editorial Comares.

Sanders, José. 1994. *Perspective in Narrative Discourse*. Unpublished Ph.D. Dissertation. Discourse Studies Group, Tilburg University.

Sanders, Ted J.M., Wilbert P.M. Spooren and Leo G.M. Noordman. 1992. Toward a taxonomy of coherence relations. *Discourse Processes* 15: 1–35.

Sanders, Ted, Joost Schilperoord, and Wilbert Spooren (eds.). 2001. *Text Representation: Linguistic and Psycholinguistic Aspects* (Human Cognitive Processing 8). Amsterdam and Philadelphia: John Benjamins.

Sapir, Edward. 1958. *Selected Writings of Edward Sapir in Language, Culture and Personality*. Edited by David Mandelbaum. Berkeley: University of California Press.

Saussure, Ferdinand de. 1966 [1916]. *Course in General Linguistics*. Edited by Charles Bally and Albert Sechehaye, in collaboration with Albert Riedlinger. Translated, with an introduction and notes, by Wade Baskin. New York, Toronto, and London: Mc Graw-Hill.

Schiffrin, Deborah. 1987. *Discourse Markers*. Cambridge: Cambridge University Press.

Schiffrin, Deborah. 1994. *Approaches to Discourse: Language as Social Interaction*. Oxford: Blackwell.

Searle, John R. 1969. *Speech Acts. An Essay in the Philosophy of Language*. Cambridge: Cambridge University Press.

Searle, John R. 1979. *Expression and Meaning: Studies in the Theory of Speech Acts*. Cambridge and New York: Cambridge University Press.

Shopen, Timothy (ed.) 1985. *Language Typology and Syntactic Description. III. Grammatical Categories and the Lexicon*. Cambridge: Cambridge University Press.

Spencer, Al. 1991. *Morphological Theory*. Oxford, U.K. and Cambridge, Mass.: Blackwell.

Sperber, Dan and Deidre Wilson. 1986, 1995². *Relevance. Communication and Cognition*. Oxford: Blackwell.

Strauss, Jürgen. n. d. *Geoffrey Chaucer. The Canterbury Tales: The General Prologue*. Trier: Multimedia Editions of Medieval English Texts (MEMET).

Talmy, Leonard. 1988a. Force dynamics in language and cognition. *Cognitive Science* 12: 49–100.

Talmy, Leonard. 1988b. The relation of grammar to cognition. In: Rudzka-Ostyn, Brygida (ed.) *Topics in Cognitive Linguistics*. Amsterdam and Philadelphia: John Benjamins, pp. 165–205.

Talmy, Leonard. 2000. *Toward a Cognitive Semantics, Vol. I: Concept Structuring Systems; Vol. II: Typology and Process in Concept Structuring*. Cambridge, Mass.: The MIT Press.

Taylor, John R. 2003. *Linguistic Categorization*. Third edition. Oxford: Clarendon Press.

Taylor, John R. 2002. *Cognitive Grammar*. (Oxford Textbooks in Linguistics). Oxford: Oxford University Press.

Thornburg, Linda and Klaus-Uwe Panther. 1997. Speech act metonymies. In Liebert, Wolf-Andreas, Gisela Redeker and Linda Waugh (eds.) *Discourse and Perspective in Cognitive Linguistics*. John Benjamins: Amsterdam; Philadelphia, pp. 205–219.

Traugott, Elisabeth C. and Ekkehardt König. 1991. The semantics-pragmatics of grammaticalization revisited. In: Traugott, Elisabeth C. and Bernd Heine (eds.) *Approaches to Grammaticalization*. Vol. 2. Amsterdam: John Benjamins, pp. 189–218.

Trudgill, Peter. 2002. *Sociolinguistic Variation and Change*. Washington, D.C.: Georgetown University Press.

Turewicz, Kamila. 1997. Cognitive grammar for contrastive linguistics: A case study of indirect speech in English and Polish. In Hickey, R. and S. Puppel (eds.), *Language History and Linguistic Modelling: A Festschrift for Jacek Fisiak on his 60th Birthday*. Berlin and New York: Mouton de Gruyter, pp. 1859–1886.

Uehara, Satoshi. 2003. 'Zibun' reflexivization in Japanese: A Cognitive Grammar approach. In Casad, Eugene H. and Gary B. Palmer (eds.), *Cognitive Linguistics and Non-Indo-European Languages*. Berlin and New York: Mouton de Gruyter, pp. 389–404.

Ullmann, Stephen. 1957. *The Principles of Semantics*. Oxford: Blackwell.

Ungerer, Friedrich and Hans-Jörg Schmid. 1996. *An Introduction to Cognitive Linguistics*. London and New York: Longman.

Ushie, Y. 1986. Corepresentation. A textual function of indefinite expressions. *Text* 6: 427–446.

Vanderveken, D. 1990. *Meaning and Speech Acts*. Vols. 1 & 2. Cambridge: Cambridge University Press.

Van Dijk, Teun A. and Walter Kintsch. 1983. *Strategies of Discourse Comprehension*. New York: Academic Press.

Van Hoek, Karen, Andrej A. Kibrik, and Leo Noordman (eds.). 1999. *Discourse Studies in Cognitive Linguistics: Selected Papers from the 5th International Cognitive Linguistics Conference, Amsterdam, 1997* (Current Issues in Linguistic Theory 176). Amsterdam and Philadelphia: John Benjamins.

Verhagen, A. 1986. *Linguistic Theory and the Function of Word Order in Dutch*. Dordrecht: Foris.

Van Langendonck, Willy and William van Belle (eds.). 1998. *The Dative*. Vol. 2: *Theoretical and Contrastive Studies* (Case and Grammatical Relations across Languages 3). Amsterdam and Philadelphia: John Benjamins.

Verschueren, Jef, Jan-Ola Östman and Jan Blommaert. 1994. *Handbook of Pragmatics: Manual*. Amsterdam and Philadelphia: John Benjamins.

Verschueren, Jef. 1987. *Linguistic Action: Some Empirical Conceptual Studies*. Norwood, N. J.: Ablex.

Vonk, Wietske, Lettica G. M. M. Hustinx and Wim H. G. Simons. 1992. The use of referential expressions in structuring discourse. *Language and Cognitive Processes* 7: 301–333.

Weinreich, Uriel. 1953. *Languages in Contact*. The Hague: Mouton.

Whorf, Benjamin Lee. 1956. *Language, Thought and Reality*. Edited and with an introduction by John B. Carroll. Cambridge, MA: MIT Press.

Wierzbicka, Anna. 1988. *The Semantics of Grammar*. Amsterdam and Philadelphia: John Benjamins.

Wierzbicka, Anna. 1991. *Cross-cultural Pragmatics*. Berlin: Mouton de Gruyter.

Wierzbicka, Anna. 1992. *Semantics, Culture, and Cognition*. New York: Oxford University Press.

Wierzbicka, Anna. 1996. *Semantics, Primes and Universals*. New York: Oxford University Press.

Wierzbicka, Anna. 1997. *Understanding Cultures through their Key Words*. New York: Oxford University Press.

Williams, Raymond. 1976. *Keywords: A Vocabulary of Culture and Society*. London: Flamingo, Fontana.

Winters, Margaret E. 1992. Schemas and prototypes: Remarks on syntax change. In: Kellermann, Günther and Michael D. Morrissey (eds.) *Diachrony within Synchrony: Language History and Cognition*. Frankfurt: Lang, pp. 265–280.

Zlatev, Jordan, Tom Ziemke, Roz Frank, and René Dirven (eds.). In preparation. *Body, Language, and Mind,* Vol. 1: *Embodiment.*

# Index

For each item, the first figure in bold type indicates the page where the term is explained in context.